ANYTHING BUT THE TRUTH

MICHAEL O'CONNELL

LOCKE ISLAND BOOKS

Published by Locke Island Books

Distributed in the United Kingdom and Ireland by
Country Books, Publishers & Booksellers,
Courtyard Cottage, Little Longstone,
Bakewell, Derbyshire DE45 INN
Tel/Fax: 01629 640670
e-mail: dickrichardson@country-books.co.uk

ISBN 0 9547750 0 7

British Library Cataloguing in Publication Data.
A catalogue record for this book is available from the British Library.

Printed and bound in England by:
The Cromwell Press

DEDICATION

This book is dedicated to the following: First to the memory of my parents, James and Mary O'Connell, and to the memory of Patrick J. McGrory, LL.B., solicitor in Belfast, scholar and writer, who knew only of the highest traditions of the legal profession, and sought to follow them every day of his working life.

Second, to the Rt. Rev. Bishop Edward Daly, D.D., the former Bishop of Derry, whose personal courage and prayerful goodness are both shining examples and deeply inspirational to everyone who meets him. He, and others, including myself hope and pray that the truth about the Bloody Sunday shootings will soon be told. Without truth there can be no justice.

AUTHOR'S NOTE

Many people have helped me with the writing of this book. I thank them all, most especially my two friends and colleagues Phil Huxley LL.M., LL.B., and Professor Terence Walters LL.M., LL.B., whose combined knowledge of criminal law, evidence and procedure is profound. I also wish to thank my two sisters, Mary and Patricia and my brother Charles for their help and encouragement over the years. Finally I express my love and gratitude to my wife Eileen, last in this list, but at the forefront of my life now and always.

CONTENTS

PROLOGUE

This year, 2004, marks the 30th anniversary of some of the most bloody murders and destructive incidents of terrorist bombing in the United Kingdom of Great Britain and Northern Ireland, and the Republic of Ireland, since the end of the Second World War. In that year of 1974, 166 civilians and 50 members of the Security Forces in Northern Ireland were murdered. In Britain 12 people died in a bombing of a coach on the M62 motorway in February, 5 died at Guildford in October, 2 at Woolwich and 21 died in Birmingham in November when the Provisional IRA bombed public houses intending to kill and maim soldiers and civilians alike. It is my view, shared by others, that in revenge and retaliation for that most dreadful and unforgivable massacre of the innocents on the coach – 9 soldiers were amongst the dead – that some elements in the security forces colluded with Loyalist para-militaries to bomb the city of Dublin and the town of Monaghan in May 1974. A recent judicial inquiry conducted into the bombings by Mr. Justice Henry Barron, a former High Court judge in Ireland, concluded that "… there are grounds for suspecting that the bombers have had assistance from members of the security forces….ultimately, a finding that there was collusion between the perpetrators and the authorities in Northern Ireland is a matter of inference."

These episodes are connected. In December 1973 there was a tripartite conference at the Civil Service Staff College in Sunningdale, Berkshire at which the heads of Government of Britain, Northern Ireland and the Republic of Ireland met for the first time together since 1925. The outcome was the Sunningdale Agreement that resulted in the formation of the Council of Ireland made up of a

1

council of Ministers, and a Consultative Assembly. There was bitter opposition to that, or indeed any idea of power sharing with the Nationalists and Republicans, on the Unionist side. On 10 December 1973 Loyalist paramilitaries formed the Ulster Army Council saying they would support any loyalist politician who opposed movement towards a Council of Ireland. On 4 January 1974 the Ulster Unionist Council, the governing body of the Unionist Party, rejected the proposed all Ireland council settlement by 427 votes to 374. On 23 March 1974 a new Loyalist group, the Ulster Workers Council, threatened widespread civil disobedience and on 15 May called for a general strike; those who did not wish to support it were intimidated and assaulted by armed groups of masked men at road blocks if they tried to go to their workplace.

On the afternoon of Friday 17 May 1974 four car bombs exploded in the centre of Dublin, instantly killing 22 people and injuring hundreds. All four cars had Northern Ireland registration numbers. Another car bomb in Monaghan killed five and injured more than 20. The eventual death toll for both atrocities was 33. The Press Officer of the Ulster Defence Association and of the strike co-ordinating committee in the North, Sammy Smyth said, "I am very happy about the bombings in Dublin. There is a war with the Free State, and now we are laughing at them". Such a stupid and insensitive remark, in the face of a most terrible mass murder of innocent men, women and children, two of whom were only 17 months and 5 months old, is unforgivable. It may have cost him his life, for on 10 March 1975 Mr. Smyth was murdered at his sister's home in Belfast by the Provisional IRA.

On 19 May the Northern Ireland Secretary, Merlyn Rees, declared a State of Emergency pursuant to section 40 of the Northern Ireland Constitution Act. Faced with the threat of power cuts in the electricity supply and the breakdown of public services the Labour Government in Britain did what it does best when defeat is inevitable. It surrendered quickly and called it a concession rather than a defeat. There already was talk in the political establishment of elements in the Army and the Security Services being ready to plot the overthrow of Harold Wilson's Government, and in any event the politicians have never been entirely sure that they can rely on the support and loyalties of the Army to move against the Unionist population of the North. There was a mutiny in 1914 over the issue of Home Rule there and it could happen again.

The Chief Executive Minister of the Northern Ireland Assembly, Brian Faulkner, known without the slightest affection to the so called landed gentry and the multitude of retired army officers as "the little shirt maker" resigned and direct rule of the Province of Ulster was restored. Africa may be the Continent of the Wind of Change. To the Unionists, Northern Ireland is all wind and no change.

Amidst all the carnage there were other casualties, amongst them the concept of Truth in politics and the fair and effective administration of the criminal justice system in England and Northern Ireland. One Tory politician, a minister in Mrs. Thatcher's government who has now returned to the obscurity from which he never should have emerged, once said that "loyalists who kill Catholics are playing into the hands of the terrorists". That was not just the party line, it is part of the political philosophy of a colonial power that purchases one part of the civilian population and intimidates the other. It meant and was intended to mean that only the IRA were the terrorists in Northern Ireland. The loyalists killers were nothing of the kind, and they were adopting a defensive or retributive reaction to the Republican armed struggle to achieve a united Ireland. That is the first colonial lie. The second is that the Troubles in Northern Ireland are the manifestation of a sectarian conflict between Catholics and Protestants, with the British Government standing on the sidelines attempting to act as some kind of neutral umpire in keeping the peace. The combination of these two indicates a desire to place the responsibility for the murder of innocent Catholics at the door of the very community that is being targeted for sectarian assassination.

In October 1996 the then Chief Constable of the Royal Ulster Constabulary, Sir Hugh Annersley, a native of Dublin, claimed that Loyalist violence was reactive and not proactive and implied that if the IRA ceased their violent campaign, the Loyalists would likewise cease theirs. If the ceasefires of that year broke down, he anticipated that the Loyalists might, if they were pushed back into violence by a renewal of the IRA armed struggle, attack the Irish Republic as well as resume violence in the North. He seems to have found that acceptable and understandable, and this view is not far removed from the proposition that when the Catholic population of Northern Ireland resisted Loyalist and State violence, they were provoking their oppressors to kill them.

Politicians at the highest level also find some problems with facing up to the truth at a personal level. On 1 November 1993 the then Tory Prime Minister, John Major, told the House of Commons in answer to a comment from the Labour MP Dennis Skinner that "people outside Parliament understand only too well that the government have dealt with terrorists over the decades," that "if the implication of his remarks that we should sit down and talk with Mr. Adams and the Provisional IRA, I can only say that would turn my stomach and those of most honourable members; we will not do it." It later transpired that the British Government had a secret channel of communication with the IRA for three years and had been in constant contact since February 1993. John Major, who very few take seriously now that he has given a new meaning to the phrase "going for a Curry," tries to explain his statement in his autobiography, saying that he would not sit down and talk with the Provisional IRA because that would have conferred legitimacy on them. "But it was necessary to have a link. That is very different from face-to-face negotiations." Whispering together at arms length seems to be acceptable, but actually sitting down and each confronting the other with argument and dialogue, would not be.

John Major seemed to have lost his propensity for sickness in the stomach when, on 26 July 1996 he greeted and shook hands with John White at 10, Downing Street in London on that day. He had been convicted in 1978 of a double killing committed on 25 June 1973 and spent 14 years in prison. The murder victims were Senator Paddy Wilson and Irene Andrews. He was a member of the mainly Catholic Socialist Labour Democratic Party in the North and election agent for John Hume M.P. Miss Andrews, reputed to be a beautiful ballroom dancer, was employed as a clerk working in the Ministry of Education. White stabbed and slashed him with a knife 32 times and her 19 times in a frenzied attack. On his release from prison John White joined the Ulster Democratic Party, the political front of the banned Ulster Defence Association, and was elected to membership of the Northern Ireland forum. When he met John Major in Downing Street Paul Wilson, Paddy's son, posed the question, "how can the British Prime Minister shake hands with a man who knifed my Father to death 30 times?" The answer is simple – in Britain's case, it comes with the job.

This book is not about politics, it is about justice and truth. I endeavour to concentrate on the abstract concepts of law rather than the personalities of the lawyers involved in some of the cases described. Chapter 1 begins with the description of the attempt by a retired judge to encourage the security forces to use extreme violence against women in Northern Ireland. Some might consider they don't need that much encouragement, but in any event the newspaper he approached refused to print his inflammatory and dangerous rubbish. After his retirement Michael Argyle reverted to his former Army rank of Major, and frequently referred to himself in that way. I regarded him, both on and off the judicial bench, with considerable distaste. I understood that he was a Catholic. If his approach to women was in accordance with the principles and teaching of the Roman Catholic faith, then I am in the wrong Church.

The bulk of the chapter is however concerned with the killings in Gibraltar, on 6 March 1988, of three members of an IRA active service unit by members of the SAS. I know of no case over the past 30 years where the SAS has ever captured alive any republican terrorist following an ambush, and this was no exception. Where a soldier is involved in a police operation, his conduct is governed by the general principles of English law and he has the same rights and responsibilities as any private citizen. Any use of force must be proved to have been in lawful self defence or have a statutory authority which establishes the circumstances in which the use of force may be justified.

Domestic and International Law recognises the necessity of protecting the public from the consequences of unlawful violence, and there are circumstances where the use of lethal force is justified and therefore lawful. The use of such force is however subject to the rule of law. The approach is a dual one: first the force used must be within the limits set by domestic law, and that itself is subject to international standards.

Where a soldier, as a servant of the British Crown, uses lethal force, his conduct is examined by those standards. Article 6 of The International Covenant on Civil and Political Rights, adopted by the United Nations provides: "Every human being has the inherent right to life. This right shall be protected by law. No one shall be arbitrarily deprived of his life."

Article 6 cannot be derogated from even in times of emergency. The United Nations Human Rights Committee considers that Article 6 sets two standards; first that the use of force in law enforcement must be in proportion to the circumstances of each case, and further that the degree of force used must be in proportion to the objective.

In the case of Stewart v United Kingdom, the European Commission of Human Rights decided that the effect on law enforcement of the European Convention of Human Rights (which came into effect in September 1953) may be stated as follows: "In assessing whether the use of force is absolutely necessary, and strictly proportionate, regard must be had to the nature of the aim pursued, the dangers to life and limb inherent in a situation, and the degree of risk that the force used might result in loss of life."

Article 2 of the Convention, which applies to Gibraltar, provides that the right to life shall be protected by law. There can be no derogation under Article 15 in peacetime. It does not primarily define instances where it is permitted intentionally to kill an individual, but describes the situations where it is permitted to use force which may result, as an unintended consequence, in the deprivation of life. If the force used in defence of any person from unlawful violence or in order to carry out a lawful arrest or to prevent the escape of a person in lawful custody is no more than absolutely necessary, then it is lawful and does not conflict with Article 2.

The expression "absolutely necessary" indicates a stricter and more compelling test of necessity than that normally applicable when determining whether action by the State is necessary in a democratic society. As will be seen in Chapter 1, Britain was found to have violated Article 2.

In the planning of the counter terrorism operation, the security forces made a number of errors. According to the Intelligence Service it was anticipated that the three IRA members would blow up a car bomb brought across the border into Gibraltar from Spain by remote control – a button job. This was based on the premise that the discovery in January 1988 of some Semtex explosives in a lock up garage in Brussels were to be detonated by a remote control device and this was a tactic that the IRA were going to use there and elsewhere. In fact this was very wide of the mark. The Belgian police did consider that the Semtex was connected with the IRA simply because the device to be used for exploding that substance were not of the remote control variety, but the standard timing devices.

Other errors included the belief that the three would be armed when in fact they were not. And that they would not use a blocking car, that is using another vehicle parked in the assembly area in Gibraltar in order to reserve a space there for the car containing the bomb. In fact they did.

Chapter 2 deals with the killing of 16 year old John Boyle. To the Lord Chief Justice of Northern Ireland, Lord Lowry, he was an innocent boy. To a British Army general he was a terrorist. It is not a civil wrong in English Law to publish a false and defamatory statement about a person who has died. In a case in 1975, a young woman known to the court as Miss X sought an injunction to prevent a friend of her dead father from publishing a book about him. In it, the friend described the father's private life, portraying him as a man who was utterly depraved and who indulged in sordid and degrading conduct. Lord Denning refused to grant the injunction, saying amongst other things "The law of defamation does not permit any such proceedings. It says simply that no action lies for a libel on a dead man, on the ground that on balance it is in the public interest that no action should lie." I call for such a public interest argument to be abolished, and for a private interest to prevail, and give the right to the immediate family of a deceased to bring proceedings to challenge or deny any false statement made about their loved one.

Chapters 3, 4 and 5 are all inter-connected. In the twenty five months between February 1974 and March 1976 eighteen innocent people were arrested, charged and imprisoned in Britain in the so called "Irish" cases of the 1970's. The convictions of all eighteen were eventually quashed by the Criminal Division of the Court of Appeal in London. The damage done to the reputation of the British Criminal Justice System is beyond doubt and beyond measure. The traumatic times in which those innocents were convicted must never be allowed to return. One of them, Patrick Maguire, the son of Irish parents from Belfast, was only 13 years of age at the time of his arrest and detention in a London police station. He was questioned by the police in the absence of any appropriate adult, who should have been there to protect his interests. He claimed the police assaulted him and his 16 year old brother whilst both were in custody. If the police had not deliberately and cynically disregarded the Home Office Administrative Directions attached to the Judges' Rules that give a child or young person that right, the truth would have been available to the tribunal of fact in the case. He was charged with other members of his family, including his parents and his brother, with the unlawful possession of nitroglycerine. A trace was said to have been found under the fingernails of his right hand. When he was found guilty by the jury the trial judge ordered him to be detained for four years.

The treatment meted out to him can be compared to that in the case of Victoria Aitken. Her father, Jonathan Aitken, was a former Tory politician in John Major's Government, whose licence to lie was over extended when he claimed that his wife had paid the hotel bill at the Ritz Hotel in Paris in September 1993, when in fact it was paid by an Arab friend. A fact which he wished, as a Government Minster to conceal. On 17 June 1997, in the midst of an action for damages for libel, he procured his daughter Victoria, then aged 17 years, to make a statement that on 16 September 1993 she and her mother drove from Sandwich to Dover, took the ferry to Calais and the train to Paris where they stayed. She knew very well, as he did, that statement was an outright lie, for she and her mother had flown from London's Heathrow Airport directly to Geneva where she was to attend school, and the journey to Paris in the fashion described was entirely false. She was clearly committing a criminal offence and she knew it. When her father was prosecuted and jailed for his lies, the case against Victoria Aitken was dropped. This is quite understandable to lawyers, if not others, since the instigator of the offence was her father and she would not have been involved in its commission but for him. Why did not the same principle apply to Patrick Maguire and his 16 year old brother. If they were involved in any criminal conduct, and I stress that they were not, that would only have come about because of the involvement of others in their family in the same way as Jonathan Aitken involved his daughter.

The year 1974 marked the beginning of the undermining of the trust and belief many had in the fairness and efficacy of the British judicial system. From that year onwards, it became almost common-place in this country for innocent people to be jailed and guilty people to remain free.

After the convictions of the 18 innocents were quashed there began a whispering campaign in the police, political and legal establishment that some, if not all, of the 18 were in fact guilty as charged. These are the 18.

First, there was Judith Ward. She was charged with 12 offences of murder and 3 of causing explosions likely to endanger life or damage property. She was convicted in November 1974 and sentenced to life imprisonment and 30 years imprisonment, those sentences to run concurrently. She remained in prison for 18 years until her release in May 1992. Her case is considered in some detail in Chapter 4.

Next there was the Guildford Four. They are Paul Michael Hill, Gerard Conlon, Patrick Armstrong and Carole Richardson. Their case really begins with the arrest of Paul Hill in November 1974. The detail of his case is set out in Chapter 3, for his was the first arrest and consequent upon that he and Gerard Conlon implicated others. Included in them was a Catholic priest, Father Patrick Carolan, the chaplain and administrator at a Catholic hostel in London used by young Irishmen. Fr. Carolan was taken to Guildford police station and there questioned by the police. He claimed that one of the officers was very rough with him and he told that officer he was the greatest bastard he had ever met. Another policeman later told him that that particular bastard was the only Catholic amongst them. If a priest was likely to treated that way at that time in that place, what hope was there for others equally innocent?

The Four were charged with bombing, on 5 October 1974, the Horse and Groom public house in North Street and the Seven Stars public house in Swan Lane, both in Guildford, and murdering five people. Hill and Armstrong were also charged with bombing, on 7 November 1974 the King's Arms public house in Woolwich where 2 people died. They denied these offences. Whilst in custody awaiting trial for the above matters, Paul Hill was charged on 15 April 1975 with the murder of Brian Shaw in Belfast. That case is examined in Chapter 3 in some detail. After the convictions of the Four the trial judge, Mr. Justice John Donaldson, (described by a journalist as Mrs. Thatcher's favourite judge) mused aloud: "I feel it is my duty to wonder aloud why you were not charged with treason to the Crown, a charge which carries the penalty of death by hanging. A sentence I would have no difficulty in passing in this case." Whether he has ever reflected on those words and his intended consequence, if it had been available to him, of consigning three innocent young men to the lime soaked grave of the prison yard for offences that they admitted, but did not commit, is unknown. (Carole Richardson was only 17 and would have escaped the death penalty by reason of age.)

In July 1990 the legal journalist Joshua Rosenberg wrote in *The Guardian* newspaper that "…behind closed doors senior members of the legal establishment are alleging that the Guildford Four – or some of them – may have been involved in the bombings after all. Even as Lord Lane quashed their convictions, he still believed they were guilty. From conversations I have had with members of the judiciary, I can say that he would not be the only judge to think so…."

The case of the Guildford Four has been well documented in several books about them. Theirs is the classic example of a legal system that thinks it cannot fail and proves constantly and consistently that it can. In October 1977 others, self confessed members of the Provisional IRA, voluntarily admitted on oath in open court to being responsible for the Guildford and Woolwich bombings. They were never charged with those admitted offences, let alone convicted of them. It is an exceedingly strange system which relies on forced and false confessions and then ignores the voluntary profession of the truth.

Paul Hill and Gerard Conlon both implicated the latter's aunt, Anne Maguire in the bombing of the Guildford public houses. She could establish her innocence by proving her movements on 5 October 1974. She, her husband Paddy, her two sons, Patrick and Vincent, her brother, Sean Smyth, brother-in-law Guiseppe Conlon (Gerard's father) and a family friend, Patrick O'Neill, known collectively as the Maguire Seven, were convicted of possession of nitroglycerine under such circumstances as to give rise to a reasonable suspicion that he (or she) did not have in their possession or under their control for a lawful purpose. Their cases too have been well documented. The only evidence against Mrs. Maguire was a minute trace of nitroglycerine on the gloves she used for washing up in the kitchen. The scientists whose evidence helped to convict Judith Ward were destroyed at her appeal hearing. It was their evidence, given at the Maguire Seven trial some months after Judith's conviction, which convicted the Seven. They served their time. They are innocent. Anne and Paddy Maguire were sentenced to 14 years imprisonment, the maximum available. Donaldson made it clear in his worthless homily before passing sentence that he wished it could have been more. Their two sons, Vincent then 17 and Patrick then aged 14, were sent into custody for 5 and 4 years respectively. The three others were also sent into custody for 12 years. Guiseppe Conlon died there. Patrick O'Neill's sentence was reduced to 8 years on appeal. On release he was served with an Exclusion Order under the Prevention of Terrorism Act 1974 which returned him to his native Northern Ireland, branded as a terrorist.

On 21 and 22 November 1974 six innocent men were arrested. They are, John Walker, then aged 40, married with seven children. Noel Richard McIlkenny, then aged 41, married with six children. William (Billy) Power, then aged 30, married with four children. Robert Gerard Hunter, then aged 29, married with 3 children. Hugh Callaghan, then aged 45, married with one child and Patrick (Paddy) Joseph Hill, then aged 30, married with 6 children. Collectively they are known as the Birmingham Six.

They were put on trial between 9 June and 15 August 1975 and were convicted of multiple murder. It is now largely forgotten that they appeared in the dock with three other men, James Kelly then aged 32 and unmarried, Michael Bernard Sheehan, then aged 47, married with four children, and Michael Joseph Murray, a married man with 6 children. The trial judge described him as "a mysterious figure, an isolated figure, a figure who sits by himself."

The Six were charged with bombing two public houses, the Mulberry Bush and the Tavern in the Town, in the centre of the city of Birmingham on the night of 21 November 1974. 21 people died and 162 were injured. There were one hundred witnesses who gave evidence at the trial of the nine accused. I have spoken to some of those involved in the search and rescue of those innocent victims of unjustified terror. Their recollection of their spontaneous attempts to resuscitate the barely living and locate the dead remains undiminished after 30 years.

This case too has been extensively written about, and well documented. On any view was there not something strange about these six family men suddenly, for no apparent reason, taking part in one of the most horrific murder cases of all time? Did someone not pause to think of the clear lack of uniformity in the confession evidence made by four of the Six to be police? The unique method of obtaining confession evidence in some other cases, as well as that of Hugh Callaghan, is examined in Chapter 5 of this book.

In their statements, Power said there were seven plastic bags used, Callaghan said there were six plastic bags, Walker mentioned three parcels (the trial judge said that John Walker was somewhat squeamish about referring to bombs and preferred to call them parcels). McIlkenny said there were four plastic bags. Unbeknown to the Six, but known to the police, was the fact that an unexploded device was discovered on the same night outside Barclays Bank on the Hagley Road, about one mile from the centre of Birmingham. That was placed inside two plastic bags. These were frequently used by the IRA in this way. A scientist told the trial jury however that in his expert opinion plastic bags had not been used to contain the bombs in the case, but they had been placed in some sort of suitcase, brief case or holdall. No identification parades were ever held, though there must have been people inside both public houses who might have seen the actual bombers placing the devices. Six working class men, all of them rather poorly paid, might have attracted attention to themselves if they were carrying briefcases or holdalls in that area on that night.

It was not clear from the confession evidence, all of which was claimed by each individual responsible to have been beaten out of them, who had brought the bombs to the city centre. Power said Walker brought two, Hunter three, McIlkenny one and Callaghan one. Walker said he, Hunter and Hill had one bomb each. McIlkenny said Walker, Hunter and Hill and himself had one bomb each. Power said he alone placed two bombs in the Mulberry Bush; Callaghan said he did it with Hunter. McIlkenny said he placed bombs in the Tavern in the Town with Hill while Walker said he did it with Hunter. He seems to have been able to be in two places almost at the same time.

The Six were charged with 21 offences of murder, and further jointly charged that they, with the remaining three accused, Murray, Sheehan and Kelly, conspired together with James McDade and persons unknown, between 3 August and 30 November 1974, to cause by explosive substances explosions in the United Kingdom of a nature likely to endanger life or to cause serious damage to property. The details of the eleven explosions were listed in Schedule 91A exhibited at the trial.

The evidence against five of the Six on that conspiracy charge was sparse in the extreme, so much so that the trial judge directed the jury that if they acquitted five of the Six, not including John Walker, of the 21 murder charges, then they must also acquit them of the conspiracy charge i.e. all stood or fell together.

This begs the question: why were all nine men tried together? It did help the prosecution in two ways to have a joint trial. First because of the most unusual defence that Kelly was running that he, an Ulster Protestant Unionist, at one time a member of the Orange Order, hated the IRA. He came to Britain at the age of 19 and joined the Army. He deserted because he was not allowed to do the job he thought he was going to be allowed to do. Thereafter he changed his name to Kelly, and made himself out to be from the Republic of Ireland in order to obtain a national insurance number and card.

In May 1974 he met his co-accused Michael Sheehan who told him he was a member of the IRA. He decided to worm his way into Sheehan's confidence, intending at a later stage to infiltrate that organisation and obtain information that he would pass onto the police. He claimed that he was asked to store weapons and at a later stage three men, including two his co-accused Michael Murray and John Walker, whom he knew initially only as "Big John", came to his house with bags containing detonators, ammunition and a pistol. On any view that must have been damning evidence against John Walker, in spite of the fact that Kelly never actually got round to telling the police about these activities until after his arrest on Friday 29 November 1974. He said that he had been on the point of contacting the police on several occasions, but his courage failed him and he did not do so, because he feared reprisals not so much against himself, but against his partner and their children. This seems extraordinary since he stayed silent for a week after the pub bombings in Birmingham, when he must have known that John Walker was amongst those arrested on suspicion of being responsible.

He was convicted, as he was bound to be on his own evidence, on count 23 in the indictment, the unlawful possession of explosives. Sheehan was charged with that offence in count 24, but surprisingly neither Murray nor Walker were charged with that offence. The trial judge made his thinking perfectly clear about the possession charge that Kelly virtually admitted, for he told the jury that if they acquitted him of the conspiracy charge then his guilt on the possession charge was relatively trivial, almost a technical offence and one which would not carry a heavy penalty. The jury took the hint and acquitted him of conspiracy and convicted him on count 23 only. True to his word, the judge imprisoned him for 12 months, which meant his release on the Saturday of the following week because of the time he had spent in custody awaiting trial. His counsel called his conduct "well intentioned foolishness". As noted above, Mrs. Anne Maguire who denied all connection with acts of terrorism and who was convicted on the basis of forensic evidence said to prove the existence of nitroglycerine on her kitchen gloves, was sentenced to 14 years imprisonment.

As for the "isolated" Michael Murray, he really took no part in the trial at all. His counsel asked very few questions in cross-examination and Murray did not give evidence in his own defence. He did one extraordinary thing however. He made an admission in writing that he was a member of the Irish Republican Army. Such an admission defies comprehension. It was not a criminal offence at the relevant time to belong to that terrorist organisation and one wonders why he did it. Its effect was clear. It contaminated the Six in the dock with him, branding them as members of the same organisation to which he said he belonged. He was not charged with the Birmingham pub bombings although on very many occasions he has been accused, and has not publicly denied, that he was one of the bombing team on 21 November 1974. His role, so it is alleged was never proved, was to make the telephone call to a local newspaper giving a coded warning of the planted bombs. Would it not be one of the tragic ironies of this case if, in the event, the police had arrested one of the bombers and not even charged him, whilst at the same time illegally obtaining evidence in order to convict the innocents?

It is clear from the trial transcript that the trial judge was almost beside himself in his admiration for the stance that Murray adopted, which he considered was akin to that of a prisoner of war. He told the jury, most unusually, that he had contemplated stopping the case against him altogether. When the jury convicted Murray of conspiracy to cause explosions they were then told something the judge knew all the time, that he was serving a 12 year term of imprisonment for a separate similar conspiracy. In this case he was sentenced to nine years in prison, that sentence to run concurrently with the existing sentence, which meant that he would not have to serve a day longer in prison as a result of that second trial. Compare the situation of a self confessed member of a violent terrorist organisation, already convicted of terrorist offences and serving a long sentence of imprisonment, who gets 9 years for another equally serious offence, with that of a woman aged 39, of good character, with no connection with, or convictions for terrorism, respectable and hard working with three part time jobs, married with four children, the youngest of whom was only 9 years of age, who was imprisoned for 14 years for a lesser offence, as Anne Maguire was.

The Six appealed against their convictions and sentence. The other three men jointly tried with them did not appeal. There were four grounds. First, that the trial judge displayed excessive hostility towards their case and gave a clear indication of his view of the facts and the witnesses as to deprive the jury of the chance to form an independent opinion. Second, that he overstepped the bounds of his judicial function in his criticism of certain defence witnesses, including a doctor and forensic scientist. (He described the doctor as "a most unsatisfactory and evasive witness".) Third, that he failed to sum up the six men's cases adequately on the scientific evidence and also on the evidence of the doctor about injuries that he said he found on them. Fourth, that he wrongly allowed certain witnesses to be called by the prosecution in rebuttal.

Their application came before the court on 30 March 1976. The three judges were Lord Widgery, the Lord Chief Justice of England and Wales from 1971 to 1980, Mr. Justice Thompson, a dour Scotsman known to some lawyers as "the wee scruple", and Mr. Justice Lawton, a former member of the British Union of Fascists and supporter of the racist agitator Sir Oswald Moseley. Widgery, a former brigadier in the British Army, had presided over the Bloody Sunday Inquiry into the shootings in Derry on 30 January 1972 where 14 innocent people died. Some claim that as a result of that inquiry, where he exonerated the Parachute Regiment from blame, that he gave his name to a new word in the English language. To "widger" is to "whitewash". (According to the journalist Joshua Rosenberg, Widgery was very ill towards the end of his judicial career, suffering from the early stages of a degenerative nervous disease that got so bad that he could no longer cope with his judicial work. When he spoke he did so in a barely audible voice, and tended to fall asleep in court in the midst of a case. For at least a year, lawyers and fellow judges closed ranks in order to protect him. On occasions those judges who sat with him in court had to write his judgments for him. For some considerable time before he resigned he was visibly and distressingly half senile).

Few expected much sympathy for the Six from this Court of Appeal. The Six had complained that they were badly beaten by the police and by prison officers at Winson Green prison in Birmingham when they were remanded in custody there by the court shortly after their arrests. Lord Widgery's treatment of their allegations of brutality is worthy of note. He said there was no evidence that the men had experienced knocking about "beyond the ordinary". Just how far police officers were allowed to go before their ill-treatment of suspects in custody became "extraordinary" was not set out by the Lord Chief Justice of England and Wales.

On 10 June 1976, 14 prison officers from Winson Green faced trial on charges of assaulting the Six at that prison. The Six gave evidence of the assaults upon them. The 14 defendants exercised their right to stay silent and did not give evidence in their own defence. They did however make unsworn statements from the dock saying they had seen violence used, but denied using it themselves. They did not wish to implicate others not before the court and they might have been compelled to do so if they gave sworn evidence from the witness box and been subject to cross examination. To the surprise of no one, since

15

it was said that the Six were bombers who had made lying accusations against the police to explain their "true" confessions, all 14 were acquitted by the jury. The result seems to indicate that the Six were assaulted at the prison, but not by the men charged with doing so, but by others. Why, it must be asked, were those others not identified and charged?

A most interesting insight into the case of the Birmingham Six was given by the Labour MP Chris Mullen, in the House of Commons on 27 February 1996. He was the former journalist whose untiring and unselfish dedication to the pursuit of truth led to the quashing of their convictions in 1991. He told the House that no less than some "2,000 statements judged by the West Midlands police to be non-material simply disappeared." In the light of what is known now about them, that seems to be quite significant.

He went on to relate how in November 1975, four months after the Six were sentenced to life imprisonment, and while their appeals against convictions were pending, a number of genuine members of the IRA in Birmingham were arrested, and at least one of them gave the police a detailed account of the organisation in that city, including names of those involved in terrorism. He gave the police the name of a man said to be one of those who placed the bombs in the pubs. The Special Branch compiled a long witness statement from the man. That remained in police archives until 1990, when someone sent a copy of it to Granada Television. They, with Mr Mullen, had made a documentary about the case. He described how at the 1991 Appeal Court hearing when the Six were freed, that amongst the documents disclosed was a statement from a scientist, a colleague of Dr. Frank Skuse, who had obtained a positive test on a swab from the hand of a passenger on the Liverpool to Belfast Ferry on the same night that five of the Birmingham Six had been tested by Dr. Skuse following their detention at Heysham. The Liverpool passenger had been released after he was found to have been innocently contaminated. If that statement had not been concealed it would have made a significant impact on the prosecution's case against the Six. The Attorney-General, in a letter dated 17 May 1991, told Mr. Mullen that "it is most probable that an oversight or administrative error was responsible for what was undoubtedly a most unfortunate error". There may be some who believe this was not a deliberately concealed piece of relevant evidence, I am not one of them.

It is also my view that the Birmingham pub bombings were not a spontaneous response to the death of James McDade, but was planned because of the significance of the date, 21 November, in republican folklore and to coincide with the anniversary of the events of 54 years previously. (The date of September 11, so highly emotionally charged in modern American history because of the bombings of the Twin Towers in New York in 2001, is the anniversary date of the regime change in Chile when they engineered the removal from office of the democratically elected President Allende).

On the morning of 21 November 1920, a Sunday, a group especially selected and trained, taking orders from the Irish leader Michael Collins, visited 8 different addresses in Dublin and there shot 19 intelligence officers, in what was to be called the first "Bloody Sunday". The victims were collectively known as the Cairo Gang because of their experience in the Middle East theatre during World War 1. Following those killings, the military response was swift and brutal.

In the afternoon of that same day various Army units, including the Auxiliaries and the Black and Tans and officers of the Royal Irish Constabulary, surrounded and then forcibly entered Croke Park, the headquarters of the Gaelic Athletic Association. A football match was taking place between Dublin and Tipperary at the time. Without warning the Army opened fire inside the crowded stadium, killing 12 people and injuring 60. Amongst the dead was one of the Tipperary team, Michael Hogan from Grangemockler. Hundreds were crushed in the panic that followed the shooting. The State's explanation, just as it was in Derry on 30 January 1972 was that the Army was fired on first and was only returning fire. In both instances, the Army suffered not one single casualty. What suffered most of all was the Truth.

At the conclusion of the trial when the Birmingham Six were convicted and imprisoned for life, the judge sent for two senior police officers, the Chief Constable of Lancashire, Stanley Parr (five of the Six had been arrested in Heysham by his officers) and the Assistant Chief Constable of the West Midlands police, Harry Robinson. He commended them both saying that the investigations were carried out with scrupulous propriety by all your officers. Whether he still considers that to be the case in the light of the subsequent activities of the West Midland Serious Crimes Squad, many of whom were at the forefront of the case against the Birmingham Six, remains unclear.

The congratulations heaped upon the head of Stanley Parr did not linger for too long. In March 1977 he was suspended as Chief Constable on full pay whilst Sir Douglas Osmond, the then Chief Constable of Hampshire, carried out an investigation into an allegation made by a Blackpool police officer, Sergeant Harry Roby, that Parr had misused his position to show favours to certain individuals. Further allegations were made that he had given preferential treatment to his friends accused of road traffic offences such as speeding and illegal parking.

The most serious allegation of all however was that Stanley Parr had altered a charge brought against a motorist whose car had mounted the pavement, killing two young mothers, on the main Blackpool to Preston Road. That happened in August 1975 and whether if was before or after the trial judge commended Parr is not known to me.

The Report of Sir Douglas Osmond was never published. After its receipt however, Stanley Parr was dismissed from his post as Chief Constable of the Lancashire police in January 1978. He was as rotten and corrupt as some of the officers who served under him.

This book may make uncomfortable reading for some. If it does, it will have served one useful purpose. In it, I have striven for accuracy and truth, for Justice deserves nothing less. No one should be afraid of the truth, except the purveyors of lies.

Throughout my life I have kept at the forefront of my mind the following words written by Pastor Niemoeller, a victim of the Holocaust. I commend them to those who do not agree with this book or its contents, and would prefer that I remain silent.

"First they came for the Communists and I did not speak out,
because I was not a Communist.
Then they came for the Jews and I did not speak out,
because I was not a Jew.
Then they came for the Trade Unionists and I did not speak out,
Because I was not a Trade Unionist.
Next they came for the Catholics and I did not speak out,
Because I was not a Catholic.
Then they came for me,
And there was no one left to speak out for me."

CHAPTER 1

LET'S SHOOT THE WOMEN

On 26 August 1994 the *Nottingham Evening Post* newspaper stated under the heading "Judge's terrorist comments trigger fury" that the former Old Bailey judge Michael Argyle Q.C. urged that Northern Ireland security forces be allowed to come out with all guns blazing to deal with terrorists. This was with reference to an article written by him under the title "Let our guns speak" and submitted to the *Belfast Telegraph* obviously with a view to publication by that newspaper. Having regard to the content and its purpose, they declined to do so. Apparently Argyle, who lived in Nottingham at the time, then decided to publicise his views in his local paper instead and they printed some, if not all, of what he had written.

His self-description is self-explanatory: "A Conservative and Unionist who was defending the actions of the security forces in the Province". He wrote: "The terrorists are the enemy" – in itself that is something most would regard as not being a very profound statement, but he added "there are not many of them and they must be met, fought upon their own ground, if necessary by using their own methods, beaten and crushed. The terrorists could not long survive without the active support of their womenfolk. These women who applaud and congratulate their men and their supreme courage in murdering children, nurses, ex-servicemen, OAPs and so on are also every bit as much the enemy as their men, and must be treated as such". What he meant was clear: shoot to kill any woman in Northern Ireland who could be regarded, presumably by him and others like him, as supporters of terrorists. So much for the rule of law in his simplistic view of life.

When Alex Atwood, at the time the SDLP councillor for West Belfast, was told of his published comments he said that Argyle was "ignorant, dangerous and reckless".

The families of the innocent women, none of whom were Conservatives and Unionists, and who were shot in Northern Ireland in the circumstances now described may well agree with that description of him.

Maire Drumm was aged 57 years at the time of her murder. She was a mother of five children; she held sincere but strong political views. She shared those views with her husband Jimmy. She had at one time been the vice president of Provisional Sinn Fein. She was a strong believer in community politics. When, at the outset of the Troubles, the British Army, acting without any legal authority whatever, imposed a curfew on a large part of the Lower Falls Road area in West Belfast from 10 p.m. on Saturday 3 July 1970 until 9 a.m. on the following Monday 5 July in order to carry out house to house searches, Maire Drumm marched down the Lower Falls Road at the head of a procession of hundreds of women carrying food, mostly bread, piled up in prams. The soldiers, not knowing what to do, simply looked on as the curfew was broken. It is widely accepted now that as a consequence of the violent and vicious conduct of some elements of the Army over that first weekend in July, especially that of the Black Watch Regiment, which brought to Northern Ireland all the violent sectarian loathing and hatred which surrounded and sustained them in their native Scotland, that the British Army entirely lost and never recovered the sympathy and support of the Catholics and Nationalists in Belfast and throughout the North of Ireland from that date onwards.

On 10 December 1974, almost three weeks after the Birmingham public house bombings in which 21 people died and 160 were injured, she and other republicans had taken part in a meeting in Feakle, County Clare in the Irish Republic, with eight Protestant clergymen who had put forward a plan to end the violence throughout the Island of Ireland and Britain. That meeting broke up in some disarray when the Special Branch of the Irish police, an Garda Siochana, arrived at the scene. Although the personal contacts were found to be useful, no agreement was reached about anything.

Sometime in 1976 Mrs. Drumm was told that she was in urgent need of medical treatment on cataracts in both her eyes and that failure to receive it would result in the loss of her sight. She sought a visa from the American Government to travel to the United States to receive the required treatment there. It is said, without any hard evidence, that the British Government lobbied against her being granted a visa, and in the event it was refused.

Although she was fearful of entering any hospital in Northern Ireland, but even more fearful of the consequences if she did not, and no doubt with a sense of foreboding and apprehension, she decided first to make a will in favour of her family and she then went into the Mater Hospital on the Crumlin Road in Belfast. Late in the evening of 28 October 1976 a British Army unit which had been surrounding the hospital was discreetly withdrawn. No explanation for that course of conduct has ever been given. Just before 10. 30 p.m. Maire Drumm was in a small room next to Ward 38 on the second floor of the hospital when two men wearing white laboratory coats and armed with a revolver, entered the building. They knew exactly where to find their victim, they needed to speak to no one seeking her whereabouts, but went immediately to the second floor. It is likely that Mrs. Drumm never saw her killers as one of them shot her three times in the chest from point blank range. She died almost immediately. There was not a hint of condemnation of the conduct of those cold blooded killers anywhere in the British press that reported her brutal murder. One London newspaper, the *Daily Mirror*, described them as "an execution squad".

Was this the kind of conduct the former judge Michael Argyle had in mind when he wrote "let our guns speak" in the *Nottingham Evening Post*?

Another women shot dead in equally horrific circumstances was Mrs. Miriam Daly, a lecturer at Queen's University Belfast. Considering the discriminatory policy of that University, exercised over many years and ultimately costing the British tax payer many thousands of pounds in compensation when those discriminated against won damages at various tribunal hearings, it is a tribute to her immense talent that she was employed there at all, notwithstanding that (a) she was a Catholic, (b) she was a Republican, i.e. she wanted to be Irish in Ireland and (c) she was a woman.

Miriam and her husband were devoted to their adopted children, Donal and Marie, who were at the time only ten years of age. On the afternoon of 26 June 1980 she received word that the security forces were engaged in a sweep though the nationalist area of Andersonstown in West Belfast where the family lived. Since her husband was away from home on that day, and because of the political tension at the time on account of the efforts of the National H-Blocks committee to obtain political status for prisoners in Long Kesh and elsewhere in Northern Ireland, Mrs. Daly decided to return home. She was known to be alive at about 2 o'clock in the afternoon when she called at a small shop to buy a load of bread.

Just after 3 o'clock her daughter Marie reached the house and found her mother lying face down in the hallway. There was blood everywhere. Miriam's hands and feet had been tied, probably to a chair. A pillow had been used to deaden the sounds of the six shots fired into her face and head at point blank range. The gun used was a 9mm semi automatic pistol, the standard issue small firearm used by the British Army. The telephone line had been so manipulated that it could still take incoming calls, but it was not possible to make an outgoing call on that telephone, so if she had wanted, or even tried, to seek outside help from anyone by its use, she could not have done so. No one telephoning the house would have appreciated that something there might be wrong.

It must take a special kind of deep pathological hatred to kill a defenceless woman in the circumstances in which Maire Drumm and Miriam Daly died. In both cases the killers arrived at, and departed from, the death scene where only a short time previously the security forces had been present in some numbers, yet they apparently saw no one or heard nothing in connection with either murder. There exists a haunting picture of Marie and Donal Daly clutching large wreathes in their tiny hands standing near their Mother's coffin on the day of her funeral. This scene has been replayed many times over in Northern Ireland, as the tears of the children fail to soften the hearts of the heartless.

When Mrs. Drumm was buried in Belfast the *Sun* newspaper in London published a picture of her two weeping daughters, with the caption "the bitter harvest of hate that was sown by Maire Drumm is reaped by her two grieving daughters". There cannot be too many occasions when the victim of an horrific murder is blamed for the grief of her surviving family.

Bernadette Devlin McAliskey was born in Cookstown, County Tyrone into a staunchly Catholic family. Her father, a carpenter, was branded a political suspect and was unable to get work. Bernadette became a political activist at Queen's University Belfast. In 1969 she was elected as the Independent Unity Candidate for Mid Ulster, to the

House of Commons at the age of 21 years. Neither her political philosophy, nor her cause of a United Socialist Ireland endeared her to her Parliamentary enemies, of whom there were many, and not always to her friends, of whom there were few. She remained in the House until her defeat in the General Election in February 1974.

On the morning of Friday 16 January 1981 she was at her home in Derryloughan near Coalisland in County Tyrone, getting her three young children ready for school when three men broke down the back door with a sledge hammer. They were also armed with a ·38 revolver and a 9mm semi-automatic pistol. One man shot her husband Michael four times as he tried to bar their progress in the kitchen; another went to the bedroom where Bernadette was dressing the children. She moved the three of them back to the far wall of the bedroom and faced her attacker without flinching. He fired eight shots at her at point blank range. He only stopped firing when the magazine of the 9mm gun was exhausted.

All three men, Andrew Watson, aged 25, Thomas Graham, aged 38, and Raymond Smallwoods, aged 31, ran from the house towards a waiting car. They never reached it, for these three armed men ran straight into the arms of four members of the SAS who were waiting for them outside. Not a shot was fired during the arrests by the Army. It later emerged that the four soldiers had been dug into a hide in a copse near the house. They left the scene quickly with their captives. They claimed their radios were inoperative and as the telephone wires at the house had been cut, they were unable to summon help for the grievously wounded McAliskeys inside it.

In a book *Biting the Bullet* by Jenny Simpson, the author describes her husband, an SAS soldier, being ordered from Belfast to County Tyrone the night before the attempted murders to cover Bernadette Devlin McAliskey "because the police had been given a tip off that Loyalist paramilitaries might be planning to make a move on her". That may account for the presence of the soldiers at the time but it does not explain why they did not detain the three gunmen before they entered the house, rather than when they were leaving it. In the event, soldiers from the locally based Argyll and Sutherland Highlanders arrived shortly afterwards at the house and saved the lives of Michael and Bernadette Devlin McAliskey. Andrew Watson, who fired the shots at Bernadette, was a former member of the Ulster Defence Regiment which, before its demise, was the largest Infantry Regiment in the British Army.

Mairead Farrell was only 31 years of old when she died. She was shot dead in Gibraltar at about 3. 42 in the afternoon of Sunday 6 March 1988. She once said "I am a socialist and I am a Republican. I believe in a united Ireland; a united socialist Ireland, definitely socialist. Capitalism provides no answer at all for our people, and I think that is the Brits main interest in Ireland".

She was born on the Stewartstown Road area of West Belfast, the only girl in a family of six children. Neither of her parents were involved in politics, but her maternal grandfather had been a Republican and interned without trial in Ballinamore, County Leitrim in the Irish Republic by the British. She was regarded by her teachers as a bright and well behaved student at the Rathmore Catholic grammar school in Dunmurry, on the outskirts of the city. She was aged 15 years at the time of the Bloody Sunday shootings in Derry, where the British Army opened fire on a peaceful anti-internment demonstration, killing 14 civilians. She later said that it was the images from Derry that confirmed what she saw as her future. She joined the Provisional IRA. She was the first woman to be imprisoned after the abolition of political status for prisoners in 1976, after her conviction for planting a suitcase bomb in the dining room of the Conway Hotel in Dunmurry on 6 April 1976. She was caught whilst leaving the premises. Two men were with her at the time. One of them, Sean McDermott, was shot dead by the RUC during the incident. The other, Kieran Doherty, later died in jail on 2 August 1981 after 73 days on hunger strike. He had been elected to the Irish Parliament in Dublin on 11 June 1981 for the Cavan-Monaghan constituency.

After a trial that lasted only one day Mairead Farrell was sentenced to fourteen years imprisonment. (The sentence in her case can be compared and contrasted with those passed in the cases of Colin Doak, aged 19, a deserter from the Royal Air Force, William Orr, aged 21 and Stephen Watson, aged 23, both natives of Lurgan in County Armagh. They were also former members of the Ulster Defence Regiment. Any attempt to discover the date of their departure from the Army, which departure enabled the authorities to describe them as former members, rather than serving members, is inevitably met with a stonewalling silence. These three killers had spent the evening of Easter Sunday 3 April, 1983 drinking in Lurgan when one of them suggested they should go out and beat up a Catholic. At about 1.15 a.m. they randomly alighted upon John McConville, a 22 year old

Catholic on his way home after an evening out. He was stopped not far from his home on a predominately Catholic housing estate, set upon and ferociously assaulted. A crash helmet wielded by one of the three was used in the attack, breaking the victim's jaw. The assault was accompanied by shouts of "fenian bastard".

On 11 January 1984 all three were convicted of manslaughter at Belfast Crown Court after the prosecution had accepted pleas of not guilty to murder but guilty to manslaughter. Doak was jailed for five years, Orr for seven and Watson for five years. Apart from the fact that if the roles had been reversed, and the Catholic had killed the RAF deserter and the two former soldiers thereby making it more likely that he would have been convicted of murder and sentenced to life imprisonment, what was it about Mairead Farrell's criminal conduct where no person died that attracted fourteen years imprisonment, when in the case of a brutal and premeditated killing of an innocent, the killers receive a sentence substantially less than that imposed upon her?).

On Mairead Farrell's release from prison in 1986 she decided to resume her studies and enrolled as a student to read for a B.A. degree in politics and economics at Queen's University, Belfast. She did not however sever her links with the Republican movement. She was now 29 years of age.

She was a member of an IRA Active Service Unit and the first woman to die "on active service" in 12 years.

In March 1988 Mairead was in the British Colony of Gibraltar, on the southern tip of Spain, with at least two others in order to plan the commission of a most terrible and unjustified atrocity against the British Army stationed there. Two men, Sean Savage and Daniel McCann were also shot dead at the same time in the same area as she was. Mairead Farrell and Daniel McCann were walking together past a Shell petrol station approaching the border crossing between Gibraltar and Spain when they were shot dead by members of the SAS. Two bullets hit Miss Farrell in the face. She had a bullet exit wound in the back of her neck and below her left ear. As she began to turn and fall to the ground she was shot again, three times, in the middle of her back. Her heart and liver were pulped, her spinal column was fractured. Two litres of blood flooded into her chest cavity. The bullets exited in the region of her left breast. One pathologist thought that she might have been conscious after being hit for a maximum of 10 or 15 seconds but she would have been stunned and bewildered.

Daniel McCann was shot twice, once in the face and then in the top of the head causing multiple fractures, laceration of the left cerebral hemisphere and extensive brain damage. Two more bullets in his back caused damage to his liver, heart and left lung. Sean Savage heard the shots and broke into a run pursued by at least one soldier. He opened fire and Sean Savage was hit by between 16 and 18 bullets, resulting in a total of twenty seven wounds He had a broken arm and extensive brain damage and multiple fractures to the skull.

It was the joint intention of these three to plan to place a bomb in a car in a parking space on a side street known as Ince's Hall about one hundred yards from the residence of the Governor of the Colony, and where on Tuesday mornings the band of the Royal Anglian Regiment assembled before and after the changing of the guard ceremonies. The whole of the parking area is overlooked by a set of buildings at the end of the yard, one of which is a branch of Hambro's Bank. Officers of the Gibraltar police watched from the window of the Bank as a white Renault car was driven into the area and parked by Sean Savage. It is a fact that Hambro's Bank has close links with the security services in Britain. One of its chair persons, Sir Charles Hambro, had been the head of the Special Operations Executive during World War II and has worked for the security intelligence agency M.I.6.

Later that Sunday afternoon, at 4.45 p.m., the Ministry of Defence in London issued a statement saying "a suspected bomb has been found in Gibraltar and three suspects have been shot by civilian police." By 9 p.m. there was a change of detail. A further statement recounted: "security forces were involved in the shootings and military personnel dealt with a suspected bomb". It was a variation on the detail of the first statement and was equally untrue.

On BBC radio the following morning in the *Today* programme on Radio 4, Ian Stewart, the Armed Forces Minister in the Conservative and Unionist Government headed by Margaret Thatcher said that a car bomb had been found in Gibraltar and had been defused. That statement was false. The presenter of the programme Peter Hobday spoke live on air to the BBC's correspondence in Gibraltar, Joe Paley. He said "tell me about the bomb which was finally defused. What sort of damage would it have done, had it gone off during the parade on Tuesday?" Mr. Paley replied, "It would have done an enormous amount of damage. It was something like five hundred pounds of explosives, packed with bits of metal, shrapnel and so on." The British newspapers repeated that falsehood; all eleven national daily newspapers reported the existence of the bomb, and eight of them quantified the bomb as being 500 lbs of explosives, one described it as being 440 lbs and another as 400 lbs. The *Sun* newspaper, dedicated to accuracy as always, described it as a "massive car bomb". Some of the newspapers reported that the three people who had been shot were armed and that there had been a shoot-out before they died. *Independent Television News* said "a fierce gun battle broke out".

On Monday 7 March 1988 the then Foreign Secretary Sir Geoffrey Howe Q.C. made a short statement in the House of Commons. He said that he was confident that the House will wish him to extend the British Government's gratitude to the Spanish authorities, without whose invaluable assistance the outcome might have been very different. He also told the House that "shortly before 1 p.m. yesterday afternoon, one of those subsequently shot brought a white Renault car into Gibraltar and was seen to park it in the area where the band for the guard mounting ceremony assembles. Before leaving the car he was seen to spend some time making adjustments in the vehicle. An hour and a half later, the two others subsequently shot were seen to enter Gibraltar on foot, and shortly before 3 p.m. joined the third terrorist in the town. Their presence and actions near the parked Renault car gave rise to the strong suspicion that it contained a bomb, which appeared to be corroborated by a rapid technical examination of the car. About 3. 30 p.m. all three left the scene and started to walk back towards the border. On their way towards the border, they were challenged by the security forces. When challenged they made movements which led the military personnel operating in support of the Gibraltar police to conclude that their own lives and the lives of others were under threat. In the light of this response they were shot. Those killed were subsequently found not to be carrying arms. The parked Renault car was subsequently dealt with by a military bomb disposal team. It has now been established that it did not contain an explosive device".

In a very short space of time there had been a fundamental change in the facts. It was now admitted at the highest level for the first time that the three dead were unarmed and there was no bomb in the car in Inch's Hall.

The killings raised more questions than answers. One thing is however quite clear. The security forces and their political masters knew in advance of the plan to bomb Gibraltar, when it was to take place, and who was involved in doing it, for the three deceased had been betrayed by an informer within the Provisional IRA.

Jack Holland is a distinguished Irish journalist who was asked by Susan Phoenix to write the biography of her late husband, Ian. He died on 2 June 1994 in a helicopter crash on the Mull of Kintyre in Scotland, with 29 others, mostly members of the Intelligence services serving in Northern Ireland. Holland and his wife were on friendly terms with Ian and Susan Phoenix, although they were given the impression that he was a hearing aid salesman or something similar. It was not until after his death that they discovered the truth that in fact Ian Phoenix was a Detective Superintendent in the Royal Ulster Constabulary.

In their book, *Policing the Shadows* (at page 198) the joint authors claim that on the evening of 26 August 1987 Daniel McCann and Sean Savage, accompanied by a third man, walked into the Liverpool Bar on Donegal Quay in the dockside area of Belfast and there shot dead two Special Branch police officers, Detective Constable Ernest Stanley Carson, aged 50, married with two children, and Michael Philip Malone, aged 35, also married with two children. A detective sergeant who was with them was shot and wounded but survived his injuries. A customer who was playing pool in the Bar was also wounded. The book then makes this further astonishing claim. "The police had discovered earlier (thanks to Operation Sedative, perhaps,) that McCann and Savage were to be involved in an even bigger operation – a bombing attack in Gibraltar using a massive quantity of the Semtex that PIRA had so recently acquired from Colonel Gaddafi. Also involved in the plot were two women members of the Provisionals – Mairead Farrell and another who had been under surveillance by the police since about 1983." If the claim is true that McCann and Savage were the killers who had left at the scene at least two eye witnesses who might have identified them, one is bound to ask why they were not arrested, charged and put on trial for a double murder. It might also explain why they were both shot dead in Gibraltar on 6 March 1988 in such disputed circumstances if someone had decided that in their case the death penalty should be carried out without the necessity of calling evidence and proving guilt.

It is clear that the United Kingdom, Spanish and Gibraltar authorities knew that the Provisional IRA were planning a terrorist attack on Gibraltar. They also knew who was to be involved – Sean Savage, Daniel McCann and Mairead Farrell. According to *Policing the Shadows* they had this information before 26 August 1987. In order to ensure that the authorities rather than the terrorists could dictate the timetable of events, it was decided that the usual Tuesday guard changing ceremonies should be cancelled whilst a small guardhouse in front of the Governor's Residence, known as the Convent, was repainted. The parade was not held on 8 December 1987 and only resumed on 23 February 1988 when it was announced that the ceremony would take place as usual on subsequent Tuesdays. Eleven weeks to repaint a small building seems an extraordinarily long time, but its effect was clear – without the parade taking place, neither would the planned bombing. The journalist David McKittrick, long recognised as the most authoritative modern writer on the Northern Ireland Troubles wrote in his book *Lost Lives* that even before the announcement of the resumption of the band parades, which some may regard as baiting the trap, that a nine men and two women surveillance team, probably members of MI5 had been using a hotel in Gibraltar since 19 February and members of the SAS arrived on the Rock and stayed at the same hotel from 26 February 1988.

Sometime prior to 4 March 1988 Joseph Canepa, the Gibraltar Commissioner of Police formed an advisory group with his Acting Deputy, George Colombo and a Special Branch Detective, Chief Inspector Ullger, a number of security service officers and at least three members of the SAS. The Ministry of Defence in London had already briefed the SAS and issued them with military rules of engagement for the Military Commander in Operation Flavius. The purpose of the SAS being in Gibraltar was to assist the police there to arrest the IRA active service unit should the police request such military intervention. The SAS were instructed to operate as directed by the Commissioner.

The rules of engagement specified the circumstances in which use of force by the SAS would be permissible. They were not to use force at all unless requested to do so by the senior police officer designated by the Commissioner, or unless it was necessary to do so in order to protect life. Even then, no more force could be used than was necessary to protect life.

The SAS could open fire against a person if they had reasonable grounds for believing that a suspect was currently committing, or about to commit, an action which was likely to endanger life, and there was no other way to prevent this. A warning need not be given if to do so, or a delay in doing so, could lead to the death or injury of any person, or if the giving of a warning was clearly impracticable. In other circumstances than that, a warning was necessary before firing, and it was to be as clear as possible and to include a direction to surrender and that fire will be opened if the direction was not obeyed.

On Friday 4 March 1988 the three members of the active service unit were seen in Spain by the authorities. That information was relayed onwards to Gibraltar. Mairead Farrell had left Belfast two days earlier and flew from Dublin to Brussels, arriving in Malaga on the Costa Del Sol on the Friday. She used the names Mary Johnson and Katherine Alison Smith, using false documents, on the flights. Sean Savage was driven to Dublin and whilst en route the car was stopped by an Army patrol. He could have been detained there on suspicion of the two murders mentioned above, assuming he was involved at all, but he was not detained but allowed to go on his way. He and Daniel McCann, both using false names and documents, flew from Dublin to Paris and then onwards to Malaga arriving there on the Friday also. They motored down to Torremolinos and it is probable that the three met up and stayed in a hotel on the Costa Del Sol.

They did not of course know it, but the next day, Saturday 5 March, the Commissioner draw up an operational order stating that it was suspected that a terrorist attack was planned in Gibraltar and the target was highly probably the band and guard of the Royal Anglian Regiment during a ceremonial changing of the guard at Inch's Hall on 8 March. The method to be used was by means of explosives, probably a car bomb. The objectives of the plan and the intention of the civil and military authorities were fourfold. First, to protect life. Second, to foil the attempt. Third, to arrest the offenders. Fourth, the securing and safe custody of the prisoners. It was stressed that minimum force was to be used during the arrest, the offenders were to be disarmed and evidence was to be gathered for a court trial. Also included, as an annexe to the order, were the firearms rules of engagement and a guide to the use of firearms by the police.

Because of the wealth of information known about the Provisional IRA's planned bombing, the time, the place and the personnel involved (their photographs were shown to those present) and the fact a car bomb was to be employed, an evacuation plan was drawn up and prepared on 5 March by Chief Inspector Lopez. It had been written by Chief Superintendent McGuinness and typed up by himself. Both officers had been told by the police Commissioner, Mr Canepa, that there was to be a suspected terrorist attack by car bomb and only the three of them knew about the evacuation plan. It was to be put into effect on Monday the 7th or Tuesday the 8th March. It included arrangements to evacuate and cordon off the area around Ince's Hall for a radius of some 200 metres. The roads to be closed were noted and any consequent diversion of traffic detailed, and the personnel to carry out these tasks were identified. For reasons that have not been explained however, this plan was not distributed to other police officers.

All these matters were raised at a briefing held by the Commissioner very late in the evening of Saturday 5 March for the SAS, the security services and a number of his own officers, including Detective Constable Viagas. Mr. Capena explained the rules of engagement and firearms procedure, covered the intelligence aspects of the operation and emphasised to his officers the importance of gathering evidence for a subsequent trial of the terrorists. The head of the surveillance team outlined their role. The meeting was told that the three terrorists were dangerous and would almost certainly be armed and likely to use their weapons in a confrontation with the security forces.

It was known that a car would be used to convey a bomb into Gibraltar and the possibility that a "blocking" car would be used was considered but thought unlikely. That would involve using another vehicle not containing the bomb to get a space in Ince's Hall, remove it and replace it with the car which did contain the bomb. It seemed to have been the view of Chief Inspector Lopez, who for some inexplicable reason was not present at this briefing, that he would not have conveyed the bomb in on a Tuesday since it would be busy and difficult to find a parking space on that day. The security forces however considered that the terrorists would not make two trips in separate vehicles, and that parking spaces would be available on Monday night or Tuesday morning.

Three possible methods of detonation of the bomb were discussed. The Senior Security Services Officer present at the briefing took the view that a remote control device was most likely to be used, rather than a timing device or a command wire. That failed to take into account the fact that there was effectively only one way in and one way out of Gibraltar, across the wide landing strip of the Colony's airport and runway and then through two sets of adjacent crossing points, one manned by the Spanish and the other by the Gibraltar police. Nothing could be easier than to seal off that border and anyone attempting to get through following the detonation of an explosive device would face the utmost difficulty. The SAS were however convinced that it was made clear to them that it was thought to be virtually certain, at this briefing and elsewhere, that any one of the three terrorists could be carrying a device, a button, which would enable them to detonate the bomb. So much so that at a later stage (at the inquest) one soldier admitted that there were discussions amongst his colleagues and himself that there was more chance that they would have to shoot to kill in view of the very short time factor which a "button job" would impose. The SAS were warned that the suspects were highly dangerous, dedicated and fanatical. At least one of them was led to believe that the equipment that the IRA had was capable of detonating a radio controlled bomb over a distance of a mile and a half.

The recollection of some of the police at the briefing differs. Some thought that both a timer and a remote control device were being discussed. The Commissioner and his Acting Deputy thought that they should expect either type of device. Chief Inspector Ullger, on the other hand, recollected that there was specific mention of the fact that the most likely method to be used was the remote control device. The officers who made up the surveillance group agreed with him.

There is strong evidence that on the morning of Saturday 5 March Sean Savage hired a white Renault 5 car from Avis Car Rentals in Torremolinos. Either on that day, or perhaps on the previous day, Friday, a red Ford Fiesta car was hired, also in Torremolinos, by a person whose true identity is not known. That vehicle was used to collect 141 lbs of Semtex-h explosives and at some stage they were transferred into the white Ford Fiesta hired by Mairead Farrell on the Saturday evening and collected by her from the car hire company, the Marbessol Agency in Marbella on the Sunday morning. The white Fiesta car was found by Spanish police in an underground car park in Marbella at 6 p.m. on Tuesday 8 March, two days after the shootings in Gibraltar. Officers of the Malaga bomb disposal squad discovered five packages of Sextex explosives in the spare wheel compartment of the vehicle. Four detonators were attached and packed around them were 200 rounds of ammunition. There were two timing devices, not primed or connected. This had not been "a button job".

Sean Savage drove the white Renault car down the coastal road from Malaga to Gibraltar on Sunday 6 March 1988. Mairead Farrell and Daniel McCann used the red Fiesta to drive down the Spanish mainland until they reached the border with Gibraltar. They left the vehicle in La Linea some short distance away and started to walk towards the border crossing. The London *Times* newspaper reported two days later that "Spanish security forces kept track of three cars used by the IRA squad and passed on the information to the British. On the Rock, the SAS team watched as a terrorist went across the border in a white Renault 5." The London *Independent* said on the same day that the Spanish police tailed the Renault right up to the gate, and Spanish security services confirmed that fact on a number of occasions. According to Roger Bolton, the broadcaster and Editor of the programme *This Week,* there was much confirmation of this and it was set out in a documentary about this case entitled *Death on The Rock* transmitted by the Independent Television Company, Thames Television on 28 April 1988. In his book named after his programme, Roger Bolton relates how the television journalist Julian Manyon and the London *Times* journalist Harry Debelius interviewed Augustin Valladolid in Madrid on 21 March 1988. He was at the time spokesman for the Spanish Security Services. He confirmed to the journalists that the white Renault 5 car was under Spanish surveillance all the way down the coast road until its arrival in Gibraltar. He states that the newspaper journalist recorded the meeting in his notes, and included the facts that four or five police cars leap-frogged each other on the road to avoid suspicion and that the police were in constant contact with both their headquarters and the British authorities on the Rock during the journey, during which a helicopter was used to target the car. Sr. Valladolid confirmed that the British were aware of the car's arrival at the border and permitted it to enter Gibraltar.

When Sir Geoffrey Howe Q.C., gave his Government's version in the House of Commons on Monday 7 March 1988 he received at first a fairly friendly reception from the Opposition Labour Party spokesman, George Robertson, whose response was not entirely accurate. He said "the very fact that this enormous potential bomb was placed opposite both an old folks' home and a school underlined the cynical hypocrisy of the IRA". He failed to define what a "potential" bomb was, but he was blissfully placing it in a position where Howe had said it was not. (In the unlikely event of this book ever being read by George Robertson, now the Secretary-General of

NATO, can it be emphasised again for his benefit that there was no car bomb found in Gibraltar on 6 March 1988. The bomb did exist alright, and was found by the police on the Spanish mainland in a Marbella car park on 8 March.)

After that, the less than friendly questions began to be asked. At the outset, the Labour MP for Liverpool Eric Heffer asked the Foreign Secretary in the House of Commons to explain why the three people killed were shot dead when it was admitted that they did not have guns and had not planted any bombs in Gibraltar. The reply was that the security forces could not have acted in any other way in the circumstances. More questions followed in the subsequent few days. First, why had the IRA been allowed to bring a bomb into Gibraltar, risking the lives of many in the narrow and restricted streets on the Rock? The authorities there believed, so it was claimed, that Sean Savage's car contained an explosive device. Second, why was the car not stopped in the vast expanse of the airport runway below the face of the Rock of Gibraltar and the driver not arrested there and then, caught in the very act of terrorism and attempted murder on a large scale? After all, there has never been a case of a suicide bomber being involved in an IRA operation, so that even if the theory about "the button job" was accurate, it was most unlikely that Savage would have killed himself, especially if he was challenged at a distance by an armoured vehicle and some of the numerous soldiers and police who were in the area at the time. The only answer to such difficult questions was to change the scenario of events. Someone decided that the story would be that all three members of the active service unit had slipped into Gibraltar without being seen to do so by anyone, and not spotted until later when they surfaced on the Rock. The main problem with this new and indeed novel approach was that the British Foreign Secretary had told the House of Commons, as noted above, on 7 March that shortly before 1 p.m. the white Renault car was brought into Gibraltar and seen to park and "… an hour and a half later, the two others subsequently shot were seen to enter Gibraltar on foot".

It is known that Detective Constable Charles Huart of the Gibraltar police took up an observation position on the border to look out for two males and a female, all members of the active service unit, at 8 o'clock on the Sunday morning, 6 March. He had seen their photographs and he knew their real names and their aliases, Katherine Harper, Robert Reilly and Brendan Coyne. He was met by a Spanish police officer and put into a computer room at the Spanish Immigration post. More importantly the Spanish police had photographs of the three terrorists and knew their names and aliases also. It is claimed that on the Gibraltar side of the border the police and customs officers were not informed or involved in the surveillance because to tell them would involve information being provided to an excessive number of people. This is difficult to understand. Were not the same number of people involved on both sides of the border? Does it mean it was alright to tell the Spanish of the observation operation, but not their counterparts on the other side? The Detective Constable was not however the only look out. There was a separate surveillance team at the border, and in the area of the airfield nearby, an arrest group. All seem to have failed to see the suspects entering onto the Rock, or so it was now claimed. Indeed a senior MI5 officer later swore on oath (at the Inquest) that "the car was not seen to cross the border…. Neither the people nor the car were under surveillance at the time they crossed the border". As for Sean Savage, the constable did not agree that he would be inclined to pay more attention to Irish passports in the name of Coyne, "I do not know" he told Mr. McGrory. When it was pointed out to him that Savage came though the border with an Irish passport in the name of Coyne, he replied "It was not my fault; it was the Spanish officer". Mr. McGrory said: "The Spanish authorities were very alert for an Irish passport in the name of Coyne, and the Gibraltar authorites were very alert for an Irish passport in the name of Coyne and yet he was missed." He replied: "That is not what I am saying, that is what you are saying".

One of the soldiers involved in Operation Flavius, Soldier F, contended that a policy had been formulated by an Advisory Group that their preferred option was to arrest the terrorists when they were on foot in Ince's Hall, to disarm them and then to defuse the bomb. There were, he said, a number of key indicators formulated by the Group for the guidance of the Police Commissioner. These included the possibility that the car would be driven to the Assembly area without prior warning and that there might be other unidentified members of the IRA on the Rock. The timing of the exercise of the preferred option of arrest was to identify all the terrorists who were present and thereafter when the car was parked and they headed for the border, intending to leave Gibraltar, they should then be arrested. Any earlier action, it was thought, might result in tipping off other unidentified terrorists and no evidence being left available for the police to use in court. All of this of course begs the question, if Mairead Farrell, Daniel McCann and Sean Savage had been arrested and not killed in Gibraltar, where was the evidence then known to the authorities that they were committing an offence in that jurisdiction? It was hardly likely that the informer who had betrayed them would ever attend court to give evidence in any prosecution against them for conspiracy to cause explosions and conspiracy to murder.

There was one major difficulty with the rewriting of the events in this case. When Chief Inspector Ullger was asked (at the Inquest) about the failure to take more scrupulous measures on the Gibraltar side to establish the movements of the terrorists and their time of entry onto the Rock he replied: "In this particular case, we are talking about dangerous terrorists. We were talking about a very, very major and delicate operation – an operation that had to succeed. I think the only way it could have succeeded is to allow the terrorists to come in and for the terrorists to have been dealt with in the way they were dealt with as far as the surveillance is concerned". Is it not abundantly clear from this sworn evidence from a Special Branch senior police officer that there never was any intention of detaining or arresting any of the terrorists at the Gibraltar border or just inside it? If the answer is yes, then the authorities willingly allowed the three active service members of the Provisional IRA into Gibraltar on 6 March 1988 either suspecting, knowing or believing that a car driven by one of them contained a bomb, putting at risk the lives of the people of Gibraltar for several hours whilst evidence sufficient for an arrest was being gathered.

Other difficulties for the "official version" began to surface a year later. First, on 13 March 1989 the Spanish Government publicly decorated and honoured twenty two police officers for the their role in the surveillance of the IRA terrorists. Then on 15 March 1989 Spanish police were reported (in the Irish Times and the London Independent dated the next day) to have claimed that British intelligence knew that the IRA team of Daniel McCann, Sean Savage and Mairead Farrell were not carrying arms or explosives when they were shot dead in Gibraltar. Highly placed sources in Spain's Foreign Intelligence Brigade claim that on the day of the shooting their officers alerted British authorities on the Rock that the IRA team had left their hotel in Torremolinos and were heading for Gibraltar, without explosives. Spanish officers are said to have crossed into Gibraltar with the terrorists. Miguel Martin, the head of the Special Branch and president of the Professional Policemen's Union said "I don't doubt that Spanish police would have crossed over into Gibraltar following the IRA. It isn't logical that they would have stopped at the frontier". The surveillance sources who worked with a Belfast anti-terrorist expert known as "F5" claimed that the British authorities were given advance warning of the IRA's arrival in Gibraltar and were told that the would-be bombers had left their weapons and explosives in Spain. "We knew that the explosives weren't in Gibraltar", Mr. Martin said. He added that as early as November 1987, when McCann and Savage were first spotted in Spain, the British Government were alerted. Britain immediately dispatched an agent from Belfast to help the Spanish with surveillance.

Did the British know on 6 March 1988 that the terrorists were not on a bombing mission but on a preparatory mission? To avoid answering the question "if you knew they had a bomb, why did you let them in," it was then claimed that the three terrorists were not allowed in, they evaded the Spanish surveillance and were not seen by anyone at the border crossing. Another difficult question, not answered then or now was, if the terrorists were allowed in because it was known they were unarmed and had no bomb, why shoot them dead?

All the evidence indicates that it was known that the three would enter Gibraltar on that fatal Sunday. There had been the late night briefing on the Saturday evening involving the SAS and the Gibraltar police. At the very same time as Detective Constable Huart was taking up his position at the border at 8 a.m. on the Sunday morning, an operations room opened with the police Commissioner on duty there from 10.30 a.m. until 12.30 p.m. when his Acting Deputy George Colombo took over. SAS soldiers in plain clothes were patrolling the streets of Gibraltar in pairs, each one armed with a 9mm Browning pistol and each carrying a radio. One of the pair was in radio communication on the tactical net and the other on the surveillance net.

At about 12.30 p.m. Detective Constable Viagas, who was on surveillance duty in Hambro's Bank overlooking Ince's Hall, received a report over the surveillance net that a car had parked in a parking space. A member of the Security Service commented that the driver had lingered in the vehicle and fiddled with something between the seats. Constable Viagas then saw the man lock the car and walk away towards the Southport Gate. Four people, including him, attempted to identify the driver at that time but could not.

A person, known to be a member of the security services team, with the designation "N" when on surveillance in the car park in Ince's Hall, though that it was 12.45 p.m., that he saw a white Renault car park in the assembly area and the driver leave the vehicle after two to three minutes and walk away. For reasons never explained that person seems not to have been followed by anyone. How were the missing 45 minutes to be accounted for? It was not until 2 p.m. that a young man was spotted in the area and was identified without difficulty as Sean Savage by Officer "H". Ten minutes later the officer "N" reported over the radio to the operations room that he had identified Savage as well and confirmed he was the man who had earlier parked the car in the assembly area. The question arises, if it was the preferred option to arrest the terrorists, why not alight upon Sean Savage when he was isolated and on his own? He was followed thereafter by a number of people and was using what was later described as anti-surveillance techniques, namely using devious routes through the side streets and stopping round the corner of alley-ways to see who followed him. He could easily have been arrested at the time, and, if the purpose of the active service unit was to kill British Army soldiers on the Rock of Gibraltar, would he have had any reason to detonate the bomb (which was not in the car, with a button he didn't have) when there was no reason to believe that a single British soldier was in the assembly area near the car at that time?

The Acting Deputy Police Commissioner George Colombo, who was in the operations room, seems not to have been told of this sighting. At 2.30 p.m. Daniel McCann and Mairead Farrell were thought by officer "M", who was leading the surveillance at the border, to have crossed over onto the Rock on foot, although they were not clearly identified. The Commissioner was immediately informed of this sighting, but he was not told that Sean Savage had been positively identified twenty minutes earlier and the circumstances in which the identification had taken place.

These two were followed in spite of the claim of no positive visual identification. Since their aliases were known, could there not have been a check with the police officer who had checked the passports of those walking through? Miss Farrell was also, so it was claimed, using anti surveillance techniques – she looked back frequently. It has to be said that she, like Sean Savage, obviously failed to see that they were being followed, so at the very least their so called techniques did not amount to much.

At about 2. 50 p.m. the operations room were told that the three terrorists had met up and were looking at the white Renault car parked in Ince's Hall. George Colombo claimed that it was only then that he was told that Sean Savage had been identified as being in Gibraltar. According to Constable Viagas he saw the three meet up in the assembly area and he put the time at 2. 55 p.m. That was the moment, so he claimed, that the MI5 officers made a positive identification of all three.

Recollections differ on what happened next. Mr. Colombo stated that he was asked whether he would hand over control to the SAS for them to arrest the three. But when he inquired whether there was a positive identification he was told it was 80% but not 100% certain. (This is clearly in conflict with the evidence of Constable Viagas). At that moment the three moved away from the car through the Southport Gate. There then followed a discussion that it was possible that the active service unit was on reconnaissance and might return for the car, and therefore it was decided not to arrest them at that time.

At 3 p.m. George Colombo telephoned the Commissioner to inform him that it seemed more and more likely that McCann and Savage had been identified. When he arrived at the operations room at about 3.10 p.m. his Deputy, the Commissioner, told him that the three suspects had met up and an arrest had almost been made. Joseph Canepa asked for proof of positive identification of the three and that was provided at 3.25 p.m when it was reported to the operations room that the three had returned to the Ince's Hall area and had walked past looking at the white Renault car again. Two members of the SAS maintain that the Commissioner passed control over to the Army at that time, but it was almost immediately rescinded when Mr. Canepa again asked for confirmation of the identity of the three terrorists. If this happened it defies comprehension. In any event the confirmation of the positive and correct identification was received in the control room almost immediately. Even then the Commissioner did not hand over control to authorise the arrest by the SAS. There is little point now in speculating why he did not. According to one of his officers, Constable Viagas, the MI5 officers had identified all three terrorists about half an hour before, at 2.55 p.m.

Mairead Farrell, Sean Savage and Daniel McCann, in spite of their use of the so-called anti-surveillance techniques, seemed to have behaved in a most extraordinary way whilst in Gibraltar. If Sean

Savage had not been seen parking the car in the assembly area as indeed he was, the three would have led their followers and observers back to the vehicle in Ince's Hall when they returned there, assuming it is true that they did. Why did they congregate in a group together, making themselves an easy collective target and spend so much time looking at the empty Renault 5?

Whatever the answer they moved together away from the assembly area and this gave the watchers an opportunity, clearly not the first, to examine the suspect car. Soldier G went forward and conducted an examination from the exterior without touching the car. He was subsequently described (at the Inquest) as a bomb-disposal adviser who had experience of dealing with car bombs in Northern Ireland. He later admitted however that he was neither a radio-communications expert nor an explosives expert. For about two minutes he stood adjacent to the vehicle, looking at the interior where he saw nothing suspicious or concealed under the seats. Whether he was suitably dressed in protective clothing, such as a helmet and a suit of toughened protective fabric is not known. Why he spent so little time carrying out the cursory examination may be understand-able but hardly justifiable. No less than 9 MI5 officers had been in Gibraltar since 23 February in anticipation of a terrorist bombing attack. Is anyone expected to believe that all the paraphernalia available to the British Army in Northern Ireland for detecting, disposing and destroying car bombs for the previous 18 years were not flown to the Rock for use there? Was there not available to the army a device used by explosives officers known as the Explosives Ordnance Disposal Remote Equipment? This was called by its users "a wheelbarrow" because it carried tools and other equipment right up to the suspect car. There was almost always a television camera in place on the wheelbarrow, helping the explosives officer to use his equipment more accurately. Was Soldier G not familiar with the military philosophy, "if you don't know it, you blow it." In the event, after the shootings on that afternoon there was no attempt to use a controlled explosion in Ince's Hall in order to safeguard life or protect property.

During that time Soldier G was near the vehicle did he wonder if any of the three terrorists might trip or fall to the ground, press the button and detonate the bomb? Of course if it was known all along that there was no button and there was no bomb, he could safely have stayed near the car as long as he wished. It would have been a gross neglect of duty not to have examined the vehicle at all – it might have contained suspicious objects, including firearms, unlikely though it would have been to leave them where they could be seen, but it could have been done differently and more effectively.

What he did notice about the vehicle, which was photographed (though there are apparently no photographs of the three terrorists in the assembly area or near the car) was that the aerial of the vehicle was old and rusty and out of place with the age of the car. He went back to the operations room and reported to the Commissioner that he regarded it as "a suspect car bomb". What he failed to do, and could have done, was to remove the aerial from the car so that it was unable to receive a remote controlled signal and therefore make it safe. When asked about this he said he had not thought of de-activating the suspect bomb by unscrewing the aerial from the car, although he later said that to do so would have been potentially very dangerous. Whether it was any less dangerous than standing next to the vehicle to examine it is not known.

The photographs of the Renault car give no indication that there was a bomb inside it, for there was no noticeable weight on the rear axle, one of the giveaway signs that are looked for in suspect vehicles.

From the moment that Soldier G made his report, two things should have happened. First, the entire area in and around Ince's Hall should have been cleared, and the assembly area and the nearby roads should have been sealed off and closed, and any buildings within 200 metres should have been vacated of every living thing, humans and animals. As noted above, there was an evacuation plan drawn up by Chief Inspector Lopez already in existence. It would appear that it was not until about 4.10 p.m., some 28 minutes after the three terrorists had been shot dead that steps were taken to clear the area and examine and make safe the Renault car. It is one of the unanswered questions about Operation Flavius for which no one has ever provided an answer.

Second, the SAS should have been told that steps were being taken to evacuate and make safe the entire area around Ince's Hall and they would be further informed when that operation was completed. Such information could well affect the timing and method of confronting the active service unit members. That was not done. Instead Soldier A was told over the radio that it was 100% certain that there was a bomb in the assembly area, that the suspects had remote-control devices and were probably armed. Soldier C was told of the indication of the old

41

aerial on a new car and claimed that it had been confirmed by Soldier E that there was a device in the Ince's Hall area which could be detonated by one of the three suspects. More likely than not this would be Savage because he had been seen fiddling with something in the car earlier.

Soldier D said Soldier E confirmed to him that there was a bomb in the car. That Soldier considered that as far as Soldier G could ascertain from a cursory visual examination he could confirm the suspicion that they were dealing with a car bomb. Soldier F was impressed by the fact that Soldier G had reported it was a suspect car bomb because there was an old aerial situated centrally on a relatively new car and accordingly it should be treated as a possible car bomb.

At 3.40 p.m. Joseph Luis Canepa, in his capacity as Commissioner of Police signed a form which had been provided in advance by the army. It said "......having considered the terrorist situation in Gibraltar and having been fully briefed on the military plan with firearms, request that you proceed with the military option which may include the use of lethal force for the preservation of life".

The word "arrest" is conspicuous by its absence in content of that form. It is on any view a most extraordinary document whose legal standing is doubtful. The police, the civil power, were calling upon the SAS to assist them, rather than handing over control of the operation to them. That control should have been retained by the police and they should have directed the operation, keeping all options open. Was the purpose of the document however to induce the Commissioner to believe that he would no longer be responsible for what happened to the three IRA terrorists within his jurisdiction? In addition the senior military adviser to the Commissioner, a permanent member of the advisory group appointed to act against the IRA active service unit, told the Inquest that the certificate of authority for the transfer of control from the police to the military was drawn up in advance and agreed by all parties. But, he added, the purpose of the army operation was to assist the Gibraltar police in arresting the Provisional IRA bombing unit and it was made clear that under the rules of engagement they were subject to the instructions of the Police Commissioner. Consequently in their plan they were mindful of the priorities they had laid down and that in the execution of that plan they had to bear in mind the sequence of arrest, disarm and defuse. The military option had been refined to a preferred foot arrest in the assembly area.

According to the evidence given at the Inquest, there was however an understanding and indeed rehearsals about how the arrests should be effected. The soldiers were to approach the suspects to within a short distance, cover them with their firearm and should "Stop. Police. Hands Up" or words to that effect. The suspects were then to be put on the floor with their arms away from their body until the police moved in and carried out the formalities of a valid arrest. It is clear beyond a shadow of a doubt that there never was an intention to arrest the three terrorists at a point which provide the people of Gibraltar maximum protection from death or injury, namely on the airfield runway, but in the assembly area of Ince's Hall, thereby allowing some or all of the three, supposedly with a car bomb, to travel the narrow streets to a destination almost a mile and a half away.

What happened next is the subject of a bitter dispute between differing sides. The three terrorists were seen by the SAS to be standing talking together for a short while at the junction of Smith Dorrien Avenue with Winston Churchill Avenue. Sean Savage then turned and started to walk south towards the Landport tunnel. Mairead Farrell and Daniel McCann started off in the opposite direction along Winston Churchill Avenue.

The majority of witnesses to the events of that afternoon say that just before the soldiers approached them, the siren of a police car was sounded. A number of those witnesses thought that both Farrell and McCann reacted to that sound and that it was the siren that caused them both to stop and turn.

The most senior officer in that police car was Inspector Joseph Revagliatte. When he gave evidence (at the Inquest) he set his stall out fairly and squarely. Counsel for the SAS, Michael Hucker asked him "when you came on shift at three o'clock or thereabouts did you know anything about the operation at all?" He replied: "Nothing at all". "You thought that life in Gibraltar was totally normal, that what was happening was the same as happened any other day of the week?" "Exactly" was the Inspector's reply. In an area the size of the Rock of Gibraltar, only some two miles long, with its population of about 29,000 people, it seems to defy belief that a senior police officer would not be aware of the existence of an anti-terrorist operation in force at this time. Did he not ever see or hear of the presence of armed members of the SAS, and members of MI5 staying at the same hotel on the Rock?

He related how when he first heard the shots his instinctive reaction was to duck down inside the car and instruct the driver to carry on quickly. As he returned to the scene he radioed to control that there had been a violent incident at Winston Churchill Avenue. A lot of people were gathering and he ordered the officers with him to stop the traffic and the people coming near the bodies. There was blood dripping from the woman's head so he called for ambulances, manpower, scenes of crime officers and other additional resources. Another Gibraltar plain clothes officer told him "It's okay, its our operation, everything is under control."

He added an interesting piece of information. He searched the bodies and Farrell's handbag, which was lying on the ground, looking for a detonation device or a weapon but he found nothing. Assuming someone else told him to look for these items, since he claimed to know nothing of the operation going on in the Colony, one might ask whether he carried out the search carefully, lest he should detonate at a push the button which, of course, was not there anyway.

According to Roger Bolton however the truth is substantially different. He and his team discovered a secret operational order prepared by Commissioner Canepa for Operation Flavius. Inspector Revagliatte was named in the document as the officer in charge of two Gibraltar police firearm teams, each containing three armed policemen, in that operation.

That officer gave evidence at the Inquest that he and the other officers were at the traffic lights in Smith Dorrien Avenue on routine patrol when a radio message was received calling them back to the police station immediately and urgently. He instructed his driver to move from their position in the stationary traffic and drive down Winston Churchill Avenue. The driver put on the vehicle's siren and the blue beacons in the midst of the heavy traffic as they passed the Shell Service Station where the shootings happened. As they drove along the carriageway they heard shots and went back to the Garage. One may question why in the middle of a combined MI5/SAS/police operation the nearest police car to the central players should be called away from the very scene where the fatal action was being played out, to return to the police station urgently. According to the journalists James Adams, Robin Morgan and Anthony Bambridge in their book *Ambush* (at page 165) "The message calling him back to HQ was so that there would be a car available to take the terrorists to jail after they had been arrested. In fact by turning on his siren, the policeman may well have caused the deaths of the terrorists". The difficulty about being persuaded by that view is not diminished by their acceptance, on the previous page, that the officer was "in his own words, in charge of routine policing on the Rock. Operation Flavius is most definitely not routine and no one had told what is going on." That means presumably that even in that role he would not have been told of the whereabouts on that day of at least one of his officers, Detective Constable Huart, positioned on the Spanish side of the Gibraltar border, waiting to identify three terrorists.

If however the Inspector's role was different from that which he and others would have us believe, and he really was in charge of two police firearms teams on that Sunday, was the turning on the siren a signal for an ambush and for the shootings to begin?

Three armed police officers, P, Q and R were members of one of the two teams under the command of Inspector Revagliatte on that Sunday. They were photographed forming a circle around the crumpled bodies of Mairead Farrell and Daniel McCann immediately after they were shot dead. As Roger Bolton commented: "This leads to the interesting conclusion that the authorities expect us to believe that policemen P, Q and R knew about the operation but that their commanding officer put in charge of them did not, or that P, Q and R arrived at the scene of the shootings at precisely the time they occurred entirely by accident, and that the Inspector did the same.'

After the three IRA members split up at the junction, Sean Savage walked passed Soldiers A and B, brushing shoulders with the latter. Knowing that Soldiers C and D were in the vicinity, it was decided not to arrest him there and then but to leave it to those soldiers, whilst they proceeded to follow Mairead Farrell and Daniel McCann. He was walking on the inside of the pavement, she on the outside nearer the road. According to Soldier A, McCann turned and looked back over his left shoulder and a smile left his face as if he realised he was under threat from that soldier. Soldier A drew his pistol from his waistband went to shout stop but he couldn't honestly say whether that word came out because events overtook the warning. He claimed that McCann's hand moved suddenly and aggressively across the front of his body, creating the impression he was going for the button to detonate the bomb. He fired once into McCann's back from perhaps three metres distance, or even closer. He saw Farrell make a half turn to the right, inwards towards McCann, reaching for her handbag that was under her left arm. He similarly thought she was reaching for the button, so he fired one round into her back from a very close distance. Soldier A then fired again at Daniel McCann, hitting him once more in the body and twice in the head. He fired a total of five shots.

Soldier B likewise claimed to have seen a movement by Mairead Farrell after he saw the turn of the head by Sean Savage and the shout from Soldier A, which he thought was the beginning of the arrest process. She made a sharp movement to her right, drawing her handbag across her body. Soldier B opened fire at her, hitting her in the back. He then turned to McCann and fired several rounds into his body, before shooting Farrell again. In total he fired seven shots. After the shootings they put on berets so that they would be recognised by the police. Both soldiers denied hearing the sound of the siren of the police car.

Officers P and R placed their jackets over the two bodies. Officer Q and Chief Inspector Revaliatte carried out a search of the bodies. No weapons or detonating devices were discovered there or in Mairead Farrell's handbag. Two of those officers, P and Q, had a clear recollection of hearing the words "Police, stop" or words to that effect – words which the alleged speaker never actually claimed to have managed to say. Another witness, an off duty police officer whose residence overlooked the killing scene, was able to support the version put forward by Officer P. The Inquest jury knew the name of the former, Constable James Parody, but not the latter. Counsel for the Army hinted at the fact that they might know each other. They certainly did, for Officer P was police Sergeant Harry Parody, the police constable's brother.

Sean Savage was shot as he headed towards the Landport tunnel. Soldiers C and D were on opposite sides of the road. They closed in on him and when he was about eight feet from the tunnel entrance there was the sound of shots. According to Soldier C Savage spun round, the soldier shouted "stop" and drew his pistol. Sean Savage moved his right arm down to the area of his hip and jacket pocket and was threatening and aggressive. The soldier opened fire at him from about five or six feet away, firing six shots as Savage's body spiralled downwards. As he fell a bullet hit him in the neck and the back. Solder D fired nine rounds at Savage, the last two of which hit him the head. Both agreed that they were shooting to kill but denied they had shot him whilst he was on the ground.

No effort was made at the Shell garage to preserve the scene properly for examination. The positions of the bodies were not marked, no police photographs were taken, the site of the shell cases and cartridges were not recorded. Officer Q was one of two local police officers, both armed with Smith and Wesson revolvers and 18 rounds of ammunition each, who followed the IRA trio through the Gibraltar streets. After the shootings Q searched the bodies of Miss Farrell and McCann and found no weapons. Then, on instructions from Chief Inspector Wilger, he collected the spent cartridges off the ground. He later returned to the central police station.

At the scene of Sean Savage's shooting, some cartridge positions were marked and Inspector Revagliatte made a chalk outline of the position of his body, but no police photograph was taken. Within the chalk outline there were five strike marks, three in the area of the head. This seemed to indicate that the shots were fired at the deceased as he lay on the ground.

At 4. 06 p.m. the SAS handed back control to the Civil Power. The SAS soldiers were permitted by the authorities to leave Gibraltar in the evening of the same day. They were not asked to, and did not make, any witness statement about the day's events. (In the result these came into existence sometime after 15 March 1988, by which time there was ample opportunity to discuss and discover the recollections of all interested parties who might be required to give evidence at the subsequent Inquest).

The next day Professor Alan Albert Watson of the University of Strathclyde at Glasgow flew to Gibraltar to carrying out a post-mortem on the three deceased. He gave evidence of his findings at the Inquest opened there by the Coroner Felix Pizzarello, sitting with a jury of eleven people, (all male, since only men are eligible to sit on inquest juries in Gibraltar) on 6 September 1988. The purpose of that procedure was to establish who the deceased were and how, when and where the deceased came by their deaths. The range of verdicts open to the jury ranged from an open verdict to accidental death or death by misadventure, suicide, or killed lawfully or unlawfully.

A Belfast solicitor, Paddy McGrory, was asked by members of the families of the deceased to represent their interests at the Inquest and he agreed to do so without a fee for his professional services and he paid his own travel and living expenses. The SAS were represented by Michael Hucker and the Governor of Gibraltar and the Commissioner of Police were represented by John Laws. Both lawyers were members of the Bar of England and Wales.

Mr. McGrory, a brave, dedicated and formidable lawyer faced

immense difficulties from the very outset. First he was not given any advance disclosure of the evidence that an MI5 operative, police officer or army witness might give, whereas the other two lawyers had advance copies of their statements in their possession. This prevented him from cross-examining on any inconsistencies or contradictions between their written statements and their sworn evidence. In addition, the order in which the witnesses were to be called was also decided by the Coroner Mr. Pizzarello. An MI5 officer, a military adviser, the police Commissioner, the pathologist, then the Commissioner was recalled, then Soldier G and the SAS soldiers were called, followed by eye witness accounts from the surveillance teams and the police. Then came the civilian eye-witness testimony and the forensic evidence. It followed from all this that any evidence which a witness might put before the Inquest contrary to that given by an earlier witness, could not be used in the cross examination of that earlier witness. To make things even more difficult for Mr. McGrory, faced with limited financial resources himself but confronted by the unlimited resources of the State in every area, the cost of a transcript of each day's proceedings was increased from 50 pence, the amount fixed under the 1984 Coroner Ordinance to £5 per sheet. Since a day's transcript would generate at least 100 pages of evidence, that increased the cost to £500 per day. The Inquest lasted for nineteen working days.

At a preliminary hearing on 5 July 1988 the Coroner accepted terms of reference put by counsel for the Crown, conforming with Section 8(2) of the Coroner Ordinance, that the Inquest should be limited to three specific matters. First, the circumstances of the deaths themselves. Second, the nature of a perceived threat apprehended in Gibraltar and which led to the transfer of responsibility for the arrest of the three deceased into the hands of the military, and third, the resulting apprehension on 6 March and the state of the soldiers own minds of the kind of danger involved and their responses and reactions to it.

Professor Watson told the Coroner and the jury in evidence that contrary to common practice he had not seen the bodies clothed and he had not been given access to the forensic or ballistic reports. This made it more difficult to determine entry and exit wounds, the direction of the shots, the distance from which they were fired, and whether the deceased were standing or lying down when they were shot. There were no X-ray facilities at the Royal Naval Hospital where he carried out the post mortems between 3.30 p.m. and 8.30 p.m. on 7 March and he had not been later provided with a full set of photographs for reference. He had reservations about the experience of those present at the post-mortem and the facilities available to him. Two members of the Royal Navy were present: neither of them had participated at a post mortem before. He would not call them morticians or technicians. He added that two doctors were also present, but he did not know in what capacity.

Professor Watson agreed with Mr. McGrory that it was the normal practice to have two forensic pathologists in Scotland if there were any suspicious circumstances and where the evidence was to be adduced at a trial, since it had to be corroborated. The forensic evidence was of fundamental importance because this can frequently establish where the shooter was standing, the distance of fire, and sometimes the sequence of shots.

He described that on examination of Mairead Farrell's body he noted that she was only five feet one inch in height. There were three bullet wounds in her back and four in her face. The cause of her death was haemorrhage due to gunshot wounds of the heart and liver. He considered that a reasonable explanation would be she was first shot in the face whilst facing the gun and then was hit by further bullets to her back. If it had been the other way round, the three shots in the back would almost certainly have knocked her to the ground and she would have had to turn her face back towards the shooter. That conflicts with the versions of Soldier A and B as to how she was shot. The pathologist further damaged their credibility when he said that the bullets to her back appear to have an upward trajectory and might indicate that she was down on the ground when she was shot, for either the shooter was down or she was. She might have been falling forwards, or downwards or even down on the ground on her face. She had been shot eight times.

A forensic scientist, David Pryor from London gave evidence on 27 September 1988, that is nineteen days after Professor Watson. It would have been better for the interests of justice if he had given his evidence immediately after the pathologist. Mr. Pryor's expertise was in the use of firearms. The blood soaked clothing of the three deceased had been sent to him in bags. It was in such a condition that accurate determination of which was an entry or exit site of a bullet was most difficult. He also examined the clothing for the presence of powder depositions which would indicate that shots had been fired from close

49

range. He found signs of partly burnt propellant powder on the upper right back of Mairead Farrell's jacket, and carried out tests which established that the density was such that she was shot with a Browning pistol from a muzzle to target range of three feet. The soldiers who shot her only had to reach out in order to touch her with both hands. Since she was dressed in a skirt and jacket if she was carrying "a button" why did the nearest one to her not reach out and hold her arms away from her body to prevent her reaching it, or opening the handbag that she was carrying?

Daniel McCann ended up, like Mairead Farrell, face down on the ground. Professor Watson considered that one of his head wounds was superficial, possibly caused by a ricochet or a bullet exiting from Farrell's back. He had been hit from the front and it was not the lethal shot. It was the other head wound that led to the massive damage to the brain. When he was asked "What about this one at the back of the head? Is the explanation or the only explanation for that that he just had to be lying down when that was inflicted or at least very low down?" He replied "Yes, I think so. That is my explanation. It suggests that the chest (exit) wounds came before the head wound". The shots to the body were at about a 45 degree angle. He had been hit by a total of five bullets. He was wearing trousers and a white shirt, without a jacket. In his case, where was "the button" supposed to be concealed?

In relation to Sean Savage it took more than 15 minutes for Professor Watson to read out from his report the long list of wounds sustained by him. The cause of death was gun shot wounds to the head. He had multiple damage to the brain and the skull, including considerable loss of tissue; he also had gun shot wounds in his lung as well. His arm had been broken and so had his leg. There was a fracture to the ninth vertebrae. But death was due to the head wounds. The others would have contributed to his death. When asked "was he riddled with bullets?" he replied "I try not to use these words. I concur with your word. Yes, like a frenzied attack one would say." Of the sixteen bullets that hit him, they caused seven wounds to his head and neck, five on the front of the chest, five on the back of the chest, one on the top of each shoulder, three in the abdomen, two in the left leg, two in the right arm and two on the left hand. The position of the entry wounds suggested that some were received as he faced the shooter.

Anyone for justice may have difficulties in reconciling a frenzied attack with the use of reasonable and proportionate force in the prevention of crime. Professor Watson and another pathologist, Professor Derek Pounder, Professor of Forensic Medicine at the University of Dundee, who was instructed by the families of the three deceased, had information from the crime scene that three of the bullets that entered Sean Savage's head left clear strike marks on the pavement. This seemed to indicate to them that he was shot in the head whilst on the ground. Professor Pounder said that the evidence from strike marks on the ground and the angle and state of the wounds indicated that Sean Savage was struck by bullets when lying on his back on the ground, with the person shooting by standing towards his feet. He maintained that view when cross-examined by counsel for the SAS. He said the three strike marks on the ground within the chalk outline corresponded with wounds to the head. In his professional opinion "those wounds must have been inflicted when either the head was on the ground or very close to the ground indeed." He amplified on that and said that the head may have been "within inches of the ground" when the shots were fired. In his view, Sean Savage would not have been able to draw a gun or press a switch.

It was the Army's case, put over and over again, that in the case of all three terrorists, each independently had made threatening movements which led the soldiers to believe they were going for a firearm – which, it had eventually to be conceded, they did not have, or to press "a button" which they did not possess, to detonate a bomb which did not exist in Gibraltar.

The shooting of Mairead Farrell and Daniel McCann happened in an area overlooked by two housing estates. Few eye witnesses were found by the police. Detective Chief Inspector Correa, who somewhat surprisingly combined the roles of Coroner's Officer and investigating officer on behalf of the Commission of Police, said there had been house to house inquiries on two occasions and that the Attorney General had made three appeals for witnesses in the press. No incident room was set up in the area on that Sunday afternoon, so that potential witnesses could come forward then.

Strangely enough the British journalist Julian Manyon found several witnesses when searching the area with colleagues, especially Bob Randall from the television programme *This Week*. It does seem extraordinary that they, both outsiders, should have found such relevant and controversial witnesses when the Gibraltar police could not.

51

Mrs. Carmen Proetta, who lived in a flat overlooking the Shell garage on Winston Churchill Avenue, claimed that the first two terrorists to be shot had their hands raised in the air. She said on the Thames television programme "they (the soldiers) didn't do anything, they just jumped with their guns in their hands, and they just went and shot these people. That's all. They didn't say anything, they didn't scream, they didn't do anything. These people were turning their heads back to see what was happening, and when they saw these men had guns in their hands, they put their hands up. It looked like the man was protecting the girl because he stood in front of her, but there was no chance. I mean they went to the floor immediately, they dropped."

That was evidence of the most damaging kind against the SAS. Two days after the transmission of the programme the *Sun* newspaper published Mrs. Proetta's photograph on their front page with the heading "The Tart of Gib". That heading, and some of the text that followed, calling this courageous and honest witness "an IRA witness" and "ex-prostitute who runs an escort agency" eventually cost the *Sun* £50,000 in libel damages.

Another witness, Mrs. Jose Celicia, said that she heard gunshots and saw McCann and Farrell on the ground. Then she heard further shots and saw a man by the bodies with his hands extended downwards. The man she thought was shooting appeared to put something inside his jacket.

A bank clerk, Kenneth Asquez, was said to have approached Bob Randall, who was a customer at the bank, and presented him with a two page handwritten statement which was eventually used in the Thames Television programme. Also used was an unsigned affidavit prepared by a lawyer to whom the bank clerk had repeated his story. Mr. Asquez claimed that whilst in a friend's car on the way to the Gibraltar border he passed the Landport tunnel. He heard what he described as "crackers" and saw a man bleeding considerably on the floor. He saw another man, with an identification card and wearing a black beret, who had his foot on the dying man's throat and was shouting "Stop, it's o.k. It's the police". At that moment the man fired another three or four shots. If this was the truth, Mr. Asquez had witnessed the murder of Sean Savage by an member of the SAS.

On Friday 23 September 1988 Kenneth Asquez went into the witness box at the Coroner's Court to give evidence. He was accompanied at court by a lawyer, the former Chief Minister of

Gibraltar, Sir Joshua Hassan Q.C.

The Coroner asked him to read aloud his statement and he did so. He then said that at the time he had given the statement to Mr. Randall he was under pressure and the latter was phoning him every day. When asked if this statement was true, or parts of it correct and parts of it not true, he replied "At the moment I'm a bit confused, because my mind is not so clear." Attempts to clarify what he meant were not particularly successful. He appeared confused and contradicted himself. When it was pointed out to him that it had not become known anywhere in the media until it was disclosed in evidence at the Inquest that the soldiers wore berets, he said that he must have heard it in the street. When he was asked to explain why he should make up such a statement he responded by claiming that he was previously ill and under pressure at work.

He was asked by Mr. McGrory in a most effective cross examination: "It is a vital part of that statement that the man with the black beret had his foot on the dying man's throat; he shouted stop and then fired three or four shots..... did you make that up?" The reply was "probably", which some may regard as somewhat unconvincing. He was then asked: "Of all the people present in this room, only you know if you made it up or not, and what you are saying. There are eleven of your fellow citizens of Gibraltar, tell them whether its true or not." Asquez weakly replied "I can't say yes or no. I was probably still confused."

When it appeared that perhaps more weight might be given to his original versions of the events of 6 March rather than his retraction of them, it was of some interest that at the end of the Inquest it emerged that the Coroner's Officer had interviewed the driver of the car in which Mr. Asquez was a passenger at the time he claimed to have seen the shooting of the bleeding man on the ground. The driver apparently said they were travelling in a direction that would have precluded Mr. Asquez from seeing the events he had described. Unfortunately the driver was never called to say this in evidence, it was not on oath and it was not tested at the Inquest in cross examination. There were two other people, both young women, in that car who could have supported either the version of the driver or that of Kenneth Asquez. All three should have been called to resolve the unsatisfactory self-induced conflict of evidence of an eye witness who saw nothing, or perhaps everything, of the events of the last moments of the life and death of Sean Savage.

Mrs. Carmen Proetta, who had provided the main interview for the TV programme *Death on the Rock,* was the next witness. She explained to the Coroner and the jury that she had been at the kitchen window of her flat in Rodney House when she saw a police car on the opposite side of the road to the Shell service station. Four men, one of them in police uniform, got out of the car. Asked by the Coroner what they did she replied: "They came very quickly out of the car and then jumped the intersection barrier which crosses over to the petrol station. When they jumped I noted they had guns in their hands – not the uniformed policemen but the other three. At least I saw guns in their hands…..Well at that moment my attraction, my eyes were attracted to the right side of the road and I saw this couple walking….. they were walking right past the front of the petrol station. They had just passed it and I noticed that, as they saw these three men jump it made them look in a startled way towards them. At this very moment, they raised their hands up, both of them." Asked by the Coroner how high, she demonstrated with her hands above her shoulders with the palms outwards and said "open hands, like this…..I heard a shot and almost immediately the girl went to the ground……she fell to the ground and the man made a gesture of either to hold her or protect her. At this moment I realised he pulled his arm down when he was going to pick her up or help her or shield her, one of the three things. At this very moment he also went down immediately after her." She heard one shot, she said, "and then all of a sudden a fusillade of shots, and he was immediately after her on the floor. Then my attention was drawn to a blond or fairish-coloured haired man who crouched in front of the fallen bodies and by holding his hands like this (she demonstrated her hands clasped in front at waist level) was pointing at them. Then I heard more shots." Anyone who might be tempted to think that Mrs. Proetta confused the plain clothes SAS soldiers with the police officers in Inspector Revagliatte's vehicle and telescoped the two events mistakenly into one should read the Daily Telegraph dated 30 April 1988. That was two days after the transmission of the *Death on the Rock* television programme, and the favoured newspapers like the *Telegraph* were being fed information by official but anonymous sources upon which they could safely rely. In that report, under the by line of the defence correspondent James Keegan, it is recorded that "Gibraltar Police vehicles may have used their siren after the shootings. The car carrying the SAS team would certainly not have done so beforehand." This is astonishing in the light of the sworn evidence of all the SAS soldiers who claimed that they had followed the IRA terrorists on foot to the Shell service station. If this was not untrue, what else in their testimony was also untrue?

Like her statement in the TV programme, this evidence greatly damaged the truthfulness and accuracy of the version of events put forward by police and the soldiers. If Mrs. Proetta was right, both Mairead Farrell and Daniel McCann were finished off whilst they lay helpless, defenceless and wounded on the ground.

At the end of her evidence Mr. McGrory asked her, "have you been attacked and abused in certain sections of the press?" "Very badly, sir" she answered. "Have you suffered from telling what you saw?" She replied with a great deal of emotion in her voice: "Not only me but my children and my family as well." "Are you aware that there are many, many other people in Gibraltar who saw this but who have not come forward?" Mrs. Proetta replied, "Let me tell you one thing; if this had to happen again, I would not be here to give evidence again."

It may be that the message she was conveying was listened to and acted upon in Northern Ireland and elsewhere, that the price of standing up and telling the truth against the State can be very high indeed.

On 13 September 1988 Soldier G gave evidence to the Inquest jury. He described his role in examining the white Renault parked by Sean Savage in Ince's Hall and his conclusion that it contained a bomb. He related how the Police Commissioner had asked him to inspect the suspect car the three IRA members had been seen watching, he ran down to the assembly area and then calmly walked across to the car. He accepted that when he reported they saw nothing out of place inside the vehicle, but still considered it contained a suspect bomb, he did not advise that the area should be cleared.

Although in many ways he was acting as an expert witness, there was no real effort to cross examine him on the extent of his expertise and experience, because the importance of his evidence lay elsewhere in that evidence. In any event it was really a question of him relying on his knowledge of explosives and their disposal gathered in the front line in Northern Ireland which seemed to carry considerable weight. Unbeknown to Mr. McGrory, a person called Alan Faraday had prepared a report for the Crown, whose counsel, John Laws, had decided he would not use and he did not propose to call Mr. Faraday as a witness. In the event counsel for the SAS decided to do so. It may not have been one of his better decisions.

That situation arose in this way. Mr. McGrory was given leave by the Coroner to call as a witness Dr. Michael Scott from Dublin. He gave evidence on 27 September 1988. He has a Master's Degree in electrical and electronic engineering and holds a Doctorate in Control Engineering and is an expert in long distance radio transmission. He has given evidence as an expert witness in IRA bombing cases. He effectively demolishes the evidence of Mr. Faraday in his article published in the magazine *Fortnight* in October 1989, as well as explaining his own role and evidence at the Gibraltar Inquest.

Alan Faraday was a principal scientific officer employed at the British Government's Royal Armament Research and Development Establishment (RARDE) based at Woolwich, South London. (RARDE and its scientists is frequently mentioned in the case of Judith Ward and others). Although Michael Hucker, counsel for the SAS, insisted on referring to him as "Professor", in reality Mr. Faraday was not even a graduate of any university, let alone holding a Chair there. He was in fact the holder of a much more modest Higher National Certificate in physics with electronics. That was his highest and indeed only academic qualification.

Mr. Faraday had been asked to given an opinion on possible firing distances of radio controlled IRA devices and the effects of intervening buildings. He wrote in reply that in considering that with particular regard to Gibraltar he was mindful of the fact that he had neither visited the Rock nor been provided with any detailed scaled map of the area. That did not prevent him for giving an opinion however. However he accepted that radio controlled devices were meant only for line of sight operation, but the actual operation range for any device might well extend beyond line of sight and in theory there is no limit to their operating range.

Dr. Scott's response to this was two-fold. First, any departure from line of sight working is a serious design flaw for the bomber. It serves no purpose and made the bomb more vulnerable to "scanning." That is a process developed by the security forces in Northern Ireland whereby a high powered transmitter moves through all frequencies emitting all possible tones, hoping to hit on the correct combination. If it does, there is an explosion, which in some circumstances can be highly detrimental to the health and appearance of the bomb maker.

Mr. Faraday did concede however that any buildings between the receiver and the transmitter will not only obscure the line of sight but was also likely to reduce the effective operating range of any radio controlled linkage. Without carrying out any detailed on the spot trials it would be impossible to guarantee whether a particular radio controlled device would or would not work because of the intervening buildings.

Dr. Scott went to Gibraltar and carried out a field test. He walked as straight as possible between Ince's Hall and the Shell Service Station. He walked along level ground, along very narrow streets with tall buildings on either side. Then the ground began to rise gradually. After about 15 minutes he was faced with the Moroccan quarters which he described as an impressive barrier. Beyond that were the old city walls, some 40 feet thick. The descent was then rapid down to the petrol station. The route was very heavily built up all the way.

After that Dr. Scott examined a large scale map of the area. The Shell garage was 1·4 metres above sea level, and Ince's Hall where the Renault car was positioned was 8·6 metres above. The line joining the two points passed through a corner of the Rock which abutted into the town. The maximum height attained along this line he conservatively estimated at 100 metres. In other words, the ground-wave signal would have had to negotiate a 100-metre hill, through a densely built up area, over a range of some 1500 metres leading into an enclosed square. The terrain could hardly have been worse.

From his professional experience in IRA cases Dr. Scott knew that the Provisionals used a tone encoder-decoder system. This involves using an encoder that is attached to the transmitter and emits a tone at a particular frequency. It is this signal which is transmitted. The receiver/decoder, when it is sure it has heard this sound, described as a whistle, detonates the bomb. In order to avoid random signals or noise causing a premature explosion, the decoder insists it must receive a loud, clear and unambiguous signal before it will detonate the bomb. A signal meeting this criteria would be best generated by an uninterrupted light of sight signal. A noisy tone, which might be acceptable and recognisable to the human ear, would not satisfy the decoder.

Mr. Faraday produced as an exhibit an ICOM IC-2E hand held 144MHz transceiver – colloquially described as "a walkie-talkie". It was compact and could easily be concealed. He told the Inquest that "….it must be possible for a radio controlled linkage of the type frequently used by the IRA could work from anywhere in this colony".

Mr. McGrory asked him about the car aerial, which was a bent piece of wire 30 inches long, on the white Renault. "Would the signal given by the ICOM be able to be received by the aerial on that car?" He replied: "It would certainly be received by it but its efficiency would be fairly poor in the sense that it is not the correct length as far as this particular frequency was concerned."

Dr. Scott's response to that was that the optimal length of the aerial was the simple function of the frequency used; the higher the frequency the smaller the aerial, and vice versa. The aerial on the Renault, given its mounting and orientation – it was in the middle of the roof and sloping back over it, would not be optimal at any frequency. That aerial was designed more with the aerodynamics of the car in mind rather than its reception capabilities. It would be expected only to receive strong signals from powerful radio stations. He considered that the Army and the police did not have to be specific about the frequency used because of course no transmitter or receiver was used by the active service unit. The site of the car in Ince's Hall was also a relevant factor in his view. It was positioned in an area surrounded by three high walls, the worse possible position for the reception of weak radio signals. As the car aerial was pointing in the direction of the Shell petrol station some 1500 metres away, this was the worst possible direction from which to receive radio transmissions.

Mr. Faraday did not agree with this. He said he could not rule out the possibility that with that car aerial and the hand held device which was exhibited, that it would not detonate a car bomb of the type being described. That may be regarded by some as falling somewhat short of actually saying it would, or might probably, happen. He was apparently claiming that it was possible.

Dr. Scott carried out some tests on the Rock. Mr. Faraday did not. Using a IC-2E and his own IC-2A hand held portable receivers, a system with two matched aerials at both ends and therefore superior to any car aerial. From the Shell service station a marginal – noisy but audible – signal could be heard in Ince's Hall, probably due to the signal bouncing off the Rock. Even these signals disappeared however, if the receiving aerial was titled towards the petrol station as the car aerial was at the time it was parked. The signals also disappeared if the transmitting device was held close to the body, as a concealed one would have been.

Dr. Scott's field tests led him to the conclusion, which he stated in evidence to the Inquest jury, that signals transmitted from a concealed transmitter would almost certainly not have registered at all on a receiver connected to the car aerial. Even if a signal had registered it would not have been of sufficient strength and quality to cause a detonation.

Dr. Scott gave his expert view on the evidence of the SAS soldiers who conveyed the impression that all the active service unit members had to do was to press a single switch on a transmitter to detonate the explosive device. This was not the case. The transmitter had to be turned on, the send button pressed and activating the encoder. If the device was pre-set, so that only one touch would be sufficient to set it off, there was a high risk that it would go off by accident if the person carrying it bumped into another person or object, or fell down awkwardly. It was of course the SAS soldiers' case that they honestly and firmly believed that Mairead Farrell, Sean Savage and Daniel McCann, or at least one of them, had a transmitter that they reached for when confronted so they opened fire. Firing shots into their bodies, however, causing them to fall to the ground would propel them into achieving the object which the soldiers shot them to prevent them doing, namely transmitting the signal to detonate the bomb.

At the conclusion of Dr. Scott's evidence Michael Hucker told the Coroner that he was considering calling his own expert witness. That same night soldiers from the Royal Corps of Signals were ordered to carry out tests that had previously been avoided. They did not carry out a test using the car aerial in conjunction with a tone decoder, although this was readily available to them. A more powerful transmitter was used than the device that was exhibited and used by Alan Faraday. This involved a bulkier battery pack which would have been more difficult to conceal. What Dr. Scott describes at "a cleverly misleading elaboration" was used, where a recording was made of a tone onto a tape recorder. The tone was then transmitted by holding the tape recorder up to the transmitter. The first tests, at 156 MHz, were a failure. No signal was received despite matched aerials being used. Finally, using a slightly lower frequency, voice signals and the tone were picked up, again using matched aerials.

Dr. Scott left Gibraltar after completing his evidence on Tuesday 27 September 1988. The tests were carried out after his departure and the next day, the 29th, Mr. Hucker called a Captain Edwards to give evidence. He was a member of the Royal Corps of Signals and had experience in VHF/HF radio in combat net radio spectrum. He admitted that the equipment used was not identical to that of Dr. Scott. He had been tasked to establish whether or not voice communications were possible on an ICOM-type radio between the Shell garage and Ince's Hall. This was too much for one clearly technically competent member of the Inquest jury. He said to the Captain: "Am I to understand that you did not perform any digital encoded message and use a decoded digital receiver at the other end?" He could only reply: "no. The only equipment I had available were the hand-held marine-band radios, and I went just for a voice test and the signal tone put down a voice audio frequency."

Mr. Faraday was then recalled. He maintained that it was easier to transmit, receive and digitally encode a tone signal than it would be to transmit, receive and comprehend a noisy voice signal. His considered conclusion was "if one can establish speech transmission, then the bomb will work".

The persistent juror did not accept that. Neither does Dr. Scott. The juror put some 48 questions to Mr. Faraday, asking him: "So really am I right in saying that, unless you attach an encoder to that transmitter and a decoder to the transceiver at the other end, you could not really perform a realistic test, only going by voice transmission?"

He replied, "I think they are realistic tests in the sense that if voice communication is established the bomb will be set off. I do not think there is any doubt about that". When pressed further he seemed to retreat from that position. The juror asked him: "If someone tells you that he has done tests and identified voice signal deterioration, that still makes you think it would work?" He rather weakly replied: "I think it is a possibility that it would work."

His ordeal at the hands of the juror was not quite over. He was asked to estimate the frequency for which the 30 inch car aerial would be the correct length. He replied 30 MHz. Dr. Scott disagrees with him. It may be the juror did as well, for at that frequency the aerial on the white Renault car would have needed to be over eight feet long.

Mr. Faraday seemed to struggle with another part of his evidence. He accepted that Dr. Scott was theoretically correct that removing the aerial from the Renault car would make the bomb safe. However, he added, "I think it would be an extremely foolish thing to do. First of all, that is absolutely and completely against all explosive ordnance disposal procedures and teaching relating to the army. Long ago it was found at cost in Northern Ireland that walking up to any suspect device or suspect item was to a foolish thing to do, and remote means are used." Had no one told him that was exactly what Soldier G had done – he had walked up to the Renault car and visually examined the car and its aerial at sufficiently close distance to be able to see inside the vehicle?

Can there be any doubt that when he left the witness box Alan Faraday must have sighed with relief that his evidence was over. Whether it was accepted was another matter.

Prior to the commencement of the Inquest on 6 September 1988 the Home Secretary, the Defence Secretary and the Deputy Governor of Gibraltar signed Public Immunity Certificates, dated 26 August, 30 August and 2 September 1988. As a matter of law, public interest immunity, formerly known as Crown Privilege, prevents material from being disclosed and adduced in the usual way, where it is held that the public interest in non-disclosure outweighs the public interest that the courts should have the fullest access to all relevant material.

The combined object and effect of the PII Certificates in this case was, first, they were necessary to protect sources and means by which intelligence is and has been gathered by the security services, including information as to dates and times of any intelligence activity. Second, to protect the means of operation and equipment of the security forces and third, to protect the operations of the Gibraltar police. The overall effect of the Certificates was, as intended, to have a significant effect upon the breadth and detail of information before the inquest and to prevent examination of a number of key issues.

What could not be concealed however was one stark fact. As noted above, the army returned control of the operation to the civil power and this was done in a form handed by Soldier F to the police Commissioner. The note stated: "At 16.06 hours on 6 March a military assault force was completed at the military option in respect of the terrorist bombing ASU in Gibraltar." The Acting Deputy Commissioner telephoned the Central police station for the evacuation plans to be put into effect. Soldier G was also instructed to commence the clearance of the Renault car in Ince's Hall. A bomb disposal team opened the suspect car but found no explosive device or bomb. The area was declared safe between 7 p.m. and 8 p.m. (All the more surprising therefore to find a Government Minister, Ian Stewart, claiming on the radio the next morning that a bomb had been found and it had been defused.)

It follows from this that from 3.41 p.m. when the three terrorists were shot dead, that the area around the suspect car in Ince's Hall was not cordoned off and the whole area evacuated. It could and should have been done earlier than that time. It was not done until about 4.10 p.m. about half an hour after the shootings of the suspected bombers. Not to clear the area was nothing short of criminal conduct by omission, unless of course it was known that there was no reason to do it until after the shootings and the commencement of a cover up. Time and again Mr. McGrory pressed the Deputy Police Commissioner Mr. Colombo to explain why, once the suspect car bomb had been located, the area had not been cleared of people. He replied that there was not enough manpower available, and in any case the bomb was only a suspect one. The identities of the IRA unit had to be confirmed, and while the three moved south and away from the border, it was thought they might come back and drive the car away. Mr. McGrory put to him that in other areas of the world the least suspicion of a car bomb led to the area being cleared and arrests were left until later. Mr. Colombo told him that they were trying to gather evidence to put a case together and he was asked "even if this put people at risk?" His reply was most illuminating. "There was no risk because we were not certain there was a bomb there, if they had come back and taken the car away there would have been no bomb there". The manpower for an immediate evacuation was not available. Once the three were shot the evacuation plan was put into effect.

The explanations put forward for the failure to clear the area before that time are ludicrous and probably false. It was said that the police plan to evacuate the area related to the day of the band parade on Tuesday, not Sunday. There might be dangers in alerting the three if evacuation began soon after they left the area. There were insufficient resources anyway, to clear the area. The latter especially seems fanciful since there was the whole British Garrison of a least 600 soldiers stationed on the Rock, with the Gibraltar Services Police also on hand, to help if called upon to do so. In any event, how many people would be required to cordon off a small area leading into the assembly area of Ince's Hall?

Most startling of all is the evidence given at the Inquest by Chief Inspector Lopez, who, as noted above, had prepared the evacuation plan on 5 March. He said that at about 3.40 p.m. on the Sunday (6 March) he had received a call from Mr. Colombo for a car to stand by at central police station but he was not aware that the suspects had come to Gibraltar. It was "well after" 3.40 p.m. he said, that he was told of the suspect bomb at Ince's Hall. He then put the evacuation into operation and it was "a mammoth task". We are asked to believe that the very person tasked to ensure public safety by clearing an area containing a car bomb was not told of its existence at the very first opportunity, and not asked to carry out his designated duty until the 59th minute of the 23rd hour. Few people outside Gibraltar will.

The best explanation may be the truthful one. There was no bomb in the car at all, and the authorities knew it. The penalty for conspiracy to murder in Gibraltar was death and the sentence was carried out on the afternoon of Sunday 6 March 1988.

All this may have been in the minds of the jury as the Coroner summed up the facts and the law relating to their verdict. He had a type-written record of his directions available to them, but he read them so swiftly that they would have needed a substantial amount of time to examine them at length in the jury room. Their task was considerable, for they had heard evidence, which was both detailed and technical, over the previous three and a half weeks. Mr. Pizzarello left them three possible verdicts, namely, unlawful killing, lawful killing and an Open verdict. He urged them, in the exercise of their duty to avoid this open verdict. (That reflected the closing argument of John Laws Q.C., counsel for the Crown. He said that the jury had to decide whether it was lawful or unlawful killing. An open verdict was only available in an artificial situation and to return it the jury would not be doing its duty).

Mr. Pizzarello failed to make it clear to the jury that they should consider each verdict separately and further to tell them that they could add a rider to their verdict provided it was designed to prevent the recurrence of death in similar circumstances. They retired to consider their findings at 11.30 a.m.on Friday 30 September 1988.

As early as 5.15 p.m. they were recalled into court by the Coroner to report progress and to be told by him that it being his duty to allow a reasonable amount of time for the consideration of the verdict, they were reaching the edge of that amount of time, and he would like to know how they were getting on. He said to them "can you reach a verdict in the next couple of hours?" The jury foreman, Mr. Daniel Gabay, a senior Gibraltar civil servant replied: "I doubt it. Several things are being discussed". The Coroner said: "It is my duty to tell you that you can bring in a majority verdict with a minority of not more than two." The foreman replied: "We have reached a majority decision but it is not nine to two. We seem to be deadlocked." Mr. Pizarello asked him to remember that it was three inquests and did the majority apply to all three, to which the answer was in the affirmative, but with just a slight difference. When the foreman was asked if another hour would be sufficient for a majority decision to be reached, he shrugged as if unable to answer with any degree of accuracy. The Coroner then said he would recall the jury at 7 p.m., in some 90 minutes time, to check further progress. He seemed, consciously or otherwise, to give them an ultimatum that they must reach a verdict at a time he put at 7 p.m. It was their right to take as long as they required, but in the event they returned at 7.15 p.m. and recorded a majority verdict of lawful killing.

On 4 August 1991 the families of the deceased lodged an application with the European Commission of Human Rights, complaining that the killing of Mairead Farrell, Sean Savage and Daniel McCann by the SAS constituted a violation of Article 2 of the European Convention of Human Rights. That Article states that "Everyone's right to life shall be protected by law. No one shall be deprived of his life intentionally save in the execution of a sentence of a court following his conviction of a crime for which this penalty is provided by law".

On 4 March 1994 the Commission reported that in its opinion there had been no violation of Article 2. The families went to the full Court complaining that no independent police investigation took place in any aspect of the operation leading to the shootings; that normal scene-of-crime procedures were not followed; that not all eye witnesses were traced or interviewed by the police; that the Coroner sat with a jury which was drawn from a "garrison" town with close ties to the military; that the Coroner refused to allow the jury to be screened to exclude members who were Crown servants and finally that the Public Interest Immunity Certificates issued by the authorities effectively curtailed an examination of the overall operation.

On 27 September 1995 the Court ruled by a majority of 10 to 9 that the killings of Mairead Farrell, Daniel McCann and Sean Savage were unnecessary, that the three could have been arrested and that excessive force had been used. The Court conceded that the knowledge of a possible terrorist attack presented the British authorities with a dilemma over how best to protect lives and at the same time use minimum force. The security forces could not have been in possession of the full facts and were obliged to formulate their polices of the basis of incomplete hypotheses. The SAS soldiers honestly believed that it was necessary to shoot the suspects in order to prevent them detonating a bomb. The Court then ruled in relation to them that the actions of the soldiers did not give rise to a violation of Article 2.

In respect of the action of the United Kingdom authorities however, in allowing the three terrorists to cross the border into Gibraltar and whether they could have arrested them, the Court took a much more critical view. The danger to the people of Gibraltar in not preventing their entry must be considered to outweigh the possible consequences of having insufficient evidence to warrant their detention and trial.

The judgment of the Court was further critical of the United Kingdom authorities for the scrutiny of the car and their supposition that the terrorists had a remote control button. They were bound by their obligation to respect the right to life of the suspects, to exercise the greatest care in evaluating the information at their disposal before transmitting it to the soldiers whose use of firearms automatically involving shooting to kill. The majority of the judges held that "The Court is not persuaded that the killing of the three terrorists constituted the use of force which was no more than absolutely necessary in defence of persons from unlawful violence within the meaning of Article 2 of the Convention. Accordingly it finds there has been a breach of Article 2".

It was not a judgment that was well received by the United Kingdom Government. It reacted with outrage and defiance, saying the verdict was ludicrous and would give succour to terrorism. Britain was the first member State to have been found to have violated the human rights of its subjects contrary to Article 2. Since its founding in 1951 up to 1994, the Court in Strasbourg has considered 76 cases brought against the United Kingdom. In 36 of those cases there has been an adverse finding against the Government. Only Turkey has a worse record on human rights.

In what many regard as an act of revenge against the media, and in order to encourage the others, in November 1991 the Conservative Government declined to renew the broadcasting licence held by Thames Television, the Company that broadcast the documentary of *Death on the Rock*. Very few people missed the significance of the link between the transmission and the demise of Thames Television. Others who wished to continue to operate their licences undoubtedly took note.

There exists in a number of television newsroom libraries a film of the removal of the body of Mairead Farrell from the road at the side of the Shell garage near the Gibraltar border crossing into Spain. Some may recall the words of the then Prime Minister Margaret Thatcher whilst watching that film. On 16 October 1984, two days after the Provisional IRA had bombed the Grand Hotel in Brighton, almost killing her, her husband and many senior members of the Government, she is reported to have said: "People who go out prepared to take the lives of other people, forfeit their own right to live". Was that philosophy being put into practice at 3.41 p.m. on Sunday 6 March 1988?

CHAPTER 2

THE DEATH OF AN INNOCENT

In 1994, a retired British Army, General Sir Peter De La Billiere, wrote his autobiography called *Looking for Trouble*. De La Billiere was born in 1935 and received a Public School education at Harrow School. He joined the Army in 1952 and served in Japan, Korea and the Middle East. In 1956 he joined the SAS. He was in overall military command at the time of the seizure by terrorists of the Iranian embassy in London. A recent television programme showed one member of the SAS on camera stating that his clear understanding of his orders was that no terrorist was to be taken alive when the embassy was stormed by the SAS.

De La Billiere retired from the Army in June 1992. He received military decorations and recommendations not only for his own Country but from others as well.

This was not his first book. He also wrote *Storm Command*, his personal account of the Gulf War. It was, so his publishers claim, a number one best seller. He is therefore a practised and accomplished writer, but the two following instances in Northern Ireland cases show he may have little regard for the truth.

The first instance appears at page 316 of his autobiography where he writes: "The next salvo in the IRA's black propaganda attack came early in 1979, in the form of a story that an SAS sergeant had raped the wife of a doctor in Northern Ireland. The aim, as always, was to portray the Regiment as ill-disciplined and out of control, a liability to all concerned. For a while the story remained a fairly minor one, but then in the third week of March the *Daily Telegraph* ran a prominent news item, and followed it, on Saturday 17 March, with an editorial which demanded an official inquiry by Roy Mason, the Northern Ireland Minster. Immediate action was needed to prevent any further escalation of the rumours.

I was incensed. Already confident that the story was a fabrication, I made inquiries which confirmed my belief." He goes on to describe the steps he took to have issued a press release denying the story.

The reality is somewhat different. It begins in June 1978 when Amnesty International published a report about treatment of suspects in custody by the Royal Ulster Constabulary, the RUC.

Statistics of complaints made against the security forces in Northern Ireland show that between August 1971 and November 1974 there were 1,105 complaints of assault and maltreatment alleged against the RUC and 1,078 against the British Army.

In 1975 184 people complained of maltreatment whilst being interviewed by the RUC whilst in custody. In 1976 the number complaining rose to 322 and in the first eleven months of 1977 the number increased again to 515. The maltreatment alleged during that year included both mental and physical maltreatment. Physical methods included beating, attempted strangulation, pressure to sensitive points of the body, bending of limbs, prolonged standing or squatting in awkward positions, prolonged physical exercises, and burning with cigarettes. Mental pressures alleged included prolonged oppressive questioning by teams of officers, threats of death and of imprisonment, and threats to the family of the suspect, stripping and verbal abuse and humiliation. The RUC and the Army denied that these allegations had any foundation in truth.

On 2 March 1977 the BBC broadcast a programme, *Tonight*, showing interviews with a Fermanagh schoolteacher Bernard O'Connor and Michael Lavelle in which they complained about ill-treatment whilst being questioned in custody by the RUC at Castlereagh Holding Centre. The teacher described being made to stand on his toes with his knees in a bent position and hands in front of him, for about three or four hours. If he moved he was slapped. He was kicked, punched and hurled across the room. He was then made to carry out physical exercises on the spot whilst naked. He was forced to stand with his slightly soiled underpants over his head, and then made to pick up cigarette butts from the floor with his mouth. A track suit top was tied over his head, blocking his airways, causing him to faint. The purpose of this misconduct was to get him to sign a confession.

The response of the State authorities was immediate and predictable. The Northern Ireland Secretary of State, Roy Mason, a former Barnsley coal miner, told the *Irish Times* that the questioning of the two men was considered fully justified in the light of information available. I find that statement quite astonishing. It would sit more easily with the methods of interrogation used by a fascist dictatorship, rather than a civilised democracy. It is an attempt to explain unlawful and criminal assaults on the ground of justification. Does that mean that torture of suspects in custody is acceptable if it is done with the right motive?

The fact that a British politician may have considered such behaviour to be justified did not prevent the court in Northern Ireland from awarding Mr. O'Connor the sum of £5,000, with costs, in compensation as exemplary damages for maltreatment during interrogation by the RUC. Exemplary damages are awarded by a court by way of punishment of the defendant for a civil wrong.

In October 1977 a Committee of the Police Surgeons Association of Northern Ireland sought a meeting with the Chief Constable of the RUC to voice their concerns about ill treatment in custody. At the end of that month Thames Television broadcast a programme entitled *Inhuman and Degrading Treatment* which featured ten cases, eight Catholics and two Protestants, all alleging maltreatment at Castlereagh Holding Centre. Roy Mason, surely one of the worst, if not the worst Northern Ireland Secretary ever, continued to shoot from the lip. "The programme was riddled with unsubstantiated accusations. I have said it was irresponsible and insensitive, and I still believe it."

The programme which caused him so much anxiety and stress was transmitted on 27 October 1977. It was time for the London *Daily Telegraph* (or the Torygraph as it is sometimes called because of its devotion to the Tory party and all its works and pomps) to come to the aid of the Party. It did with the most incredible and farcical story, which, because it appeared in small print (as opposed to the large print, of the tabloids) persuaded people they were reading something of substance.

The journalist Gerald Barlett, under the headline, "IRA award prizes for fake claims of RUC brutality" wrote: "Prizes are given according to the degree of self-inflicted injury". He goes on to cite the case of one hard line Provisional punching himself in both eyes and then filing a complaint alleging brutality against the RUC. The prize for that was a large whiskey and a box of cigarettes. Since the newspaper itself had reported only two days previously that in the previous year, 1976, there had been no less than 648 complaints against the RUC alleging assault either at the time of arrest or during interview, that would call for an awful lot of prizes. It is also a clever piece of black propaganda, since it identifies those who complain about brutality with membership of the Provisional IRA.

In early November 1977 a group of about 30 solicitors who practised in the non-jury Diplock courts in Northern Ireland decided to set up a three-man committee to collate evidence of alleged brutality, and wrote and told the Secretary of State that ill-treatment of suspects in custody was common practice, and the object was to obtain confessions to terrorist activity.

It was against this background that the Amnesty International Team began their investigation which led to their 1978 Report. After examining some 78 cases the team concluded that: "On the basis of information available to it, Amnesty International believes that maltreatment of suspected terrorists by the RUC has taken place with sufficient frequency to warrant the establishment of a public inquiry to investigate it..... legal provisions which have eroded the rights of suspects.....have helped create the circumstances in which maltreatment of suspects has taken place.... The evidence presented to the mission suggests that machinery for investigating complaints against the police of assault during interview is not adequate."

The publication of that report by an internationally respected body (although respect for Amnesty International in Britain always depends on its targets: when it fires a broadside at an African or Balkan dictator, it is splendid, but it is otherwise when it is dealing with Northern Ireland) meant an end to the pretence that there was nothing wrong with the way the RUC gathered evidence from suspects in custody.

Thames Television wished to broadcast its *This Week* programme on 8 June 1978 to discuss the Amnesty report, but the Independent Television Authority banned its transmission. That Authority was running scared of the politicians. (It was the same Television Company, Thames, that courageously broadcast the programme *Death on the Rock* which questioned the official account of the killings of three members of the IRA, by the SAS, in Gibraltar in March 1988. The Government headed by Mrs. Thatcher was in a fury over its transmission. When the time arrived for the renewal of television company franchises with the Independent Television Companies, the franchise for Thames was not renewed. Some see a connection between the transmission of the programme and that refusal to renew.)

The Amnesty Report recommended that, for reasons relating to the protection of suspects and police officers alike, a public and impartial inquiry be established to investigate the allegations of maltreatment. Pending the establishment and reporting of such an inquiry, Amnesty International further recommended that immediate steps should be taken to ensure that suspects being interviewed by the Royal Ulster Constabulary on suspicion of terrorism be protected against possible maltreatment. Measures to this end should include access to lawyers at an early stage of the detention.

The British Government refused to set up such an Inquiry. In a statement on 8 June 1978 to the House of Commons, Roy Mason invited Amnesty to submit to the Director of Public Prosecutions in Northern Ireland the allegations of criminal conduct which they wished to make, and their evidence, so that in due course the Director might investigate those allegations and report on his general findings and conclusions. In the meanwhile, said the Minister, he was setting up a Committee of Inquiry to "examine police procedures and practice in Northern Ireland relating to the interrogation of persons suspected of scheduled offences; to examine the operation of present procedures for dealing with complaints relating to the conduct of the police in the course of the process of interrogation; and to report and make recommendations."

One can only pause to admire the competence of a Colonial Power, drawing on its many years of experience of suppressing the truth, giving every appearance of being reasonable, relying on the Parliamentary sincerity of a former Barnsley coal miner, to invite Amnesty to do something which it knew would probably not be done, and at the same time ensuring that by its terms of reference, few within the Nationalist community in Northern Ireland would co-operate with the Government appointed Inquiry.

On 16 June the members of the Inquiry were named. They were Judge H.G. Bennett Q.C., a middle ranking member of the judiciary in Britain, about whom very little was known; a senior police officer, Sir James Haughton, holder of the Queen's Medal for policing, and a doctor, Professor John Marshall.

On 16 February 1979 the Inquiry team delivered its unanimous

Report to Roy Mason. For reasons that would later become apparent, the Government seemed reluctant to publish that Report. At mid-day on Sunday 11 March 1979 events forced its hand.

On that day, at that time, London Weekend Television broadcast a programme, presented by the journalist Mary Holland, dealing with the allegations of maltreatment of suspects in custody in Northern Ireland. Amongst those interviewed by Mary Holland was Dr. Robert Irwin, a police surgeon and general practitioner. He had ten years experience of working for the RUC, including three years at Castlereagh Holding Centre. He was regarded, as Liz Curtis notes, as having a great respect for the RUC and had the reputation of being as steady as a rock. What he had to say was devastating for the authorities both within the British Government and in Northern Ireland. Dr. Irwin said that he had seen between 150 and 160 people with injuries at Castlereagh. "There are injuries which could not be self-inflicted. Ruptured eardrums, I would say, being one of the most serious, could not possibly be self-inflicted."

The authorities fought back that very evening of the transmission of the programme. Some might call their tactics damage limitation. Others would describe them as very dirty tricks.

As Liz Curtis's research has disclosed, on that Sunday evening RUC press officers began leaking a variety of smears against Dr. Irwin to journalists, suggesting he had personal reasons for discrediting the police. She cites the *Irish Times* as noting: "First indications of press office willingness to supply background detail detrimental to Dr. Irwin came on Sunday night when one reporter was told the doctor had 'got a bit of a demotion'.......You know his wife was raped a while ago"… and the suggestion was then made that Dr. Irwin had seemed to hold a grudge against the police for failure to track down the rapist.

A journalist with the *Guardian* was briefed in similar terms. A press officer told him on the telephone that "Irwin was a drunk, had lost his job in Castlereagh because he was 'foul tempered' and that he was 'sour and bitter' at the RUC." An *Observer* journalist was told by a similar source that Dr. Irwin's transfer from Castlereagh to a city centre police station had 'rankled' and that Irwin had 'domestic problems' which the journalist understood to be a reference to his wife's rape. In an interview with the Press Association, at which Dr. Irwin became distressed, he spoke frankly about the rape, saying it had been traced to a British soldier on undercover duty. He asked however that his remarks be treated in confidence and this was respected by the Press Association until the whole issue entered the public arena.

It was the *Daily Telegraph* newspaper that was responsible for this on 16 March 1979. In a story written by Gerald Bartlett (who had noted the existence of prizes for Provos who injured themselves then complained about RUC brutality), the headline was "Rape case bitterness denied by the RUC". This clearly is the "prominent news item" mentioned by General Sir Peter De La Billiere at page 316 of his autobiography, because he says it was followed on Saturday March 17 by an editorial that demanded an official inquiry by Roy Mason. It will be remembered that his description of these events were as "the next salvo in the IRA's black propaganda attack early in 1979, in the form of a story that an SAS sergeant had raped the wife of a doctor in Northern Ireland."

This was anything but the truth. For as the *Daily Telegraph* reported, some 12 hours after Dr. Irwin had made his allegations on television, Whitehall officials had apparently sanctioned 'leakage' of the details of the rape of his wife. The Bartlett story continued in terms that Dr. Irwin was alleging that his wife was raped by an SAS non commissioned officer, who was subsequently spirited out of Northern Ireland to avoid charge or inquiry.

There was an angry response in the House of Commons the day following publication of this identification of a victim of rape that both she and her husband wished to remain confidential, but the *Telegraph* journalist tried to justify it by maintaining that he had "checked and demolished this planted leak with exemplary care".

Whatever the merits of disclosing this information, what is abundantly clear is that there was a black propaganda campaign at work in March 1979 in the case of Dr. Irwin and his wife. It was not the IRA at work in its dissemination, but the dirty tricks department of the British Government. To describe it as the "next salvo" as De La Billiere does is curious, unusual and untrue.

As a footnote, on the same day as the leaked smear story appeared in the *Daily Telegraph*, March 16 1979, the Government published the Report of the Bennett Inquiry. Chapter 19 of the Report sets out in 64 paragraphs a summary of its principal conclusions and recommendations.

At paragraph 16 there is to be found three lines that might, if anything could, (which in my view is doubtful,) embarrass Roy

Mason and the British Government. The Inquiry found: "Our own examination of medical evidence reveals cases in which injuries, whatever their precise cause, were not self-inflicted and were sustained in police custody." So Dr. Irwin had been accurate and truthful all along. Was it really necessary for the British State to try to discredit him in the way it did, especially since they knew, having seen the Bennett Report in February 1979, that what he was claiming on television was supported by evidence accepted as true by that judge, a police officer and a doctor?

That is the first instance in which I take issue with General Sir Peter De La Billiere. The second relates to the killing of John Boyle.

At page 315 of his autobiography he narrates the following. "By the time I took over, at the end of 1978, the SAS had been deployed in Northern Ireland…..There had been a few minor problems – as when some men strayed over the border into the Republic – and every time something went wrong, the IRA sought to make capital out of the incident, working up a campaign of black propaganda against the Regiment.

Shortly before I assumed command there had occurred what became known as the Dunloy incident. Our soldiers had found a weapons cache in a grave, and had staked the site out, lying up for several days and nights hidden in a wet ditch at the edge of the churchyard. One night a man appeared, lifted the top of a grave and took out a semi-automatic weapon, which he pointed in the direction of the watchers. They, thinking that he had seen them and was about to shoot, opened fire and killed him."

I maintain almost every single statement of fact in that second paragraph is entirely false. The weapons were not found by soldiers, they were found by a sixteen year old schoolboy John Boyle. The soldiers were not lying up for several days and nights, but only a few hours, and then not in a wet ditch. It was not a man that appeared, it was a boy. It was not at night, it was about 10 o'clock on a summer's morning. Of the four soldiers who were at or nearby the scene of the killing, only they know whether John picked up a gun and pointed it at them.

The autobiography goes on and indeed gets worse in what I regard are false allegations, the most serious of which appears first: "Clearly the dead man had been a member of the IRA; but he was only sixteen and probably a low-grade operator. The IRA opened up a vociferous propaganda barrage, producing pictures taken seven or eight years earlier, when the youth was singing in a choir, and presenting us as having killed a choirboy." I have researched this case over a number of years, and at no time have I ever found any other reference to the use of photographs of John Boyle in this way, anywhere in the literature available. Nor have I seen any such photos. I wrote to the publishers of *Looking for Trouble* some time ago asking they provide, either themselves or through the author of the book, sufficient information to enable me to identify where these photographs were used in the way described, and where they can now be found. I have received no reply and accordingly no information.

John Boyle was the second youngest child of a family of eight children, seven boys and a girl. He was a pupil at Our Lady of Lourdes School in Ballymoney, County Antrim. He was sixteen years of age when he died.

The family lived on their farm near Dunloy, a mixed Catholic and Protestant area.

On the afternoon of Monday 10 July 1978 John and his brother Hugh had been working on the farm, saving the hay. At about 4 o'clock John decided to walk from the field across a narrow lane to an old disused graveyard in order to look for some ancestral names on the gravestones. As he searched and read and moved around he found one gravestone that had fallen forward. Beneath that headstone, which lay flat, there was a cavity which was partly blocked by another stone roughly spherical in shape, John found a plastic bag, an Armalite rifle, a revolver, an incendiary bomb, a face mask, combat jacket and black beret. This may have been left there in connection with a terrorist outrage at some time during the so-called "Marching Season" in Northern Ireland, when bands and groups from both sides of the sectarian divide march, sometimes in areas in which they are not wanted. One of the important dates in that season was just two days away, the 12th July.

John told his brother Hugh immediately about what he had found in the graveyard. He accompanied John to the scene and saw the cache. They told their father Cornelius and he too saw the weapons. No member of the Boyle family touched any of the objects found at the gravestone.

On returning home Cornelius Boyle instantly telephoned the RUC station at Ballymoney, telling them what had been found in the graveyard. He was told by a detective constable that he would have the matter attended to. Later that same day this constable and three other RUC officers went to the scene and checked the bag. They did not remove the firearms. At the very least, one would have expected them to ensure that neither the rifle nor the revolver could be fired and any ammunition would be removed from that entire area.

The RUC officers contacted an army captain at Ebrington Barracks in County Derry. A decision was made that a four man team from the SAS would move into the graveyard under cover of darkness, to keep the area under surveillance, as it was likely that the firearms would be recovered for use on 12 July. A parade organised by the Orange Order was scheduled for the area that day.

At about midnight a briefing was held at Ballymoney Police Station at which members of the SAS stationed at Ballykelly were present. First there was a conference upstairs in the police station, at which the RUC gave information to the SAS soldiers, including an officer of the rank of captain, later referred to as Soldier F. On the assumption that there was a good chance that a terrorist might return to the graveyard in the immediate future, it was arranged that a patrol of four men, consisting of soldiers A, B, D and E, and under the command of Soldier A, would go to the graveyard and keep watch, with a view to effecting his arrest.

The patrol had assembled in a downstairs room at the Police Station and on conclusion of the conference upstairs, was briefed by Soldier F and the detective constable who knew where the cache of arms was. He was also able to brief the soldiers on the surrounding geographical features and roads, and tell them something about the inhabitants of the neighbouring countryside. He also showed an army driver where the entrance to the graveyard was. According to the journalist Desmond Hamill that officer warned the soldiers no less than three times that the family of the boy who found the cache might approach the site, because they were working in adjacent fields, and that they should be very careful. He said later that he thought the soldiers did not pay much attention to what he was saying. (The army's version given to the court by the captain from Ebrington barracks was that the army did not expect any member of the Boyle family to return to the cache, and that the detective constable who briefed them told the soldiers that he had warned his informant to keep away from the graveyard, and that he would repeat this warning again. That police officer maintained however that he had told the soldiers three times at the midnight meeting that the information had come from a family with children between the ages of ten and twenty four years, and advised them to be careful, in case any one of them returned to the scene out of curiosity.) As noted by Fr. Raymond Murray in his book *The SAS in Ireland*, during the subsequent trial for murder against Bohan and Temperley, it was suggested by defence counsel in cross-examination of this police officer that he had not, as he claimed, warned the soldiers three times in the way and in the terms that he said. His witness statement was put to him and he was asked to explain why that statement contained no reference to those three warnings. The police officer replied that he had mentioned them in his original written statement, and the one produced to him in court was typewritten. It had been sent to him for signing by a person in the Department of the Director of Public Prosecutions in Belfast in February 1979, and he had assumed that it had been deleted from the statement for a legal reason.

The four man SAS patrol was driven to the graveyard in the early hours of the morning, in complete darkness. It was about 2.30 a.m. Two soldiers, D and E concealed themselves in a disused farm building on the road opposite the path that led into the graveyard. It was their responsibility to observe the movements of anyone approaching the graveyard and to contact and warn the other two soldiers. Soldier A was apparently Sergeant Alan Michael Bohan; Soldier B was apparently Corporal Ronald Joseph Temperley. (At some stage it would appear that they changed ranks. Indeed, to add to the confusion, Lord Lowry, the judge at the subsequent murder trial described Bohan as a corporal and Temperley as a trooper). These two soldiers concealed themselves in a hide between a hedge and a stone wall, about 12 yards away from the cache. They sat back to back, so that one soldier was facing the approach to the gravestone and the other was looking directly at it. Anyone approaching the cache would roughly have his back turned to where Bohan and Temperley had taken up their positions.

The detective constable who had briefed the army was on duty until the early hours of the morning of 11 July. He did not finish his work until about 2.30 a.m. The next morning he telephoned the Boyle household and asked that no member of the family should go to the graveyard. Of course he was unable to give full reasons why they should not. In any event it was too late for John and Hugh Boyle. Both boys had left the house and gone to the fields about ten minutes before the phone call was received at about 9.40 a.m.

At about 10 o'clock that morning John decided to go back to the graveyard. He left the field and drove towards it on a tractor. Soldiers D and E, who saw his approach, apparently did not tell their two colleagues inside the graveyard; in any event they too must have heard the noise of the approaching tractor. Soldiers D and E claim to have seen nothing of what happened next in the graveyard. It was alleged that their view was obstructed by the wheels of the tractor.

John walked into the graveyard after opening the gate. As he walked along the footpath he passed within nine feet of Sergeant Bohan and Corporal Temperley. They did not hinder or challenge his approach to the spot where they knew there was an Armalite and a revolver. According to them John walked straight to the arms cache, knelt down and pulled out the plastic bag and then took possession of the Armalite, the butt of which had been protruding.

According to Sergeant Bohan John was holding the rifle in both hands, with the left hand on the stock. He then turned round to the left to face the two soldiers and whilst he did so he "brought the Armalite rifle to bear on them." The two soldiers fired their rifles at John hitting him in the head, neck and trunk. He died instantly. His brother Hugh heard the shots and ran from the nearby field into the graveyard. There he was detained by the soldiers, who made him lie face down on the ground for two and a half hours. During that time he was threatened that if he looked around he would be shot. His father Cornelius went to see what was happening. He knew his two sons were working that area of the farm. As the journalist Peter Taylor describes, he had left home at about 9 o'clock that morning to visit a neighbour in a farm about a half mile from the graveyard….. "When Con arrived, the neighbour asked him if he had heard the shots. Whilst the two men were talking, the neighbour's mother came out of the house and told Con that his wife had just telephoned to tell him not to go near the graveyard." He went immediately to the area of the graveyard but stopped short of the field where his two sons had originally been working, and was surrounded by soldiers with blackened faces. They ordered him to lie face downwards on the ground and kept him in that position for about an hour. One soldier in the background was heard by him to say "we have got the bastard – he's lying over there." Eventually the father and his living son were handed over to the RUC and released by them shortly after. His dead 16 year old son continued to lay where he had fallen.

The British army issued a statement on 11 July saying that "at approximately 22.00 this morning near Dunloy a uniformed military patrol challenged three men. One man was shot, two men are assisting police inquiries. Weapons and explosives have been recovered." This was followed by a second, more detailed statement. In it the army said, with some inaccuracy: "On Monday 11 July a two man patrol operating in the area of Dunloy heard a tractor approaching the graveyard. It stopped and shortly afterwards a man ran into the graveyard, went to a gravestone and reached under it. At this point the man saw the two soldiers and he straightened up pointing an Armalite rifle at them. The soldiers fired five rounds at the armed man who was killed. The Armalite was subsequently found with its magazine fitted and a round in the breech ready to fire. In addition, a blast incendiary bomb, a revolver, a mask, a combat jacket and a beret were found under the gravestone. A man leaving the scene on a tractor was arrested by the army, and a third man who arrived shortly afterwards in a car was also detained. Both were handed over to the police."

Of the inaccuracies set out in that statement, the greatest is the claim that the Armalite was loaded and there was a round of ammunition in the breech. That claim was untrue. Also untrue was the original suggestion that the soldiers had shouted a warning, for it was later admitted that did not happen. It was impractical to do so, so the Army claimed in its revised version of the truth.

The RUC also issued a statement. It was short, to the point and true. It said simply: "An incident occurred at an old graveyard at Dunloy when a young man was shot dead and two arrested. Both have since been released. The police are satisfied that the three men are not connected with terrorism." One is bound to ask whether that statement pointing to the innocence of John Boyle carried much weight with General De La Billiere at the time he was writing his auto-biography?

The RUC began their inquiries at the scene of the killing. Sergeant Bohan and Corporal Temperley had been taken away from the scene of the killing by helicopter. Bohan had sent a pocket phone message to the two soldiers concealed outside the graveyard, Soldiers D and E, saying "Contact. Get QRF." That meant he had engaged a suspect and his fellow soldiers were to summon the Quick Reaction Force to the killing scene. Before leaving the area however, as he later admitted, he went forward and searched John's body for weapons and documents. He found neither. He did however lift the plastic bag from the ground and emptied the contents onto the grass. That conduct precluded him from claiming that the reason the cache was not examined in the early hours of the morning when the SAS arrived at the graveyard, was a fear of a booby-trap.

As the police were later to discover, the two SAS men were helped to make witness statements by a legal officer in the Army. That was clearly a privilege not enjoyed by ordinary members of the public when a crime is committed. There was no question and answer session as happens in the usual course of a police investigation. There were two sets of statements, the first were simply handed over in the afternoon of 11 July and the second, much more elaborate statements, which foreshadowed the defence of self-defence, on 7 August 1978.

On 19 July 1978 Mr. Gerard Fitt, the Northern Ireland SDLP Member of Parliament, asked questions of the Northern Ireland Secretary Roy Mason in the House of Commons about the police inquiry into John Boyle's killing, including when a report into the incident was expected and whether the coroner would be holding an inquest. He was told that the police could question anyone they believed could assist their inquiries, and it was not possible to say when those inquiries would be complete; the question of holding the inquest was one for a coroner to decide.

On 3 August 1978 Mr. Fitt tried again to extract some information from the Northern Ireland Secretary, again without success.

No further progess was made for about six months. Then someone leaked the details of the post-mortem on John Boyle to the Press Assocation. On the front page of the *Belfast Newsletter*, dated 1 February 1979, the front page headline read: "SAS accused in death report". The body of the text said that: "A secret report leaked last night suggested that SAS marksmen gunned down an innocent schoolboy and that evidence was faked to justify the shooting. The Army had claimed the boy, sixteen year old John Boyle of Dunloy, Co. Antrim was shot dead after he aimed an Armalite rifle at the soldiers. But a report prepared by the RUC reveals the boy was shot in the back, and police forensic experts could find no trace of his fingerprints on the rifle supplied by the army".

Four days after that information was published, the Rev. Ian Paisley questioned the Attorney-General, Mr. Sam Silkin Q.C., the Government Law Officer in the House of Commons, if the DPP in Northern Ireland (for whom the Attorney-General has constitutional responsibility) had sent him the papers in John Boyle's case. Mr Silkin told the House that there had been consultations between them and as a result soldiers were to be prosecuted.

The case, such was its importance, was subsequently listed for trial before the Lord Chief Justice of Northern Ireland, Lord Lowry, sitting without a jury in Belfast Crown Court. It was the first prosecution brought against soldiers serving in the SAS.

(At the outset of the proceedings on 6 February 1979 an incident occurred showing disrespect for the Ballymena court when, although there were only two accused, five other men crowded into the dock with them, supposedly for the purpose of concealing the identities of Bohan and Temperley. By the time of the actual trial in the Crown Court the two were properly identified by name in open court and both sat together in the dock.)

The case for the Crown was that John Boyle had been shot from behind. This was based on the expert opinion evidence of the Assistant State Pathologist, Dr. J. R. Press. The defence claimed, on the other hand, the shot that killed him had entered the front of his head. That was the expert opinion of a British pathologist, Professor James Cameron. He considered that John was shot in the head from the front and that his body was turned by the impact of the first bullet so that the subsequent bullets hit him in the back of his body.

Dr. Press told the court that a bullet had entered the right hand side of the back of the head and fragmented. Some fragments lodged within the skull, while the remainder passed forwards, lacerating the brain before making their exit on the upper right eyelid. Two bullets had entered the back of the right upper chest where they fragmented, and some fragments passed forwards and upwards, lacerating the right lung, the oesophagus, the throat and the right common carotid artery before lodging in the muscles on the right side of the neck; other fragments passed downwards and forwards, fracturing the fifth right rib and lacerating the right lung, the stomach and the liver, before lodging beneath the skin on the right side of the chest.

In the course of a very strenuous cross-examination by defence counsel however, Dr. Press did retreat to some extent from his original propositions. He agreed with the suggestion put to him that the wound in the back of the head did look more like an exit wound, and the wound in the eye could have been either an exit or any entry wound. In order to dispose of the issue of self-defence raised by the accused, (it was important to note that they were not required to prove it, it had to be disproved by the prosecution), the Crown really

81

had to establish that the bullet entered the head and exited through the eye.

The Lord Chief Justice described Dr. Press as a most important Crown witness, whose evidence in his report of the post mortem was a clear indication that the deceased was shot in the back. If it was right, the defence put forward by the soldiers that they were acting in self-defence could not possibly stand up. One central question in the case was, was it in fact right?

Amongst the prosecution witnesses were two RUC officers. One gave evidence of going to the British Army base at Ballykelly on the afternoon of the shooting, in an attempt to interview those who could give relevant evidence about the events in the graveyard. He made very little progress in this regard. "People were produced," said that officer, "I had never seen them before. I tried to ask who they were and things were discussed in general terms. It was a situation I had never come up against before."

The officer then read the statements handed to him, not on that first occasion, but months later, made by the two accused, and drafted with the assistance of an Army major. In his statement Sergeant Bohan said that a detective constable had taken him to the graveyard with another soldier and had briefed him about the area. He had been assured by that officer that the family who found the bundle under the gravestone would not be back to the site of the find. "I believed," he said, "we would be up against armed terrorists. Our mission was to capture the terrorists. To apprehend a terrorist would be of great value for long term intelligence." He continued by saying that as he saw John Boyle at the gravestone he thought he was a terrorist whose photograph he had seen, and who was believed to be an expert in explosives. He went on: "I did not challenge because of the possibility of other terrorists supporting him. He started to remove the rifle from the bag, and turned, bringing it to bear on us. We fired, and he fell."

It should be noted that in the first of two statements, Sergeant Bohan maintained "Believing our lives were in imminent danger I aimed and fired." Had this stood alone and he held on to that contention at the trial, he might have been in some difficulty, because as Lord Lowry noted: "one possible inference from the first statement is that (Bohan) took deliberate aim not being in a situation of emergency."

Someone clearly saw the inherent danger in that approach and it was put right in the second statement. Now the position was: "Believing our lives to be in danger, I fired." No longer was it claimed, or admitted, that he had aimed at the target before firing the shot.

In his written statements Corporal Temperley described how he saw the young man standing with the weapon at his right side, at hip level. "Sergeant Bohan stood up, and I thought he was going to make a challenge. There was a noise like the rustling of clothing or branches. The man turned round and the rifle came up, pointing towards the observation post. Sergeant Bohan fired, then I fired three shots at 'single fire'." He went on to claim that, at the briefing with the RUC, the soldiers were told that the cache had been discovered by a 10 year old child.

The other officer was the detective constable who had taken part in the briefing of the soldiers. During his evidence, according to Demond Hamill, the mutual suspicion of the police and the army came through clearly. It was put to this witness that he had suggested the name of a man wanted by the police as a possible collector of the bomb and weapons in the graveyard, and that he had mentioned any particular person to the army at the briefing in the police station. He denied on oath both these allegations. The detective constable bristled with indignation when it was suggested he told the army the name of his informant, or given personal details about other Catholic families. Time and again his answers stated with the phrase "I did not tell the Army".

This witness also denied the suggestion, put to him on Temperley's instructions by his counsel, that he had told the soldiers that the cache had been discovered by a 10 year old child. Corporal Temperley did not enter the witness box to give evidence on oath in support of that suggestion. It remained just that, an unsupported suggestion, denied by the police officer to whom it was put.

At the close of the case for the prosecution, the defence case opened. Sergeant Bohan left the dock and went into the witness box to give evidence in his own defence. Corporal Temperley did not. He was not obliged to, he had the right to stay silent without any adverse inference being drawn against him, and he did so. It was clear to him however that his evidence would have more weight if it was given on oath from the witness box and subject to the test of cross examination, rather than just relying on the recitation to the court of what he had said in written statements to the police.

The sergeant mounted a forceful defence of his action in shooting

John Boyle. His attitude varied from the petulant to the sarcastic. He maintained his position that John Boyle had stood up, turned bringing the weapon to bear on the soldiers, and he thought their lives were in immediate danger. He fired and John fell, and that as soon as he fell the sergeant stopped firing. He claimed he fired not more than twice and probably only once.

He claimed that the Soldiers D and E told him that they did not see who was entering the graveyard, as their view of him was obscured. It may be noted that some are able to see the driver of a tractor sitting in an upright position from some considerable distance away, but apparently these two "look-outs" could not. For this reason they could not get a radio message to him.

Bohan's case was that the soldiers were told that the weapons were probably to be used against a local Protestant march on 12 July, and it was expected that more than one armed man would return to collect them.

If that was so, one wonders why he stood up to challenge John Boyle, (as Corporal Temperley said in the written prepared statement to the RUC that he did) thereby presenting himself as an easier target to any gunman loitering nearby, rather than remain in a concealed position where John had obviously passed the two soldiers, without seeing either of them.

During cross-examination, when asked whether he had been told to shoot the first person who approached the cache because he was likely to be a terrorist, he denied it, saying that he did not believe that he could go around shooting people, and furthermore no one could tell him to get out and shoot somebody. He could not however remember whether he had fired at John from a sitting or standing position. (This detail was recollected in tranquillity by his fellow soldier, that he was standing and not sitting, and it is difficult to reason out why Corporal Temperley should be either lying or mistaken on this point). As a matter of law, what Temperley said about Bohan in his witness statement was not evidence against him. If he had gone into the witness box at the trial and said the same thing, it would have been. Clearly it was in his presence, whereas previously it was not, and additionally it was sworn evidence on this occasion. Did this have an influence on Temperley's decision not to give sworn evidence in his own defence?

Sergeant Bohan could not remember either whether he had fired from the hip or the shoulder (he had by this time abandoned his initial admission that he had fired an aimed shot), and he could not say at what part of the deceased's body he had fired at. When questioned about "tactics" he angrily replied, "tactics are like opinions. Everyone has one. We cannot dictate tactics to terrorists."

As counsel for the prosecution pointed out to him in the course of questions, both soldiers by their conduct had shown that they knew John was not accompanied by anyone else, and Bohan admitted that he had run forward towards the deceased after firing and hitting him, proving that he must have known there were no terrorists in the vicinity. Otherwise he would not have left cover. He accepted that photographs of the dead boy taken at the scene seem to indicate that John had just emptied the plastic bag immediately before he was shot. As noted above, it was Sergeant Bohan who had done that. When counsel suggested that Bohan was in a cool, collected state of mind when he fired at the deceased, he disagreed.

When asked how did he feel when he discovered that John Boyle was not a terrorist he replied: "His actions indicated to me that he was a terrorist…Nothing else…. I was told that the person who had been shot was not a terrorist, but I do not accept it… I cannot regard any person who points a weapon at me as being a completely innocent person."

The whole of the defence case really turned upon the witness statement of their expert witness, Professor Cameron. Clearly the defence considered that they had made enough inroads into the evidence of Dr. Press, using Professor Cameron's information from the post mortem, and his interpretation of the findings, for they decided not to call him to give evidence in the case. (Cameron claimed in his report to have found that the basic measurements of John's body and the site of the bullet wounds were inaccurate, but he did not say so in sworn evidence from the witness box). That in itself was quite a high risk strategy, but it turned out to be the right one.

Professor Cameron was a pathologist with an international reputation. So much so that the prosecution called him as an expert witness in their case against Michael and Lindy Chamberlain in Australia. The case involving these two committed Christians fiercely divided that Country when they were accused of complicity in the death of their youngest child Azaria, aged nine and a half weeks, who disappeared on the family visit to Ayers Rock in August 1980. Their trial began on 13 September 1982. The case for the Crown against Lindy Chamberlain charging her with murder was short and simple.

Sometime between eight and nine o'clock on Sunday 17 August 1980 the baby disappeared and her body was never found. It would be proved, said counsel for the prosecution, largely upon scientific evidence of the baby's clothes, that the child had lost a great deal of blood, in all probability from injury to the major vessels of her neck. She died very quickly because somebody had cut her throat. Lindy Chamberlain claimed, from first to last, that the dead child had been taken from the family tent by a dingo. That suggestion was dismissed by the prosecution as a fanciful lie, calculated to conceal the truth, which was that Azaria died by her mother's hand. Michael Chamberlain was charged with being an accessory after the fact to murder, knowing that the murder had taken place, and knowingly assisted in disposing of the baby's body and misleading the police about the circumstances of the baby's disappearance. It was claimed he also attempted to have the police and the coroner believe that the baby had been killed by a dingo.

Part of the case concerned the family's car. What was claimed to be foetal blood of a baby less than six months old, was found in that car and the prosecution said it would be preposterous to suggest that the dingo took the baby from the tent and into the car.

The Crown called Professor Cameron as a witness. He began impressively saying he had carried out in excess of fifty thousand post-mortem examinations. While not completely excluding the possibility of an attack by a dingo he said he saw no evidence he would have expected to see had that occurred.

In his report Professor Cameron said that, on his reading of the evidence, the last time the baby was seen alive was at 15. 30 hours on the day she disappeared. When his attention was drawn to the statement of another witness, Judy West, who said she had seen the child when the sun was setting, he agreed that the sun would not have been setting at half past three and his conclusion was "a false assumption if one negates, as I have apparently negated, Mrs. West's evidence."

Have you made any other false assumptions before you gave evidence? Defence counsel asked him. "Again, not to my knowledge was his reply." However, several other differences with other evidence, perhaps not of major significance, were pointed out to him.

It was substantially different however when he was shown Exhibit 90, the plate cut from under the dashboard of the Chamberlain's car, and he confirmed that the pattern appeared to be that of an arterial blood spray spurting upwards under the dashboard from a point near the firewall. Clearly the Crown were claiming that the baby had been murdered whilst Lindy sat in the front passenger's seat and held Azaria out in front of her under the dashboard. As the baby's throat was cut, an artery spurted blood at a trajectory of approximately forty-five degrees, producing the spray pattern found on the plate. It seemed impressive evidence.

Lindy and her husband were convicted and various appeals against conviction were dismissed. She was sentenced to imprisonment for life. He was ordered to enter into a good behaviour bond for three years. Many people believed in their total innocence however. Both were of excellent character, Michael Chamberlain was a pastor of the Seventh Day Adventist Church, she was a loving mother, devoted to her three children, with no motive to kill her baby.

In June 1986 a Government appointed Royal Commission , headed by Justice Trevor Morling, investigated the case again. He found that the evidence did not justify the convictions, and if the evidence put before him had been given at the trial, the judge would have been obliged to direct the jury to acquit the Chamberlains on the ground that such evidence could not justify that conviction.

The evidence about the blood in the car was demolished, almost at a stroke. There had been no blood in the car other than, perhaps, minute quantities of the kind which one expert said one might expect to find in any family car.

Even before the Royal Commission got under way, the evidence about exhibit 90 which Professor Cameron thought appeared to be in a pattern of arterial blood spray was known to be wrong. The research carried out by a scientist, Leslie Smith, established that the spray was not comprised of blood, infant or otherwise, at all, but of a sound-deadening material used in the course of the manufacture of the car.

Of course this mistaken scientific evidence given by Professor Cameron was after the SAS soldiers' trial. There is however another instance when he gave important mistaken evidence as well, and this was in the notorious Maxwell Confait case in 1972, some seven years before the soldiers' trial in Northern Ireland. Confait was a transvestite homosexual prostitute who was murdered, then incinerated, in an arson attack at his home in Lewisham on the night of 21/22 April of that year. Three youths were arrested. Ronald Leighton, then aged 15, and Colin Lattimore, aged 18, were charged with both his murder and arson, and a third, Ahmet Salih, aged 14 with arson alone. Leighton was said to be "borderline subnormal and really an immature, inadequate, simple dullard". Latimore was said to be educationally subnormal with a mental age of an eight year old. Psychiatrists who examined him said he was highly suggestible, so that the slightest indication of the expected answer would produce it. Salih was described as being reasonably intelligent, but he was the youngest of the three, and aged only 14 years.

After a trial at which they pleaded not guilty, they were all convicted of arson. Leighton was convicted of murder and Latimore of manslaughter on the ground of diminished responsibility. The entire case against the three was founded on confession statements they made to the police, admitting the offences, saying that the victim was killed within a matter of minutes of starting the fire.

The principal medical witness for the prosecution (described in the law report as "the well-known forensic pathologist") was Professor Cameron. The appeals against conviction and sentence lodged by the three were refused by the Criminal Division of the Court of Appeal on 26 June 1973.

The three families would not accept the verdict of the jury or the decision of the Appeal Court. The British State did not then recognise, even if it may do so now, that confession evidence may be unsafe. Christopher Price, the newly elected Labour M.P. for Lewisham, worked with the families who believed in their sons' innocence, and persuaded the Home Secretary to send the case back to the Appeal Court on 18 June 1975, for that Court to determine the whole of the case.

The crucial issue in the case was the time of death of the victim and the time of the onset of the fire. Maxwell Confait's body was found in the house by two firemen. Both noted the body to be cold and stiff to the touch. An attempt to pick the body up in a fireman's lift failed because the body was very stiff and awkward. One fireman's impression was that the body was not recently dead. A witness estimated that the fire began at 1.10 a.m.; another thought that might be a reasonable assumption. A telephone call for assistance had been made to the fire brigade at 1.21 a.m. and the firemen were there within two minutes.

The Crown did not dispute at the trial that Colin Latimore had an unimpeachable alibi for the hours between 6 p.m. and 11.30 p.m. on the night of the killing. He was at a Salvation Army Torchbearer Youth club and there were independent witnesses who saw him there, and some also saw him at his home at about 11.45. His father spoke to him at 12.35 a.m. at the house. Leighton and Salih were together at Salih's home from 11 p.m. until the end of the television programme at 12.50 a.m.

For the confessions to be true, the murder followed by the arson must have taken place after those times.

The Divisional Police Surgeon Dr. Bain arrived at the killing scene at 2 a.m. He examined the body. In his original report he estimated that the body had been dead for between four and six hours. That is between the hours of 8 p.m. and 10 p.m. His impression was that rigor mortis was complete. He did not take the rectal temperature.

Professor Cameron arrived at the scene at 3.45 a.m. He carried out an examination of the body. Contrary to the opinion of the Divisional Surgeon he thought that rigor mortis was then commencing. He estimated the time of death at some six hours earlier, plus or minus two hours. That is between 7.30 p.m. and 11.30 p.m.

He too failed to take the rectal temperature. As the Appeal Court observed, ".....an omission which Professor Cameron now acknowledges and regrets."

In his evidence to the jury at the trial however, Professor Cameron repeated the substance of his report but said that his estimate must be extremely vague. This was of course most helpful to the prosecution, because if the death occurred within the time span he originally set out, namely between 7.30 and 11.30, then the prosecution would have been in difficulty, having regard to the alibi evidence which stood unchallenged by them. Then he went even further, and the effect of his evidence was to assist the case of the party calling him, namely the State that was responsible was for the conduct of the case against the three accused young men. After discussing, ("inconclusively", the Appeal Court remarked later) the effect of heat in the room on the time of the development of rigor mortis, he concluded that the time of death might have been as late as midnight. This was something the prosecution team badly wanted to hear, and it convinced the jury that it was right.

However, after the reference by the Home Secretary to the Appeal Court, counsel was permitted to call fresh additional expert evidence from two distinguished pathologists, Professor Keith Simpson and Professor Donald Teare. In the light of their evidence given to the Appeal Court about the time of death, the judges were driven to the conclusion that Confait's death could not have occurred after midnight on 21 April, and most probably not later than 10.30 p.m., and possibly as early as 6.30 p.m. Accordingly the court quashed the convictions of all three young men. The version of events outlined in their confession statements, in the light of this evidence, could not be true. There was no other evidence save those confessions against them. They had falsely confessed to a crime they had not committed.

In this case, as well as in the Chamberlain case, Professor Cameron made mistakes that related to relevant and material evidence. Most importantly, he was entirely wrong about the time of the onset of rigor mortis, which led him to the vague times establishing the moment the victim had died. Had he also made a mistake in the SAS murder case in his evidence about the injury to John Boyle's eye being the entry wound, or was Dr. Press's original opinion correct that it was an exit wound? If he, rather than Professor Cameron was right, then John was shot in the head from the back after all. If that is what happened, and was proved beyond reasonable doubt, then the sixteen year old schoolboy was murdered.

In the event, in an 18 page judgment setting out his reasons, Lord Chief Justice Lowry acquitted both Sergeant Bohan (whom he refers to as Soldier A, and Corporal Temperley, Soldier B.) He had to decide as a matter of law whether the Crown proved the case of murder against either accused whose defence was justifiable homicide on the ground of self defence, and that they honestly believed on reasonable grounds that they were in danger. His decision was that the Crown had failed to discharge that heavy burden of proof of guilt.

The Chief Justice made one point abundantly clear about the Boyle family. He said this: "I should explain that no responsible person has said a word either expressly or by implication against the standing and respectability of the Boyle family, consisting of Mr. and Mrs. Boyle and five sons (one of whom, Hugh, is married and lives a short distance away from the family home. Soldier A (Bohan) however, in the course of his evidence, seemed to say that the deceased not only appeared to aim his rifle at A and B (Temperley) but was actually doing so. Considering that the weapon was not loaded, this statement may be regarded as self-justificatory and, in the context of the Boyle family's reputation, untrue."

Clearly therefore, the judge rejected the sworn evidence that the unloaded gun was aimed at the soldiers. Not merely that however; it is obvious that on this finding the Lord Chief Justice did not accept that Sergeant Bohan was being truthful when he claimed that John

Boyle aimed the gun at him. If he found him to be lying on this point, how was it possible to accept him as a truthful witness on other equally relevant points?

The judge then moved on to the pathological evidence and he accepted that the defence cross examination of Dr. Press was so detailed and effective as to cast the gravest possible doubt on the reliability of his principal conclusion, namely that John had been shot in the back. He said he considered that the most probable explanation was that "Soldier A shot the deceased in the head when the deceased's head was facing A and slightly inclined to the left, that the deceased fell forward with his left shoulder coming under his body and towards the right, that while he was in that position two bullets from Soldier B's rifle entered the deceased's back (which would cause them to make a downward track towards the fifth rib and lung) and that the deceased's body finished up roughly on its left hip and back as shown in photograph 24/7. To put it no higher, a responsible tribunal of fact is bound at least to assume in favour of the accused that something like this did happen and that the deceased cannot have been shot from behind in the ordinary sense. I say that advisedly despite the fact that defence counsel elected not to call either of the forensic medical witnesses who were identified by him as being in court and prepared to testify on lines consistent with his cross examination."

Lord Lowry then proceeded to demolish the credibility of Sergeant Bohan as a witness at that trial. "I found him to be, on the whole, an untrustworthy witness, eager to make unmeritorious points and alleging, which I am sure was untrue, that he had been told by the detective constable that a 10 year old child had found the cache. This was a natural follow up of cross examination of the same detective constable to the effect first that he had told the Army that a 10 year old child, and second that a 10 year old girl had found it. Soldier A was quite definite that the plan was to capture whoever came to the cache, but was quite vague and unsatisfactory when questioned as to the details of the plan."

Sergeant Bohan might well have considered at this stage that the case was going to be decided against him. Only the soldiers knew the truth about what actually happened in the graveyard and here was the trial judge indicating that he did not believe some central elements of the defence case.

Lord Lowry went on to make a number of specific findings and he added a number of comments. He found first that John was probably shot from the front through the head by Sergeant Bohan and as he twisted and fell, he was shot twice through the back by oblique fire from Corporal Temperley. He could not be sure that John did have the rifle in his hand held near his body at the time he was shot, but he considered he may have done. Even if he did, the rifle was not loaded and therefore Bohan and Temperly were never in any actual danger. John's head may have been inclined slightly in any plane or direction, and therefore nothing more could be inferred from the angle of the head wound.

At no stage of his judgment did Lord Lowry address the difficult point of the absence of fingerprint evidence. If John had picked up the rifle, his prints must have been impressed upon some part of the weapon, but they simply were not there. Why did the absence of such evidence not drive Lord Lowry to the inevitable conclusion that John never picked up the rifle at all?

The Lord Chief Justice did skirt around this point by remarking that, if John did get the rifle into his hands, the two soldiers must have seen him kneel or husker down at the graveside, take out the plastic bag, extract the rifle and stand up with it in his hands and, strangely enough, they must have done nothing while all this was going on. The question is bound to be posed, why did they not? If they thought that John Boyle was a terrorist, as Bohan claimed he did, why did he let him get the rifle into his hands at all, since they claimed not to know whether the weapon was loaded. In fact they assumed it was. (The initial army propaganda had untruthfully said that it was loaded with a bullet in the breech).

The judge also drew the inference that because of the presence and position of the other two SAS soldiers outside the graveyard, it was at least probable that Bohan knew that John was alone. His behaviour after the shooting (and indeed during it if, as Temperley said, he stood up to fire his weapon) supported that inference. He then went on to state that John Boyle did not attack or consciously menace A and B, but they may have believed that their lives were in danger. (One is bound to ask, from what and from whom?)

Added to this area of uncertainty, it is obvious that the crime scene was interfered with by someone. Counsel for the prosecution at the trial suggested that before the RUC arrived the gravestone was tilted up and the contents of the cache scattered to give the impression of a terrorist caught at his work. Who did that, if it happened, and why? In addition, despite a careful search by the police, one only spent case was found, although at least three shots (it had originally been suggested that it was five) had been fired, so it appeared that evidence had been removed from the scene. Again, one is bound to ask why and by whom and when? It may be however that it was the picture painted by defence counsel, (Michael Lavery Q.C.) which made the most indelible impression upon the mind of the trial judge. Counsel pointed out that this was a young boy, almost morbidly fascinated by his discovery the previous day, returning to the graveyard to inspect it at close quarters, perhaps to handle and wield, albeit innocently, the forbidden and dangerous article which he had found there. It might be argued to counter this, that John had not attempted to handle or wield the contents of the cache or indeed the rifle on the previous day, so why should he want to do so on his return there?

In the light of all the foregoing, the Lord Chief Justice ruled that the case against the two SAS soldiers was not proven and he found both men not guilty. He did not pause there however. He went on to castigate the Army and Sergeant Bohan in words that should be read and reflected on by General De La Billiere. "On looking back," he said, "it is sad to say, the Army and Soldier A and his patrol gravely mishandled the operation because they shot an innocent boy who, whether he was holding the gun or not, had no capacity to harm them. They either knew or ought to have known that the deceased was unaccompanied and one would think that they ought to have found out whether the rifle was loaded. Nothing would have been easier with better planning than to capture the deceased alive, always assuming that to be the primary object."

The overall tone of this judgment is almost one of disbelief of the soldiers' case. They were acquitted because Lord Lowry could not exclude the possibility that John Boyle did, for whatever reason and in whatever way, turn the rifle towards the defendants, and therefore it was impossible to find that the Crown had disproved the defence of self defence. My view is that the absence of fingerprint evidence shows otherwise. I find it difficult also to comprehend the finding that John may have brought the rifle to bear upon the soldiers, but he did not attack or menace them with it.

It may be of interest to note that the journalist Mark Urban, in his book, *Big Boys' Rules* quotes one barrister as saying about Lord Lowry's summing up in the case that "the language he used about Bohan was so derogatory that in any case not involving the Army, I would have thought it was virtually impossible not to have had a conviction in that court."

Does this suggest that perhaps there were two standards of justice at that time in Northern Ireland? One for the British Army, the other for the rest of the civilian population?

It is abundantly obvious from his evidence in court that Sergeant Bohan would not accept that he and Temperley had killed an innocent, even after it was proved beyond any doubt whatever that the boy he shot was the person whose initial information resulted in the Army stake-out of the graveyard. "I was told that the person who had been shot was not a terrorist but I didn't accept it" he said in evidence on oath in court at his trial. Probably nothing will ever convince him otherwise.

General Sir Peter De La Billiere, who was almost certainly not even in Northern Ireland on 11 July 1978 when John was shot, clearly defames the dead in his autobiography. But he was not the first to do so. There were others, who took refuge in anonymous press briefings to avoid being identified publicly. When the trial of the two SAS soldiers ended on 4 July 1979, Cornelius Boyle, John's father said: "I know some of the RUC and I trusted them. I did what I felt was right and they let me down. They did not give us a warning until after the boy was dead. Had the police given me any kind of warning I would have taken it and John would still be alive. I thought they owed me this much. For anything the police have done for me I thank them, and for anything they could have done and did not do, it is they and not I who have to live with it. I have little to say about the Army. They have not deviated one inch from the path trod by their predecessors in Ireland. Having killed the boy they tried to discredit him and defame him and in this they have failed miserably, as they were bound to do."

This first act of defamation was by the State, the second in a book by a former soldier. A lie does not become less of a lie by its repetition. Whatever view one may take of the verdict of Lord Lowry in the case, one fact is established beyond contradiction or doubt. On 11 July 1978, in Dunloy, two British Army soldiers shot dead an innocent school-boy, John Boyle. Anyone who claims otherwise is stating anything but the truth.

CHAPTER 3

THE CASE OF PAUL HILL

Between January and November 1974, fourteen members of the RUC, twenty-nine soldiers from the British Army, together with seven members of the Ulster Defence Regiment, and one hundred and fifty nine civilians were murdered in Northern Ireland. Amongst the civilian casualties was Brian Shaw, aged 20 years, from Mansfield in the County of Nottinghamshire. He was the second youngest of six children. He had served with the British Army as a rifleman in the Royal Green Jackets in Northern Ireland and, while in Belfast, he met and married a local girl, Maureen Ashwood, on Saturday 6 July 1974. He had bought himself out of the Army in May 1974 and had then found a job as a lorry driver with a soft drinks firm. His older brother Malcolm, also a soldier, was to say later than the only thing Brian wanted to talk about was Maureen. He was so full of love for her and for Belfast. That's why he wanted to live there. He was aware of the dangers but he firmly believed he would be safe.

The young bridge and groom lived with her family at Carncaver Road in East Belfast whilst they sought and saved for a home of their own. They were to have very little time together. Two weeks after the wedding on Saturday, 20 July 1974 Brian Shaw went to a florist's shop to pay for the wedding flowers. Shortly after 10.30 p.m., on the evening of that day, he was found lying in the hallway of a derelict house at No. 8 Arundel Street, near to the Falls Road in Belfast. He had been killed by a bullet fired into the back of his head at close range, and a second bullet had been fired into his face. The Provisional IRA later claimed responsibility for the murder and said that under interrogation the man had admitted membership of the SAS, serving with the British Army in Northern Ireland. The Army denied that claim and said the dead man had been employed as a lorry driver. That might have been acceptable to the neutral observer, but the Army spokesperson went on to add that no SAS units were serving in Northern Ireland. That latter statement might be literally true, in that units of that regiment were not there, but according to the *Daily Telegraph* journalist Toby Harnden, "part of the regiment's B Squadron had been deployed in Belfast in 1974 and SAS members had often been attached to other units..." The denial is even more difficult to accept in the light of the report in the London *Times* on 19 March 1974 under the headline "SAS men serve in Ulster as undercover agents." In the body of the article that followed, the distinguished journalist Robert Fisk wrote "in spite of the obvious political implications of the move, the decision to involve the SAS in the Ulster war was prepared at the highest ministerial level in London, although its presence here had been revealed only to a few selected senior officers". Three weeks after that the former Barnsley coal miner Roy Mason, then Minister of Defence in the new Labour Government under Harold Wilson, told the House of Commons that there was absolutely no truth in the story. There were no SAS in Ireland, he said. If anyone believed Mr. Mason's statement, which of course was based on information given to him by someone else, I was not one of them. There is reason to believe that the decision to send the SAS into Belfast and Derry had been made in January 1974 by members of the Tory Government then in power, and when Labour went into Government on 4 March 1974 no one thought fit to tell the incoming Minister of Defence that had been done.

Three men were arrested and charged in relation to Brian Shaw's murder. They appeared at Belfast Crown Court on 17 June 1975 before Mr. Justice Basil Kelly, a former Minister in a Unionist Government at Stormont, and also Attorney-General for Northern Ireland for a number of years. He sat alone, without a jury, in the so-called Diplock Court system. The three men, Hector Young, Martin Monaghan and Paul Michael Hill faced a number of charges. In the result, after a seven day trial, Hector Young was acquitted of murder, conspiracy to murder and the intimidation of Brian Shaw. His case had been that he had met up with the deceased in Mooney's public house and went with him to another, the Unicorn. It was quite safe for anyone to drink in those city centre drinking establishments, but he claimed that Brian

Shaw wished to visit the Glengeen Bar in the much more dangerous area of the Divis Flats in West Belfast and they went there together in a taxi. It was from those premises that two men abducted him and took him away to his violent death. Hector Young denied knowing either of those men, or the purpose for which they took him away. Clearly the trial judge believed him and directed his acquittal.

Martin Monaghan was convicted of intimidation and of being a member of the IRA. He was sentenced to three years imprisonment.

Paul Hill was convicted on murder and intimidation and sent to prison for life. Mr. Justice Kelly told him that although he was not the man who pulled the trigger, he had clearly aided and abetted the murder and was a willing member of the Provisional IRA execution squad sent out to kill Brian Shaw.

The case for the Crown against the three men was that Brian Shaw had been lured (rather than simply accompanied) by Hector Young from the city centre public house to a bar in the Divis Flats area and then taken to a house in Linden Street, off the Falls Road, where he was questioned, beaten and then driven by car to the house in Arundel Street where he was executed in cold blood. The only evidence against Paul Hill was contained in a confession statement he made at Guilford police station to two RUC officers between 4.30 and 5.55 p.m. on Friday 29 November 1974. He has always maintained that statement was not voluntary and that it was untrue.

Paul Hill had been arrested at a friend's house in Southampton on the morning of Thursday 28 November 1974 by Detective Sergeant Anthony Paul Jermey, on suspicion of causing explosions at Guildford. The house was searched and so was he. Nothing incriminating was found. He didn't know it at the time but, following his arrest, he was the first person to be detained under the Prevention of Terrorism (Temporary Provisions) Act 1974 which had come into law that same Thursday morning. He was also the first person to be charged with the Guildford public house bombings. He did not know at that time either that his girl-friend Gina Clarke, also from Belfast, whom he had known since 1972 and they had plans to marry, was also under arrest. She was pregnant at that time, and gave birth to a daughter, Cara, on 3 September 1975.

Why the police should have alighted upon Paul Hill as a suspect for the Guildford pub bombings is clouded in mystery. Amongst the explanations, and the probability is that none of them is actually true, was first that an army intelligence sergeant in Northern Ireland had recognised a photofit as Paul Hill. According to the London *Times* his name was given by an informer to Detective Chief Inspector Brian Richardson of the Surrey police, one of the arresting officers on 29 November. The third version was a combination of the first two – that the arrest followed a tip-off to military intelligence from an anonymous informer, who was paid off in the best Judas Iscariot tradition. One of the problems encountered with this type of information is that it is seldom accompanied by tangible evidence or proof of the commission of any criminal offence. That evidence has to be subsequently obtained and frequently it was when, following a police interview at which no solicitor or any independent person was present, the suspect suddenly provided, quite voluntarily and spontaneously so the police claimed, the confession evidence that alone proved his guilt.

The fourth version may be regarded as the most bizarre of all. It emerged on 20 January 1987 when the then Home Secretary Douglas Hurd, after making an oral statement in the House of Commons, lodged in the Library two memoranda, one dealing with the Maguire Seven case, the other with the Guildford Four. The latter states: "The security forces in Northern Ireland had received information from as early as August 29, 1974 suggesting that Hill had gone to England to carry out bombings." He had in fact left Belfast about a week prior to that date but thereafter lived openly and freely under his own name, signing on for work or unemployment benefit and yet no attempt was made to interview him or arrest him in relating to the ferocious and continuing bombing campaign waged by the Provisional IRA. The inference may be drawn that either this statement was quite untrue or, alternatively, the police were incompetent beyond belief in failing to detain him for questioning, at the very least, for complicity in causing explosions.

The fifth and final explanation was offered by Commander Bob Huntley in his autobiography published in 1977. He claimed that Paul Hill's name was given to Surrey police by an unidentified security man based in Northern Ireland, after he had seen a photofit picture which he thought resembled Paul Hill.

After his arrest he was taken to Shirley Road police station in Southampton. Whilst there, he later said, one police officer, a detective inspector, loaded his revolver in front of him and said to him that if he tried to run he would get one of these. When he arrived at Guildford police station he was treated in a hostile manner as if he was one of the public house bombers. When placed in a cell the officer who arrested him, Detective Sergeant Jermey, grabbed him by the hair and pushed his face against a cell door several times, pointed to some graffiti on the back of the door and said: "I don't want anything like this out of you, you bastard." That officer denied both the unlawful conduct and the spoken threat.

Paul Hill claimed that he was later taken from the cell and swabs were taken of his hands. A senior police officer came into the room and was generally hostile to him, but it was not until some time after that he was put back in the cell, then taken from it to the murder inquiry room on the second floor of the police station. He was still handcuffed and he was abused verbally, told he had "done" Guildford and was hit on the back of the head. From a window he was shown a police officer standing at a barricade where the press were, one person was holding a camera. He claimed that Detective Sergeant Jermey took a photograph from his inside pocket and said words to the effect that it would be worth thousands of pounds to the press. A fourth detective came into the room and spread out on the table a number of photographs showing mutilated and dead bodies. They could not have been easy for anyone to look at. Paul Hill was asked to look at them, the police saying "look at what you and your friends did, you murdering bastard! Look." An officer snatched up a picture and held it in front of me. Underwood called out the names of the victims. The photographs were of naked bodies, torn and horribly mutilated, lying on cold mortuary slabs. There was a girl with no leg, just a stump; there was a man with a wound in his stomach – a huge fleshy exploded mushroom."

Detective Superintendent Underwood, according to Paul Hill, then made reference to a man named Lennon who was found shot dead in a lane in Surrey and said "you don't want to end up like him," especially as he was only 20. This was a clear reference to Kenneth Lennon, a native of Newry, County Down in Northern Ireland, who on 10 April 1974 had told Larry Grant, the senior legal officer of the National Council of Civil Liberties in London, that he had been pressurised to become an informer for the Special Branch in Luton and he feared for his life. Only a few days previously he had been acquitted of conspiracy to effect the escape of persons in legal custody at Winson Green prison. His co-accused Pat O'Brien, aged 19 years, was convicted and imprisoned for three years. The case against him was that in broad daylight, with no attempt at concealment, he had taken a photograph of that prison. (Two months later he was freed by the Appeal Court). In truth Lennon had set up the entire escapade which allegedly was to spring three Irish men, known as the Luton Three, then serving ten years imprisonment. He was charged to conceal his role in the incident, and to help ensure his acquittal. The jury were told by leading counsel for the prosecution, Harry Skinner Q.C., (who had prosecuted the Birmingham Six) that he was a man of good character i.e. no convictions for criminal offences. In fact he had been convicted on no less than three occasions, and the police knew it, although clearly Skinner did not. Political literature was found in Pat O'Brien's home by the police and it formed a crucial part of the prosecution case against him. His counsel (Louis Blom-Cooper Q.C.) unsuccessfully attempted to have it excluded from evidence, on the basis it was prejudicial to the defence case. Harry Skinner told the jury that no political literature had been found at Kenneth Lennon's home. Both sides stated in open court that this was a strong point in his favour. Some may regard it surprising that prosecuting counsel should be making a point in this way, which greatly assists the defendant. It does happen occasionally, and it seems to carry great weight with the jury, even more than when the defence make the very same point in his favour. However, as the Director of Public Prosecutions later had to admit, this also was untrue. When Lennon's house in Luton was searched on 9 August 1973 police officers found political literature published by Sinn Fein.

The prosecution said they could link Pat O'Brien with the Luton Three, and he must have been conspiring with others to effect their escape from custody, but whether one of them was Lennon was a more difficult question, because, said counsel, Lennon had no known political involvement. Since this was patently untrue, his counsel Kevin Winstain (who was one of the defence counsel in the Maguire Seven case) looked at his instructing solicitor in amazement. The jury were also told that a sketch map of Bedford prison had been found in O'Brien's possession. It had been drawn up with the help of his co-accused Lennon, but that fact was not disclosed to the jury by the prosecution or anyone else.

Following his acquittal at Birmingham Crown Court, Lennon fled to London and sought out the singer George Melly who urged him, after hearing his story, to contact others, including the Civil Liberties Council. As he left the club where they talked Lennon said to Melly: "but you still think my story's a fantasy. If you read in the papers that

I've been found face down in a puddle or a ditch, you'll know I've been speaking the truth." Three days later, on Saturday 13 April 1974, two boys found a body lying face down in a ditch in Chipstead, Surrey. It was Kenneth Lennon. He had been shot twice in the head and once in the neck. His killer has never been found. The mystery surrounding his death, and the publicity it attracted would not have escaped Paul Hill' s attention. The police officers involved in these incidents denied they had even taken place, let alone their content not being admitted. It does seem however a most strange detail for Paul Hill to invent, but one can see the sense in denying that they mentioned the Lennon killing to him. Was it not done in such a way, that if true, it contains something approaching an admission that the State was involved in Kenneth Lennon's death; something to which Underwood could not possibly admit or confess? Was it however mentioned to Paul Hill to indicate to him what fate he might expect if he stayed silent and admitted nothing?

The Surrey police claimed that apart from one interview between him, Detective Superintendent Underwood and Detective Sergeant Jermey beginning at 4.35 p.m. on 28 November, (when the hand swabs were taken), they did not interview Paul Hill again before the arrival of two officers from the RUC who intended to question him about Brian Shaw's murder.

It was eventually admitted however that Detective Superintendent Imbert from the Bomb Squad at Scotland Yard did interview Paul Hill from 10.15 p.m. for ten minutes. Detective Superintendent Underwood was with him. The content of the interview was described as "another matter". The first named officer saw Paul Hill again the next morning, 29 November, alone, for three minutes. It was brief and its content not described.

One problem arising out of these interviews was that although they ought to have been recorded in the detained person's register, they were not. This led to later allegations that "the very jailer responsible for making the records was trying at one point to say no interviews took place with any CID officers." If that was not the purpose of failing to make the record, it is difficult to imagine what the real purpose was. The whole purpose of keeping the register was to show when, where and by whom the detained person was interviewed, as well as recording other matters such as provision of food, access to legal advice, and contact with others.

Paul Hill's account of the events of the night of his arrest differed greatly from that of the police. He said that after the upstairs interview he was taken to a cell where there was just a board but no mattress and only one blanket. His clothes were taken from him and he was given half a towel to cover himself, a small thin towel, for the rest of the night. The only food he was given at Guildford on 28 November was a packet of crisps and a cup of tea to drink. He was unable to sleep that night because the gaolers kicked the cell door, shouted in, and pulled the flap on the cell door down several times. It was cold and the light was left on. Most significant of all however was his claim that someone put a revolver in the door flap of the cell. He was later to claim that because of these assaults, threats, acts of intimidation and deprivation of food and sleep, he was reduced to a wreck and was ready to agree to any suggestions or allegations that were put to him by police officers. All this was denied by the police, who claimed that Paul Hill confessed freely and voluntarily to his part in the killing of Brian Shaw.

Detective Chief Superintendent Simmons told the court in evidence that when he heard about 11.00 p.m. on the night of 28 November that RUC officers were coming to interview Hill, he gave instructions that he was not to be interviewed until those officers arrived from Northern Ireland. If that instruction was given it was disobeyed, according to Paul Hill, by both Detective Sergeant Jermey and another English police officer who took him back to the upstairs interview room and there he was questioned again. (Presumably the instruction did not apply to Detective Superintendent Imbert from Scotland Yard. One must question why not, if it did not?) After those two interviews, only one of which was admitted to, Paul Hill was given a lunch consisting of potatoes, carrots, a piece of meat and a small cup of water. He had received no breakfast, so that was his first meal of the day on 29 November.

He said that afterwards four police officers came into his cell. Simmons and Jermey were accompanied on this occasion by Detective Chief Inspector Cunningham and Detective Constable McCawl of the RUC. He was questioned about Brian Shaw's murder and replied that he knew nothing about it and did not do it. The Chief Inspector continued to put certain information to him and he continued his denials for half an hour.

It was put to him that he had shot a policeman who had been sitting in his car near Dunville Street. Also that he had murdered a protestant man found dead in a house in Leeson Street and finally that he had been involved in the kidnapping and murder of Brian Shaw. In support of that last allegation they produced from a briefcase a gun wrapped in polythene and said it was the one used to kill him. Paul Hill denied each and every allegation made against him.

Following that, he was removed from the cell in handcuffs and taken again to the upstairs interview room and there questioned by the two RUC officers. Eventually he signed a statement written down for him by Detective Constable McCawl. Paul Hill claimed that at this stage he was frightened and wrecked and he just did not want them talking to him anymore and he agreed with their suggestions. He knew, he said, what he would get if he did not agree. He did not however, make any allegations of violence or ill-treatment against either of the two RUC officers.

His first statement began at 4.30 p.m. on 29 November and ended at 5.55 p.m. that same day. The caution at the top of the statement is quite unusual.

It states: "I have been told by Det. Constable McCawl that I am not obliged to say anything and I understand that anything I say will be taken down in writing and may be used in evidence. I clearly understand this caution and wish to make a statement."

The Judges' Rules 1964, which came into effect on 27 January 1964, were not rules of law but rules of practice drawn up for the guidance of police officers. Any breach of the rules might result in an exclusion of evidence as a matter of the trial court's discretion. Rule IV was as follows: "All written statements made after caution shall be taken in the following manner:

(a) If a person says that he wants to make a statement he shall be told that it is intended to make a written record of what he says. He shall always be asked whether he wishes to write down himself what he wants to say; if he says he cannot write or that he would like someone to write it for him, a police officer may offer to write the statement for him. If he accepts the offer the police officer shall, before starting, ask the person making the statement to sign, or make his mark to, the following:

"I........wish to make a statement. I want someone to write down what I say. I have been told that I need not say anything unless I wish to do so and that whatever I say may be given in evidence."

What is clear that these words were not followed, either in the letter or the spirit in this statement. The endorsement differs from the Judges' Rules.

The statement itself gets off to a good start. It began exactly where, if the police officer had a choice, he might have begun himself – for it gives the relevant day and date, "Saturday 20th July this year". There is no shortage of names provided in the statement. No less than eight men and one woman are implicated in this or other crimes.

When the statement was finished Paul Hill signed it. It was now five minutes to 6 o'clock on Friday 29 November 1974. He broke down and wept. It was not however the end of his ordeal on that day. According to him, the Surrey officers entered the cell and told him they wished to speak to him about the Guildford pub bombings, and that was the reason why he was there. That being so, one wonders why the RUC officers were allowed to question him first about a crime committed in Northern Ireland, which, in the absence of his confession statement, they had no evidence at all against him. Without the confession statement the RUC officers would have had to return to Belfast empty handed.

According to their evidence, Paul Hill simply said that he would tell them all he knew. He then went on to dictate a statement to Detective Sergeant Jermey, in the presence of the Assistant Chief Constable of the Surrey police and Detective Chief Superintendent Simmons. That statement is untimed, and despite the seniority of the police officers present at the taking of the statement, this was a clear breach of Rule II and III of the Judges' Rules which require that the time a statement began and ended must be recorded. That was not done on this occasion as it had been when the two RUC officers took the first statement.

This second statement begins well also, saying "About the 23rd August 1974 I came to London, after Gerry Conlon." He goes on to name a number of other people, including his sister Elizabeth, as well as his girl friend Gina Clarke, both of whom were subsequently arrested. Also arrested were his aunty and uncle Anne and Frank Keenan. He also said that he stayed at 25, Westbourne Terrace, which he describes as Conlon's uncle's house. His name, he told the police, is Hugh Maguire. He (together with his wife) was also arrested. Also named is a woman called only Marion who showed Conlon how to make bombs. He named also Patrick Joseph Armstrong from Belfast, although he claimed he did not know him there. He apparently produced a brown paper bag from his pocket containing photos of two pubs that were blown up.

Paul Hill goes on to describe two women carrying bags and

travelling by car to Guildford.

Following that second statement the arrests began. Gerard Conlon was arrested at his home in Belfast at 5.30 a.m. on Saturday 30 November 1974. Meanwhile Paul Hill was making a further statement some time on that Saturday. Detective Superintendent Imbert and Detective Chief Inspector Mundy took it from him. It is written down on a witness statement form headed "Surrey Constabulary," but also noted is that the station or section was the Metropolitan Police and the Division, CO.C1 Bomb Squad. The statement implicates Patrick Armstrong in the Guilford bombings as well as Paul himself, and narrates how he looked after the explosives used to bomb the pub in Woolwich.

It was very self-incriminating and damaging to both of them, even though what he claimed against Patrick Armstrong was not in law evidence against him, because it was not made in his presence. He had no opportunity to challenge or deny what Paul Hill was saying, that he was involved in terrorist offences.

In spite of the importance of the evidence and the circumstances in which it was obtained, here were two senior police officers taking a statement which is not timed as it should be under the Judges' Rules. The question arises why? One answer may be that this evidence had to be tailored in due course to fit in with other times, other admissions or confessions, and other suspects.

Later that evening Paul Hill saw Gina Clarke. She was crying and hysterical. She continued to maintain that on the night of the Guildford bombings she and Paul were together in Southampton. He persuaded her to change her story because, he later said, the police told him that he had got her involved and he was responsible for ruining her life, with the result that she would spend the best part of her life in prison.

When she changed her story, she was released from the police station without charge. Some may see a connection between those two events.

Paul Hill spent seven days in police custody, during which time he made a total of seven statements under caution.

The fourth of these statements was actually written by him at Guildford in his own handwriting on 1 December 1974. The times between which it was written was not recorded by anyone. The signature was witnessed by Detective Chief Superintendent Simmons.

It this statement Paul Hill described how he was told that the two pubs he had seen in photographs were being done the next day. On that day, so he wrote, Patrick Armstrong arrived with a bag with those photographs in it. Two cars were driven to Guildford. There were two women with carrier bags. One woman was called Marion, and he knew her, but he did not know the older woman whose name he was never given. She was about 30 years old. At Guildford Paul left the car and went to the railway station. Later he returned to London with Armstrong. He saw Gerard Conlon at the Quex Road hostel and he asked if everything went ok. At some stage Paul saw a report in a newspaper about the pub bombings in Guildford. He had not admitted any personal involvement in those crimes, so far. He did admit however travelling to Woolwich and, whilst there, Armstrong threw a bomb into a public house in that town. Paul Hill had, so he admitted, stored the bomb that was in a plastic container about a foot high, until it was needed. On the return to London he had gone to a public house in Camden Town for a couple of pints of beer.

The fifth statement was made on 2 December 1974. It was taken in the presence of Detective Inspector Blake and Detective Constable Lewis, but actually written by Paul Hill. This statement was timed and noted. It began at 3.55 p.m. and ended at 4.58 p.m. on that Monday afternoon. The place was Godalming Police Station in Surrey.

At the subsequent trial of the Guildford Four, counsel for Gerard Conlon, Lord Basil Wigoder Q.C., had instructions from his client to make a serious allegation against Detective Inspector Blake and he did so. It was that the police officer had persistently assaulted Gerard Conlon whilst he was in custody in order to obtain a confession statement from him. Detective Inspector Blake denied it completely, saying he had not interviewed Gerard Conlon at any time. He did admit a fact known to Gerard Conlon, namely that he was a Catholic, because Gerard claimed the Inspector said "I am a Catholic and you make me sick". He also alleged that Inspector Blake had a tattoo of a dagger on his arm, and that had been seen when he rolled up his sleeves to deliver the blows to Gerard Conlon's body. Asked in court to roll up his sleeve for the benefit of the jury, Inspector Blake did so, and there to the surprise of very few, was the dagger tattooed on the arm.

The explanation put forward by the officer was rather good. First he had told someone visiting Gerard Conlon at Winchester prison (where he was then in custody) that he was a Catholic; perhaps to the

Inspector it was an interesting piece of information that he felt he ought to share with someone else. However, the choice of a visitor to a person on remand for murder and terrorist offences seems rather strange. Second, he said, whilst he worked in the centrally heated rooms in the Godalming police station, he frequently removed his jacket and rolled up his sleeves, so anyone passing by could see the tattoo. Why Gerard Conlon should have focused on this detail and store it up presumably for future use in relation to an officer who denied any contact or interview with him seems equally unusual.

That statement of Paul Hill, after the formal beginnings, said "I am now making a third statement the first two which I made where not the whole truth but most of them were." In fact this was the fifth statement, the first had been made to the RUC officers about the Brian Shaw murder, and it seems strange that Paul Hill should regard this as the third statement he made to police officers when it was not. In it however, he claims that the two bombing teams at Guildford were "Gerry and the old bird… and Paul and Marion was another." He and Patrick Armstrong waited outside where the cars were parked whilst they planted the bombs. (Contrary to all this, at the subsequent trial the prosecution claimed that it was Patrick Armstrong and his girl friend Carole Richardson, posing as a courting couple, who planted a bomb under a seat at one of the public houses, the Horse and Groom, in Guildford).

The next day, Tuesday 3 December 1974, Paul Hill wrote down another statement in the presence of the same two officers, between 3.50 p.m. and 5.30 p.m. This time he changed an important name. Marion now became Carol, and he further identified her as Amstrong's girlfriend who lived in a squat in Kilburn. Her accent, previously Irish, now changed to English. She went with Paul to plant the bomb in Guildford, so he now said.

The other woman, whose name he claimed not to know, now acquired one. It was Annie, whom he had first met in a club in Maida Vale and again at the Carousel ballroom in Camden Town. On both occasions she was with Hugh Maguire and his wife Kitty. He went on to claim that she told him she was from Abysinia Street, Belfast and that she had a brother who was "retarted." She was the other part of the bombing team with Gerry.

It is now clear that he was pin-pointing Anne Maguire. These family details could relate exactly to her. Within hours of this statement she and the remainder of the Maguire Seven were arrested later, around 9.30 p.m., on that Tuesday. Carole Richardson was seen by the police at 6.40 p.m. at her mother's home in Iverson Road, Kilburn, where she was visiting with a friend, and taken to Harlesden police station nearby. She was only seventeen years old and she was not to see the outside world as a free person for another fifteen years. Her boyfriend, Patrick Armstrong, was arrested at 9.25 p.m. on that Tuesday night at 14, Algernon Road in Kilburn, London. Carole made a total of four statements to the police whilst in custody, Patrick made three, the last of which was to an officer in the RUC.

Gerard Conlon for his part had made a statement at Godalming police station on Monday 2 December 1974. It was timed by Detective Chief Inspector Grundy and Detective Sergeant Jermey, who were present, as being written between 2.20 p.m. and 8.05 p.m. Some may regard this as a fairly long time, and if there was a break for refreshment or toilet facilities that is not recorded.

His second statement, made on 3 December 1974 in the presence of the same two officers, began at 5.47 p.m. and ended at 7.02 p.m. So within 17 minutes of Paul Hill implicating Anne Maguire, he began to speak. Right at the very outset he started with these words: "My aunt Annie showed six of us how to make bombs. Annie is the women in the flat I've spoken about in my first statement." He went on to confess to going into the public house with "Coral", with a bomb she had in a bag, and leaving it there. Annie was also on that bombing expedition, so he said.

From having virtually no evidence against anyone for the Guildford bombings on 5 October 1974 that could justify a prosecution, the police were now, at the end of November and beginning of December, in possession of an abundance of evidence. Some of it however was difficult to reconcile, and everything depended on whether it was true.

In summary, Paul Hill and Gerard Conlon said that Annie Maguire went into the Horse and Groom and Paul (a person never identified) and Carole Richardson went into the Seven Stars. Gerard said it was he and Carole that went into the Seven Stars. Carole herself said she, Patrick and the passenger in the car, probably Gerard Conlon, went into the Horse and Groom. Patrick said he, Carole and Gerard went into the Horse and Groom, so to that extent these versions are consistent. As to the Woolwich bombing, Paul Hill said he passed the bomb to Patrick Armstrong, who then threw it through the public house window, where Patrick said he was not involved in the actual bombing itself, only in a reconnaissance of the premises.

Sometime after Wednesday 4 December 1974, Detective Inspector Blake and Detective Constable Lewis interviewed Paul Hill again, this time at Guildford police station. It is not possible to say whether the Detective Inspector was wearing his coat or had his sleeves rolled up, but in this final statement Paul suggests that Patrick Armstrong told him that Gerry and Annie were going to do the Horse and Groom and Paul and Carol the Seven Stars, and they did.

Someone on the prosecution side saw a potential difficulty with the admissibility of at least one, if not both, of these statements, because by the time they were made, Paul Hill had been charged with murder on 1 December. The Judges' Rules 1964 prohibit the interviewing of a detained person in custody after charge, except in specific limited circumstances that did not apply in this case.

It was dealt with in this way. According to the two police officers, Detective Inspector Blake and Detective Constable Lewis, Paul Hill asked to see them shortly after 2.45 p.m. on 2 December. If a detained person already charged wishes to do that and volunteeer a further statement, that is not a breach of the Judges' Rules. According to the Detective Inspector, Paul Hill said: "I feel I can trust you two. There's one or two things in the statements I have made that's not quite right and I want to put them right.' I cautioned him and he replied, "I know. Can I make another statement?" I said to him, "you realise that you don't have to make another statement and that it's a matter entirely for you." Hill replied, "Yes I know. I want to make a statement." He was then taken to an interview room, where later that same afternoon I was present when he wrote a statement himself. When he completed the statement he was invited to make any alterations or additions he wished and he then signed the statement."

As noted above, that statement started at 3.55 p.m. and ended at 4.58 p.m. The detained person's register shows, however, that Paul Hill was not returned to his cell until 5.25 p.m. and no explanation is known to exist why he was not. That record also shows that the same two officers interviewed him again that day, 2 December, from 6.06 p.m. until 6.58 p.m. but if a record of it was ever made it cannot now be found.

At 11.25 a.m. on the morning of 3 December 1974 Paul Hill was taken from the cell by Detective Inspector Blake and Detective Constable Lewis for the purpose, so it was claimed, of obtaining his fingerprints. That apparently took no less than an hour and twenty

109

five minutes. No record of anything said by anyone is available.

At 2.10 p.m. the same officers took Paul Hill from the cell for the purpose, so it was claimed, of getting his antecedent history, which would include details of his education and employment. The detained person's register shows that a third officer was there, Detective Chief Inspector Grundy. He claimed in a statement that he was however elsewhere – interviewing Gerard Conlon at. 2.20 p.m. that same afternoon.

Detective Inspector Blake's evidence of what followed the obtaining of the antecedent history was this: "Hill said 'You won't be mad at me if I tell you something.' I replied, 'what do you mean. Is it something connected with the statement you made yesterday?' Hill replied, 'yes.' I then cautioned him and he replied, 'The girl Marion, that's not her real name. It's Armstrong's girlfriend Carole. She's the one you want. I didn't tell you before as I was frightened of Armstrong.' D.C. Lewis said, 'Why are you frightened of Armstrong?' Hill replied, 'He's well up in the Provos and his minder McGuinness has a gun. Christ I'll get a head job for telling you this. Give me a pen and I'll write it all down.'

Paul Hill then wrote a sixth statement under caution in his own handwriting. It began at 3.50 p.m. and was completed at 5.30 p.m.

Assuming the question and statement set out above took five minutes, and the finding of the writing materials for Paul Hill to make another statement took ten minutes, that still leaves and hour and twenty five minutes unaccounted for. The fundamental importance of this statement is that for the first time Carole, that is Carole Richardson, Patrick Armstrong's girl-friend, is mentioned and incriminated by Paul Hill.

According to the detained person's register Paul Hill was returned to his cell at 5.55 p.m. Again, some twenty five minutes were not accounted for at Godalming police station. He would presumably have not been allowed to wander around the police station either alone or accompanied, and it is difficult to fathom why he was simply not taken back to the cell immediately after the conclusion of the statement under caution, at 5.30 p.m.

That detained person's register further shows that at 6.55 p.m. until 7.10 p.m. Paul Hill was being interviewed in his cell by Detective Inspector Brian Richardson of the Special Branch. What was said or done between them was not recorded and not given in evidence.

Sometime after that he was moved from Godalming to Guildford police station. At 10 a.m. Detective Sergeant Jermey saw him there. Whatever may have been said, nothing was recorded. At 11.25 a.m. Detective Inspector Blake and Detective Constable Lewis interviewed Paul Hill again. During the course of that interview, which began (according to Blake) with the words "Good morning, Paul, how are you this morning?" to which Hill replied, "Fine, sir. Have you got Gina here?", the police say that shortly after that he was allowed to see his girl-friend, and they discussed the time of his arrival at Southampton on the evening of the Guildford pub bombings. It was after that that Hill wrote out his seventh and final statement, beginning at 11.40 a.m. and finishing at 12.55 p.m. The statement was witnessed by Blake and Lewis.

Paul Hill's recollection now is that he saw Gina Clarke not in the morning but in the evening of 4 December. She was crying and distressed and still maintaining the version of what she had previously told the police about Hill's movements, so far as she knew them, on 5 October 1974, and that he had been in Southampton with her. He told her he had signed statements for the police and to change her story and say that he arrived later than he actually did. He believed that unless she changed her story giving him an alibi, she would be charged. She did change her story. She was not charged.

Sometime after that he identified Patrick Armstrong as the person he had implicated in his written statements (he had been arrested at 9.25 p.m. the previous evening, 3 December 1974).

In the afternoon the police took him by car around Guildford to point out various sites and, at about 5.13 p.m. at the police station, he identified Anne Maguire, Gerard Conlon's aunt, to the police, telling them "the last time I saw her was in Guildford." After his conviction and sentence Paul Hill was a hated figure. He had blighted many lives including his own. The question has to be asked, if he was innocent, why did he confess, apparently so readily and so freely, if the police were to be believed, to the most terrible terrorist crimes involving the massacre of the innocents, if he did not commit them, and why implicate others in those crimes as well?

The first break through came on 19 October 1989, after he and the three others had been imprisoned for almost 15 years. On that day, at a special sitting of the Appeal Court at the Old Bailey in London, counsel for the Crown told the Court that since the cases had been referred back on appeal by the Home Secretary, that "evidence of great significance has come to light. That evidence throws such doubt upon the honesty and integrity of a number of the Surrey officers investigating this case in 1974 that the Crown now feels unable to say that the conviction of any appellant was safe or satisfactory. The case against each appellant depended entirely on confessions to the police. There was no other evidence. Each appellant was arrested and interrogated over a number of days. Each made more than one statement in writing. Each was interviewed by units of two or three officers from the Surrey Constabulary. A total of 12 Surrey officers were involved in the interview. Armstrong and Hill were also interviewed by officers of the Metropolitan police about the Woolwich bombing, and Richardson made limited admissions to those officers about the Guildford bombing. In each case this occurred after they had already been interviewed by the Surrey officers and in each case the interviews took place during the period they were held at Guildford police station.

Secondly, the Avon and Somerset officers (who had reviewed the evidence in the case and conducted inquiries into how it was gathered) discovered a set of manuscript notes relating to an interview with Hill. The notes have been identified by one of the officers involved. (That was Detective Constable Lewis. The other officer, Detective Inspector Blake had died by this date). The interview as revealed by the notes was never tendered in evidence and had not been disclosed to the DPP or to prosecuting counsel. It relates to relevant and significant matters. It is clear from the contents of the notes that it took place two days after Hill had been charged (that was on 1 December 1974) and led to his fifth statement under caution. It is clear that these officers also seriously misled the court. The content of the notes bears no resemblance to the evidence given by the officers as to the way in which they claim Hill "volunteered" to make his fifth statement. The inescapable conclusion is that the true interview was suppressed and a false version given by the officers to the court in order to circumvent the rule that a suspect once charged must not be interviewed except under special circumstances. Hill's fifth statement was of considerable significance in the trial because in it he was the first to name Carole Richardson. During the trial the officers denied the defence suggestions that there was an interview that day. The manuscript notes are inconsistent with that denial."

If it is thought that the fabrication of evidence by the police was limited only to the efforts of two practiced and accomplished liars, that would not be correct. Counsel told the appeal court "Other records have revealed disquieting aspects of the case. The detention sheets for each appellant (which do not appear to have been either required or made available at the trial) and they record the suspects movements around the police station – reveal a disturbing difference between the number and times of interviews according to the sheets, and the number and times of interviews according to the officers in evidence. Interviews were shown on the sheets which were never given in evidence or revealed to the DPP or prosecuting counsel. Interviews are shown on the sheets as taking place at markedly different times from those given in court by the interviewing officers, and the discrepancies apply to each appellant."

Put shortly, it follows from that that the police had fabricated some evidence, concealed more, and then were stupid enough to let remain in existence the very proof that they had done both of these things. Or perhaps it was less a case of stupidity and more that they had such contempt for the criminal process that they never imagined that they would be found out. In Belfast the records were called for and shown to be wrong. If they had been called for in the London trial they would have been shown nor merely to be wrong but also to be false. The Guildford Four are entitled to an explanation as to why their defence team at the Old Bailey failed to do what had been done by another barrister only months before in Belfast, with some success.

Counsel went on with the sorry tale of police misconduct. "It is the view of the Crown that the Armstrong and Hill notes show clear *prime facie* evidence that a total of five different police officers seriously misled the court in relation to two of the four appellants."

It was clear, said counsel, that if this material had been available to the trial court, it would have contaminated the case for the prosecution as a whole. The case depended entirely upon the confessions, and in turn, the integrity of the officers taking them. Moreover it was a case where the confessions produced substantially inconsistent accounts between the appellants. The last point was hardly surprising. If the Guildford Four were entirely innocent, as indeed they were, one could hardly tell a story which was entirely consistent with that of the another, since all the confessions were false and forced from them.

The convictions of the Guildford Four were quashed on 19 October. The Lord Chief Justice, Lord Lane, said the Surrey police officers seriously misled the court. In fact they must have lied. Paul Hill was released on that day, but since his conviction relating to Brian Shaw was still outstanding, he was granted bail in Belfast in relation to that on the following day, 20 October 1989.

On 21 April 1994 the Lord Chief Justice of Northern Ireland, Lord Hutton, quashed the murder and intimidation convictions.

His counsel, Tony Gifford Q.C., relied on the material put before the appeal court in London in relation to the fabrication of interview evidence, but the matter did not end there. He was allowed, with leave of the court, to adduce further evidence from three witnesses, Witness A, Witness B and Frank Kennison. All three had been serving police officers in Surrey in 1974, but had since retired. The prosecution called Christopher Rowe, who was Assistant Chief Constable in Surrey in 1974. He also had retired.

Before these latter two gave evidence the prosecution were contending at the appeal that armed officers were not on duty in Guilford police station until further arrests of people other than Paul Hill were carried out, that is after 28 November 1974. Mr. Kennison gave evidence however that he was on duty as an armed officer in Guildford police station on that date from about 5 p.m. to 7 p.m., and it was probable that one or two armed officers replaced him for the remainder of the night. The evidence of Mr. Rowe tended to support that. Indeed some people would be surprised if, after the arrest of a terrorist suspect there were not armed officers available at the police station where he was being detained, lest any effort be made to rescue him from lawful custody.

Witness B was allowed to conceal his true name from publication as was Witness A. The reason is not known but can be guessed at. He told the court he had received firearms training and was on armed duty at Guildford police station following the arrests of persons in connection with the Guildford bombings. One armed officer would be on duty in the passage outside the cell block and the another would be in the corridor leading from the cell block to the front outer office of the police station.

During some of the shifts another officer, Constable Gerald Queen, was definitely on duty as an armed police officer, although he could give no further detail about when that actually was. On one shift however, whilst standing in the corridor, he heard the click of a hammer, at least twice, and possibly three times, falling on the chamber of a gun and he saw that the sound was coming from the hand of Constable Queen. That officer was standing in front of a cell, cell E, with his gun, a ·38 Smith & Wesson revolver, pointing into the hatch of the cell door. Queen's hands were outstretched, he had an expression on his face like a leer; the gun was pointing into the cell. He did not say anything as he did this, but eventually he turned and looked and saw that Witness B had seen what was going on. He did not speak. The witness walked away in disgust.

He made no report about the incident to any senior officer. He thought it would be pointless to do so, because of the emotion surrounding the Guildford case, and he did not feel that anything he said or did would be listened to or acted upon. He believed the feeling within the police station at that particular time was that they had arrested the people responsible for the bombings. He would, if he reported the matter, have been dealing with officers of much higher rank than himself and with people with stronger personalities. That is all very well, but did he not realise when the evidence of guilt that was given at the trial consisted entirely of confession evidence and nothing else? Did he not connect the dry firing of the gun into the cell, and its effect on the conduct of the person at whom it was directed, and hear about the allegations this had happened being canvassed by Paul Hill's defence at the trial? He knew that when the police denied this conduct, that such denials were untrue, yet he stayed silent whilst some young people were condemned to spend the remainder of their lives in prison. When pressed at the end of his examination in chief why he had not reported it he replied, "that it was nothing other than that it would probably not have helped his career at the time. He had an over riding feeling of the position in Guilford police station at that time. People had been killed and two buildings had been demolished".

He knew Constable Queen and had worked with him in the past, particularly at Gatwick Airport in January, February and March 1974. Their responsibilities included controlling the main concourse there. On a couple of occasions he had witnessed the improper use of a firearm by that officer at the airport. Queen apparently took some delight in creeping up on people when they did not know he was there. On a couple of occasions he saw Queen suddenly appear from bchind a pillar with a gun in his hand and with a silly leer across his face.

This rather bizarre sense of humour, which few would regard as funny, paled into insignificance when put into the context of mistreating a suspect in police custody and obtaining as a consequence a confession to crimes which was untrue.

Witness B also told Lord Hutton that a few days after the incident with the revolver at Guildford police station he was in the charge room at Godalming police station with at least three other police officers. (Paul Hill had also been detained and questioned there). Constable Queen spoke about how he had drawn his gun, unloaded the bullets from it, and then fired the gun dry at somebody in one of the cells in Guildford police station. The other officers present seemed not to be unduly bothered by what they had been told, and they seemed to take little notice of what Queen said. Witness B did not know if anyone believed him, and as far as he knew no action was taken by anyone.

Witness A had a variation on this evidence to give. He could not remember when, but did recall being in the custody area of Godalming police station when Constable Queen, in the presence of other officers, said words to the effect that he had been into a cell and put a gun to a prisoner's head, squeezed the trigger, and the suspect nearly shit himself. The witness thought it was at a station other than Godalming, and he placed no credence on what Queen had said, because he took it as boasting.

The prosecution were given the clear opportunity to call Constable Gerard Queen to challenge and deny each and every allegation made against him by his two former colleagues in the Surrey police. It was known exactly where he was at the time of the appeal. He was a serving police officer, with the rank of Inspector, in the London Metropolitan police. He did not attend court to explain or deny what was being said about him. In his absence from the witness box was he expressly admitting that unlawful conduct?

Paul Hill was finally set free from his past in April 1994. The ramifications of the wrongful conviction of the Guildford Four are still being felt in the criminal justice system to this day.

CHAPTER 4
CONVICTING AN INNOCENT

Judith Teresa Ward was born on 10 January 1949 at Stockport in Cheshire, the third child of a family of eight children. The two youngest members of the family were twins who were put up for adoption shortly after their birth. Judith never knew them and has had no contact with them since their adoption. Her parents divorced when she was young and, as the eldest daughter in a one parent family, much of the responsibility for helping in the house with the younger children, and doing the household chores, fell upon Judith. Her mother's health was not good, and on two occasions the children were removed from their family home and placed in a residential children's home, and then with foster parents while she was receiving medical attention.

Judith left school when she was 16 years of age, with few academic qualifications. Her first paid job outside the home was as a credit clerk with a catalogue company in Stockport. Whilst she was so employed she decided to apply for a job as a stable girl, working with horses in the small village of Semley in Wiltshire, many miles away from her Cheshire home. She got the job and stayed for about a year, during which time she passed examinations in horse management, which she needed to fulfil her then ambition to become a riding instructor. That job ended only because her employers decided to reorganise their own domestic arrangements; these did not include Judith in their plans and she arranged to return to her home in Cheshire.

Almost at once she found another job working with horses, this time in the Isle of Man. Whilst she was there she was told that a vacancy existed at a trekking centre in Ravensdale near the town of Dundalk, some 40 miles north of Dublin in the Irish Republic. She applied for that job and got it. She took the long sea journey from Liverpool to Dublin. It was her first visit to Ireland. The year was 1966. She was 17 years of age.

Judith Ward knew very little about the history of the Country to which she had travelled. She had no inkling of the fact that 1966 was a year of significance and remembrance, for that year marked the 50th anniversary of the Easter Rising in Ireland of April 1916.

It is doubtful also whether Judith paid much, if any, attention either to the politics or the politicians of the day in Ireland, North or South. In the North of Ireland the Prime Minister, Captain Terence O'Neill, was determined to ignore the past and look more to the future and end of the ancient conflict that had divided the two traditions there. His dearest wish was to end the old community divisions and encourage Catholics, Protestants, Jews and Dissenters to look forward rather than back and to work together for the prosperity of all. That was an attitude and approach not shared by everyone within Captain O'Neill's Unionist Party; they thrived on the politics of confrontation rather than consensus and rejected his politics of conciliation. To them Northern Ireland was created to be, and must remain, a Protestant State for a Protestant People. O'Neill's opponents were determined to resist change in the status quo, by the use of unlawful force if necessary. They acted under the pretence that he was seeking to bring about a reform of the constitutional arrangements of Northern Ireland within the United Kingdom, when in fact he was planning nothing of the sort.

There is no doubt now that during 1966 a number of so-called Loyalists combined together to concoct a plan calculated to deceive the security forces and their political masters in Belfast and London. It was their intention to mislead the Army and the police completely, and cause them to believe that a series of bombings and gun attacks which they carried out themselves were the work of the Irish Republican Army, the IRA. Their basic objectives were twofold: first to curtail or conclude Captain O'Neill's bridge building efforts between the two divided communities in the North of Ireland, and then even further to encourage the opposition to him within the Unionist Party to such an extent that he would be removed or forced to resign from office.

In April 1966 there was a bomb attack on the headquarters of the Unionist Party in Belfast and two shots were fired through the front door of the Shankill home of the newly elected Unionist Member of Parliament in that city, John McQuade. He was a former dock worker who had close connections with a fundamentalist Protestant clergyman, the Reverend Ian Paisley. He was also a member of the Ulster Protestant Action Organisation. Two brothers, Billy and Gusty Spence, were also members of that group. The brothers and Mr. McQuade also belonged to the same Orange Lodge in Belfast, the Prince Albert Temperance Lodge.

The gun attack on his own home, blamed of course on the IRA, was in fact carried out with the connivance of Mr. McQuade, although the Special Branch of the RUC did not discover this until 1969.

In May 1966 the first killings of the current round of the Troubles in Northern Ireland took place. They were carried out amidst rumours throughout Northern Ireland of the existence of the Ulster Volunteer Force, the UVF, a Loyalist paramilitary organisation. On May 7, a UVF member of the Protestant Action Force threw a petrol bomb at a public house, licensed for the sale of drink, owned by a Catholic family. The bomb missed its intended target and exploded in the house of an elderly woman, Martha Gould, who lived next door to the pub. She was burnt to death. No one has ever been convicted for her murder.

On May 27, four men, including Gusty Spence, drove by car to the predominately Catholic area of the Falls Road in Belfast intending to murder Leo Martin, a well known republican activist. Fortunately for Mr. Martin the four failed to find him, but undeterred, (for in such circumstances any Catholic would do) they fell upon a drunken man, John Scullion, who was singing Irish rebel songs as he staggered happily homewards. He was shot at point blank range; he died of his injuries two weeks later. With the lack of attention to detail in murder cases where the victims were considered to be nationalists or Catholics (and therefore expendable) and which was to become the hallmark of the Royal Ulster Constabulary, officers of that Force concluded that Mr. Scullion had been stabbed. It was only after his funeral had taken place that the case was re-examined and it was decided that the body should be exhumed and a post-mortem carried out. It was then discovered that he had a bullet wound and that he had been shot. (When the former Deputy Chief Constable of the Greater Manchester Police, John Stalker, carried out an investigation in 1984 into the RUC's handling of six killings by shooting which had occurred some two years previously in Northern Ireland, he found that police files were poorly prepared and presented. He expected to find a particularly high level of inquiry since all six victims had been shot by the RUC, but this was shamefully absent. The files were, he said, little more than a collection of statements apparently prepared for a coroner's inquiry. He said they bore no resemblance to his idea of a murder prosecution file.) Clearly in the intervening years, between 1966 and 1982, little or no improvement in the technique in the investigation of homicide cases could be alleged against the RUC.

On June 26, 1966 a third in the series of murders took place. On that date, a Sunday, at about 2.30 a.m. four young Catholic barmen, Peter Ward, aged 18, Liam Doyle, aged 19, Andrew Kelly, aged 27, and Richard Leppington, aged 16 years, left the Malvern Arms public house on the corner of Malvern Street and Ariel Street in Belfast. The area is centred around the predominately Protestant Shankhill Road. As the four left the public house they were confronted by a number of armed men who opened fire with revolvers. One ·455 bullet hit Peter Ward in the chest, killing him instantly. Liam Doyle was struck by two ·455 bullets in the left forearm and right ankle. He was also hit by a ·32 bullet fired by another gunman. Andrew Kelly was shot in the abdomen by two gunmen, one firing a ·455 bullet and another, different gunman from the one who shot Liam Doyle, but who also fired a ·32 bullet. As he lay upon the ground one of the killers aimed a gun at Mr. Kelly's unprotected and defenceless head. Before the gunman could fire a further shot however a young woman in a nearby house screamed at him, distracting his attention away from his intended victim, and he ran off as quickly as he could. Richard Leppington, the 16 year old, escaped uninjured from the gunmen, but he was severely shocked and traumatised by the horror of what he had witnessed.

When the news of this cowardly attack upon these innocent victims, chosen at random, was given to the Northern Ireland Prime Minister, Captain Terence O'Neill, he returned immediately to Belfast from a visit to France. He had been in that Country to attend a Battle of the Somme Commemoration Service and pay tribute to the men of the 36th (Ulster) Division who had died in action there. He condemned the outrage and announced in the Stormont Parliament the proscription of the Ulster Volunteer Force, the UVF, which was thought to be responsible for the shootings.

Captain O'Neill said he had gone to France to honour the men of the Ulster Division, many of whom were members of the original Ulster Volunteer Force formed in Belfast in 1912. He went on to say "let no one imagine that there is any connection whatever between the two bodies; between men who were ready to die for their Country on the fields of France, and a sordid conspiracy of criminals prepared to take up arms against unprotected fellow citizens."

The police response on this occasion was swift and effective, and within a few days of the shootings three men were arrested and charged. They were Hugh Arnold McClean, Robert James Williamson and Augustus (Gusty) Spence. The latter was a former British Army sergeant who had served in Cyprus at a time when the Greek-Cypriot section of the population of the Island were engaged in an armed struggle against Britain, seeking political union with Greece. When arrested however, Mr. Spence was working at the Harland and Wolff shipyard in Belfast. He was charged with the murders of John Scullion and Peter Ward.

There was a sensation in the Remand Court, and outside it, when it came to the public's knowledge that, according to the evidence of an RUC officer, District Inspector Bradley, when he charged Hugh Andrew McClean with the murder of Peter Ward, the accused replied, "I am terribly sorry about this. I am ashamed of myself. I am sorry I ever heard of that man Paisley or decided to follow him. I am definitely ashamed of myself to be in such a position."

At a later date, during the trial, another RUC officer told the court on oath in evidence that when Mr. McClean was asked in an interview why he had joined the Ulster Volunteer Force he replied: "I was asked did I agree with Paisley, and was I prepared to follow him. I said that I was."

The Reverend Ian Paisley, now head of the Democratic Unionist Party in Ulster, had condemned the murder and in a subsequent statement denied that he even knew Mr. McClean, and no evidence exists to show that he did. Not unexpectedly however, Mr. Paisley went further. He condemned the police for their alleged breach of the licensing laws at the Malvern Arms public house saying "it is a well known fact that the police themselves used this pub for drinking after hours." Some may think a minor breach of the licensing laws, if that happened, was somewhat trivial and insignificant compared to the horrific murder which was under investigation at the time.

In October 1966 Mr Spence, Mr Williamson and Mr McClean

appeared in court at Belfast City Commission before the Lord Chief Justice of Northern Ireland, Lord MacDermott, and a jury, jointly charged on an indictment containing two counts. First that they murdered Peter Ward and second that they together carried out that murder in the course or furtherance of a seditious conspiracy to create a public disturbance and disorder and to injure and murder persons who might be opposed to their opinions. The Crown claimed that the motive for the killing was that the three men, together with a fourth man not before the court, were acting in the name of the Ulster Volunteer Force and that they believed the deceased and his friends to be "IRA men". Conviction on that second count carried the death penalty. Such a penalty would not have been available to any court in England and Wales for the death penalty had been suspended there (and later abolished) in 1965. When the British Government introduced the abolition legislation in the House of Commons in 1965 the Unionist Government decided to go their own way on this issue so they introduced the Criminal Justice (Northern Ireland) Act 1966 in the Stormont Parliament. Under section 10 of that Act murder was a capital offence if done in the course or furtherance of a seditious conspiracy. The whole tenor of that legislation, and indeed that section of it, was aimed exclusively at the IRA, but in fact the first persons to be charged under the Act with capital murder were the three Ulster Loyalists.

In the event Messrs. McClean, Williamson and Gusty Spence were acquitted by the predominately Protestant jury on the capital charge, but convicted of murder and sentenced to life imprisonment. (It may come as some considerable surprise to those who support the death penalty for murder, especially those in the Conservative & Unionist Party, that section 10 of the Criminal Justice (Northern Ireland) Act 1966 was abolished by the Conservative Government in 1973, following the imposition of Direct Rule on the Province and the suspension of the Stormont Parliament.)

It was at this time in 1966 that Judith Ward, according to her biography published in 1994, began to take an active interest in the politics of Northern Ireland. She learned with some astonishment and outrage that there could be discrimination on religious grounds in Northern Ireland, and she noted the existence and objectives of the emerging Civil Rights movement there, and thereafter the split in the republican movement which led to the formation of the Provisional IRA.

It was also about this time that Judith became romantically involved with a local Dundalk man whom she had met in the course of her employment, but rather than continue their friendship she decided to return to England. Perhaps this was the first sign of her emotional immaturity and the onset of a psychiatric illness, because she began to experience feelings of guilt and depression, the very same illness that was to blight her life for many years in the future.

Once she had returned home to England she got a job at the local Woolworth store in Stockport, but she was unable to settle down to the disciplined routine that such a post entailed. Surprisingly therefore she made a decision to apply to join the British Army, and when her application succeeded she was posted, on February 5, 1971 to the Women's Royal Army Corps, doing the nine weeks basic training course at Guildford in Surrey. There then followed a four months trade training course as a communications centre operator at the Army Barracks at Catterick in Yorkshire. When she successfully completed that course she was posted to the military town of Aldershot on August 5, 1971. Judith found the atmosphere and environment of that establishment oppressive and overpowering; it began to wear her down. On October 4, just about two months after her arrival there, she obtained a week-end leave pass and once away from the confines of the Army garrison she decided not to return. Instead she travelled to Manchester, went immediately to the airport there and flew to Dublin in Ireland. From there she travelled northwards towards the border, back to the town of Dundalk and to her old friends at the riding school at Ravensdale.

Once again Judith was unable to settle down; she clearly failed to realise that the personal problems confronting her moved with her wherever she travelled. Although she makes no mention of it in her autobiography, it was at this time that she apparently formed a friendship with, and indeed became engaged to marry, a man called John McKeowan. Sadly that friendship did not last and ended as unhappily as the first. By this stage in her life Judith Ward was now a very ill woman and she began to drift around the countryside, sleeping rough wherever she could, unwashed, unwanted and always alone.

On March 22, 1972 Judith came to the notice of the police. This was within two days of a bomb explosion in Donegall Street in Belfast where the Provisional IRA murdered seven equally innocent people. Included amongst the dead were two RUC constables.

Judith made a written statement to the police officer who interviewed her. It contained a tissue of lies from first to last. A copy of that statement was sent to the Director of Public Prosecutions and retained there. Its existence, let alone its contents, was not disclosed to her defence team or to the court when she was put on trial for murder. Some unidentified person apparently decided not to disclose it on the ground it was not material to the issues before the trial court. That is a view with which not everyone would agree; one of the issues which the jury had to decide was whether Judith Ward was a truthful person when she made statements containing self-incriminating evidence to a police officer.

The statement began with two material lies. She gave her name as Teresa O'Connell and said she was aged 14 years and 8 months. In fact she was 23 years of age. More lies followed. She claimed her mother (who was in fact alive and well and living in England) had died when Judith was aged 6 years and subsequently her father, Francis O'Connell, had walked out on her and her brother in Cork city some four years previously, sometime in 1968. She and that brother, whose name she said was Eddie, aged 19 – in fact she had no such brother of that age or name – together led a wandering lifestyle, so she claimed, travelling by caravan around Ireland until the day they quarrelled. Thereupon Eddie told her he intended to travel to the North of Ireland to join the Provisional IRA.

She went on to say that she left the caravan before Eddie did and she hitch-hiked to the town of Newry, just over the border from the Irish Republic. There, so she claimed quite untruthfully, she was questioned by the RUC and said in answer to their questions that she was going further north to County Antrim to search for her brother Eddie. Instead of doing that however, she changed her mind and travelled to Belfast and then right across the Province of Ulster to Derry, still looking for that missing brother Eddie.

The imaginative lies went on. She told the interviewing police officer that she had previously been interviewed by the RUC and then the British Army; a soldier had, so she said, assaulted her with a rifle so badly that she needed treatment at a hospital as an in-patient for one night. From there she was taken to a convent, which she left as soon as she conveniently could. The search for the elusive non-existent brother Eddie went on. Soon after, in the early hours of one morning, she was lifted by the Army whilst on the street and handed over to the RUC. Arrangements were made for her to be given shelter at St. Joseph's Training School. She put the date of these events as being on or about March 20.

After the conclusion of that police interview it was decided by them that no further action was called for; Judith had not committed any criminal offence. The RUC had no reason to believe, and Judith did not disclose, that she was absent without leave from the Army base at Aldershot.

The importance of that interview of March 22 however is clear. Here was a overt manifestation of how convincingly and effectively Judith could deceive a police officer, giving him details which could easily be checked and verified, and defines her capacity to invent details of people, places and events which, although false, she probably believed herself.

It was about this time that Judith began to sink even more deeply into a depressive state. This must have been apparent when she was again interviewed by an officer of the RUC. Her recollection of that event now is that she was viewed as "an undesirable person," and, on May 22, 1972, she was put on the boat back to England. Judith arrived back in England and travelled home to Stockport. There she decided that she might as well give herself up to the police, not knowing what was likely to happened to her, but she felt she had no other choice. She went to the police station and there the sergeant to whom she spoke thought that she had run away from home, but after it was established that she was absent without leave from the Army, she was detained, but not for long. A travel warrant was obtained for her and without any supervision of any kind and entirely alone, Judith travelled by train from Stockport to Aldershot.

According to her, when arrived she was confined to barracks for 7 days, and two policemen, whom she presumed were from Army Intelligence, interviewed her about her movements in Northern Ireland. They seemed indifferent to what she told them.

Not mentioned in her autobiography, but related at her trial, was the conversation between Judith and another woman soldier at Aldershot. She has been identified as Private Blake of the Women's Royal Army Corps. At Judith's 1974 trial Private Blake told the jury that Judith had claimed to her that she was a lieutenant in the IRA; that she had been helping to "blow places up and things like that," and that she had the letters "IRA" scratched on her arm. If the volunteering of this information was calculated to impress her fellow soldier, it failed. Private Blake told the jury that she did not take much

125

notice of what Judith told her.

On May 24, 1972 Judith was interviewed at the Army barracks by Detective Inspector Ison and other officers of the Special Branch of the London Metropolitan police. Whether it was to these officers that Judith was referring in her autobiography is unclear, but it is a matter of record that on the following day the police took a written statement under caution. She was clearly suspected of the commission of a criminal offence, as evidenced by the fact she was told she was not obliged to say anything, but whatever she did say might be given in evidence against her. She was told she had the right to stay silent, but that was the last thing Judith was likely to do. She told the police that sometime between the events of Bloody Sunday on January 30, 1972 and February 22, 1972, when the Official IRA placed a stolen car containing a 50 pound explosive device in the barracks at Aldershot housing the 16th Parachute Brigade, (the bomb exploded without any warning being given, killing 7 innocent people), she had been in a bar in the town of Dundalk. Whilst there she had been invited into a back room where she was introduced to two men, one of whom was called Seamus Quigley. In the written statement which Judith went on to make to the police, she alleged that one of those two men tried to persuade her to give information about the Parachute Regiment, urging her "to be loyal to Ireland". Gallantly, so she claimed, she declined to do so.

What the interviewing Metropolitan Police officers made of Judith and her fanciful story can only be guessed at; certainly it was decided not to charge her with any criminal offence. She was however discharged from the Army on June 2, 1972. Her written statement under caution was kept on record, later to be used in evidence against her at her criminal trial.

Judith returned home to Stockport. Within a few days of her discharge from the Army she was sent £250 in back pay; some of it she gave to her mother.

From June to early August 1972 Judith tried once again to settle down at home. She worked locally doing odd jobs, including shop assisting in the local Woolworths. Eventually she left home again and set off for Ireland once more, travelling via Dublin before crossing the border into the North.

On August 15, 1972 Judith was known to be in the City of Belfast. That day was a Tuesday; it was marked by a particularly bizarre incident in the Law Courts. Four men were brought before the

Recorder's Court charged with armed robbery. All four refused to recognise the Court because, so they said, it was an instrument of an illegal and undemocratic regime. Such a proclamation would not have been unduly surprising from a republican group, but these four men were, on their own admission, members of the Loyalist Ulster Volunteer Force. Such a display of disloyalty to one of Her Majesty's Judges on the part of those who persistently profess their loyalty to Queen and Country was truly astonishing, even by the standards of Northern Ireland.

Sometime on that Tuesday, elsewhere in the City, a group of soldiers from the Royal Electrical and Mechanical Engineers were on patrol when one of them, Sergeant Reynard, saw Judith Ward jump from a ground floor window ledge and run away from the patrol – just the kind of conduct likely to attract the attention of the approaching soldiers. Judith was ordered to stop and she did so. She was detained by the soldiers, interviewed by Sergeant Reynard and then handed over to the RUC and questioned by them.

On the previous March 22 Judith had given her name as Teresa O'Connell; on this occasion she gave her own. She claimed however that her parents had been gypsies originating from the Dublin area where she had spent her early childhood. There was no reason why Judith should have been detained further by the security forces and she was released without charge. (During the course of their investigation into Judith Ward, following her arrest by them in 1974, the West Yorkshire police interviewed Sergeant Reynard and took a witness statement from him. How they knew of his contact with Judith in 1972 is a continuing mystery. In the event the police failed to disclose the existence and the contents of the Sergeant's statement, both to the defence team and the court. It was a statement very helpful to Judith's case and was not even sent to the Director of Public Prosecutions in London.)

Eight days after her detention by the Army and the RUC, Judith claimed that she managed to gain entry to Thiepval Barracks at Lisburn, a predominately Protestant town outside Belfast. This complex was (and is) the headquarters of the British Army in Northern Ireland and accordingly one would assume that high level security precautions were in place to exclude those whose presence was not welcome on the premises, more especially in the light of the murderous bombing attack on the Army barracks at Aldershot.

(The barracks gets its name from a First World War battlefield of special significance to the Protestant People of Ulster, for it was at Thiepval that the 36th Ulster Division suffered massive casualties at the hands of the German Army. On one day alone, July 1, 1916, in the Battle of the Somme, the British Army's overall casualties numbered twenty-one thousand dead or mortally wounded. At least two thousand of the dead were from the 36th Ulster Division. Of the 750 men from the Shankill area of Belfast who served on the Somme, only 76 returned alive.)

Judith Ward's explanation given at her trial in 1974 for visiting Thiepval Barracks was that she intended to visit a former friend serving with the Women's Royal Army Corps. How she eluded any security checks then in place was a mystery then and now. By August 29, 1972 however the Army had information that Judith had visited the base and detained her on that day for questioning about it.

She was also detained and questioned about this unauthorised visit to supposedly secure military premises from September 3 to September 6. The interviews took place in the presence of an RUC policewoman but were conducted by two men, Corporal Coleman and Constable McNulty of the RUC. Both gave evidence at Judith's trial in 1974. They told the jury that she gave her name as Judith Minna Ward. She discussed her family and said she had served in the British Army until she had gone absent without leave from her unit. During that time, so she claimed, she had visited republican areas in Derry and Belfast and she named various individuals to reinforce the strength of her claims. She had met various republicans, including Mickey Pierce and Mickey Moore of Newry. The latter was, so she said, an ex-internee at Long Kesh, a prison camp set up on the site of an old airfield near Lisburn.

Judith claimed she had visited him there, using the name Teresa O'Connell, bringing letters in and out of the prison, conduct which, if true, was an admission of a criminal offence.

There was much more to come. Judith told Corporal Coleman and Constable McNulty that sometime after she joined the army she returned home to Stockport on leave. Whilst there a man called at the family home. Whether he identified himself to Judith is not clear, but she said he told her Mickey Moore had sent him, and Judith was asked to obtain some information which Mickey Moore could use, presumably for terrorist purposes. Judith declined to provide any such information. The narrative however did not stop there. Judith went on to relate some information about an occasion when she had been invited into the back room of a public house, which she named as McLoughlin's Bar, in the town of Dundalk in the Irish Republic. She named two men, Seamus Quigley and Paddy McNally, one of whom was to her knowledge in the IRA. They asked her to draw a map of the army camp at Aldershot where she had been stationed, and she did as best she could.

Judith ended that narrative by claiming that, when she heard of the explosions at Aldershot in which the seven people died she didn't think that the map she had so helpfully provided had been used in that attack. It was for this reason that she had not admitted this on any previous occasion, either to the Army or the RUC. Now however she was confessing to two members of the security forces if she was truthful, that she was a party to the causing of explosions in which seven innocents had been murdered.

She was still detained; whether she was under arrest and not free to leave is not now clear. By September 6 she was still not charged with any criminal offence, when she appeared to have admitted freely and voluntarily her involvement in serious crime. What she did do however was to continue to confess, this time in a written statement under caution, which was eventually to be produced at her criminal trial in 1974 as exhibit 79. The statement was witnessed by Lance Corporal Lamb of the Women's Royal Army Corps.

In exhibit 79 Judith returned to her description of the visit to Thiepval Barracks, but on this occasion she gave much greater detail than she had previously. She added another name to the litany of names that the Army and the RUC were compiling with her help. This time she named Michael Kelly. After explaining the circumstances in which they met she claimed he asked her to look at the security arrangements at the Barracks, especially at the entry gates, and how pedestrians and civilian cars were searched, and anything else likely to be of interest to a terrorist. Judith Ward signed this statement as being true.

Once again she had confessed to the commission of serious criminal offences, but she was not charged with any of them. It seems she was not even arrested in respect of them. Could the explanation be that no one believed a single word she said? What did happen however was that the written confession evidence was retained and used as part of the Crown's case as exhibit 79 at the 1974 trial. Because it is difficult to ascertain any direct relevance to any charge levelled against Judith in that 1974 trial the jury there must have wondered why such admissions had not led to a prosecution at the time they were made, some two years earlier.

What however the jury did not know was that on the same day as she made the written confession, statement exhibit 79, Judith Ward had been interviewed again, on at least two occasions, by Detective Inspector Hyland and Detective Sergeant Speers of the RUC. The 1974 jury knew nothing of this because someone on the prosecution side deliberately decided to conceal the existence of these interviews. Judith told the Detective Sergeant that the statement (exhibit 79) she had previously made was "all true, except for the portion about her carrying out observations for the IRA". On any view this was a considerable retreat from the seriousness of what she had not long before openly admitted. Obviously Sergeant Speers wanted to know why she had made such a serious incriminatory admission if it was untrue. Judith told him, quite significantly, that she just wanted to get away from the Army because they had held her for four days and she had signed the statement in order to obtain her release.

Thus at least one person, if not more than one, on the prosecution side knew at the time of Judith Ward's trial in 1974 that she was contesting the voluntary nature of that prior confession, claiming it was induced by duress of circumstances in which she found herself, and was therefore not freely made and was not true. If her defence team had known that was the position they would have been bound to challenge, as a matter of law, the admissibility of that evidence.

Judith was interviewed again, this time by Detective Inspector Hyland and another officer. To them she repeated that her written statement (which became exhibit 79) was true apart from the fact that she had collaborated with, and furnished information about the Aldershot barracks to the IRA. When asked to explain further she said she had been with the Army for four days, and "would have admitted to almost anything to get away from them." She added however that she had no complaints about her treatment by the Army. What was clear however was that she just needed to get away from the oppressive atmosphere of questioning and detention.

The importance of these interviews cannot be over-emphasised. They not merely attack the ground of admissibility of the statement that became exhibit 79, but shed very powerful light on Judith's tendency to make false self-incriminating admissions when she felt under pressure.

More developments were to follow, of even greater significance.

Detective Inspector Hyland was asked to, and did on May 27, 1974, make a witness statement about those events in which he was involved in September 1972. The only reason he could possibly have been asked to do this was in anticipation of this evidence being given at Judith Ward's forthcoming trial – which in fact started on October 3, 1974. That officer added an observation to the content of his proposed evidence. In it he said "despite being further interviewed with regard to this aspect of her confession, she continued to profess her innocence and I must concede that I found her to be very convincing."

Someone on the prosecution side decided that no judge or jury was going to hear that evidence at the forthcoming trial, for its effect upon the jury can only be imagined now. Here was a senior police officer, who subsequently rose to the highest ranks in the RUC, with very substantial experience in dealing with terrorists, concluding that he found Judith's denials of previous incriminating admissions convincing. Would the jury have shared his view if they had been allowed to see that evidence?

When Judith's case went to the Court of Appeal in 1992 the judges noted that the proposed evidence of both Detective Inspector Hyland and Detective Sergeant Speers was not disclosed to the Director of Public Prosecutions and obviously therefore not to the defence team either. There are at least five important questions that arise out of this; first, who asked the Detective Inspector to make the witness statement (as he did) on May 27, 1974? Second, why was he asked to make it? Third, who decided to conceal its existence? Fourth, why was the Detective Sergeant not asked to make a further witness statement, since Judith had told him separately of the falsity of the admissions made in exhibit 79 in the same way as she told Detective Inspector Hyland? Finally, was this evidence deliberately concealed, but allowed to stay in existence in the belief it would never be discovered and see the light of day, in order to convict an innocent?

In any event, following the confessions to the Army and the subsequent retractions to the RUC officers, Judith was released and allowed to go on her way without a criminal charge of any kind being brought against her. The probability was that no one believed a single word of her confession statements. What, moreover, may not have been known then, but is certainly known now, since a check was carried out for the purposes of the appeal in 1992 by a senior RUC officer, that the names mentioned at various times by Judith, such as

Kelly, Quigley and McNally, could not be identified by the RUC or linked by them to any terrorist organisation. She had claimed to have met the latter two in McLoughlin's Bar in Dundalk; any person visiting that town could hardly have failed to see that establishment so prominent is its position in the town. The RUC regarded it, as did the Garda Siochana, as a probable meeting place for supporters of the Official IRA, an organisation both politically and militarily different from the Provisional IRA, which Judith claimed to support and to have worked for.

She makes no detailed mention in her autobiography about these events, save to say, "I was questioned by the RUC during this period and it has been said that I made some pretty weird statements." Clearly her recollection about them is not good.

It is now known however that in August 1973 Judith was back in England. It was a busy time for the terrorists. On Sunday August 19 two petrol bombs exploded at the Army base in Aldershot. The following day a bomb damaged a shopping centre in Hampstead in North London. On Tuesday August 21 seven book-bombs were received at various addresses in the London area, including the Central Office of Information, the Northern Ireland Information Office and various West End clubs. The Ministry of the Environment received a similar device. Ten fire bombs were received at a number of shops and stores; all failed to ignite. By Friday August 25, no less than 26 explosive devices had been located in the London area; on that same day a letter bomb sent to the London Stock Exchange exploded and injured two people. The next day a man had his hand blown off by a letter bomb received by the Economic Intelligence Unit of the Bank of England in the City of London. On that same day a secretary to a Member of Parliament working at the House of Commons was also injured by a letter bomb.

On Sunday August 26 Judith was discovered by a police officer sleeping rough on Euston station in London. She was taken into custody and questioned by two Metropolitan police officers, one of them a member of the Special Branch. True to form, Judith began to confess to terrorist crime almost immediately. She said she lived in Ireland and gave a Dublin address. She had, so she claimed, carried out assignments for the IRA, but she gave no details of them. She denied being a member of that organisation. The reason she gave for being in London was that she was looking for work. A search of her rucksack revealed documents relating to activities of the IRA.

Notwithstanding the possession of that material, her confessions and the recent terrorist activity in London, Judith Ward was released by the police without charge. She could get no one, if that was her intention, to believe anything she said. That was however a statement of affairs which was not destined to continue.

On August 28 Judith obtained a live-in job as a chambermaid at the London Park Hotel near the Elephant and Castle in South London. Another young woman, Elaine Gately, began working there the very same day and they struck up a friendship and indeed shared a room together. The job was not onerous, the hours were not unduly long and the pay and general working conditions were agreeable.

It was about this time that, on her days free from work Judith began to visit Kilburn in North West London, an area then popular with emigrants from all over Ireland. There she encountered an old friend who had moved from Dublin to London. This man was, so she claims, a member of Sinn Fein, the political wing of the Provisional IRA. She went with him to a political meeting held in a room above a public house where the main topic of discussion was the situation then existing in the North of Ireland. She saw on display political leaflets and books for sale, probably the sort of literature and documents founds in her possession by the police officer at Euston Station.

In addition Judith attended public meetings and demonstrations in support of various cases connected with Northern Ireland. On one occasion she kept vigil with others outside a London prison (which she thought was Brixton) where Marion and Dolours Price were imprisoned following their arrest and conviction for the car bombings in Central London on March 8, 1973, in which 180 people were injured and one man died following a heart attack. Judith was not to know that her fame as an innocent prisoner was to greatly surpass that of the Price sisters. (These two later went on hunger strike when the prison authorities refused their request for transfer to serve their life sentences in Northern Ireland. The Home Secretary, in a written Parliamentary answer in December 1974, had told the House of Commons "that it would not be in the public interest" to allow their request for transfer. Within the space of three months he changed his mind. On March 18, 1975, following a protracted hunger strike during which, after 39 days without food, both Price sisters were forcibly fed, they were moved to Armagh's Women Prison to complete their sentences in the North of Ireland.)

As noted above, two dates in Judith's life in August 1973 are documented and easily capable of being proved. On August 26 she was seen by a police officer on Euston station sleeping rough. On August 28 she began her employment and residence at the London Park Hotel.

At her trial in 1974 however, Judith made an astonishing and untrue claim on oath whilst giving evidence in her own defence before the judge and the jury. She said that on August 15, 1973 she had gone through a ceremony of marriage with a member of the Provisional IRA, Michael McVerry. No record of such a marriage exists, simply because it did not take place. Why she made such a claim and what effect it had on the jury trying her cannot now be ascertained, though it was hardly likely to have endeared her to them.

In her autobiography Judith poses the question herself; "why did I say that?" And then she provides an answer. "I don't even know, not even where his name came from: it has been said that it was suggested earlier but I have no memory of this. All I can say is that this is a pointer to the mental state I was in; it was just one of the many absurd statements I made at this time."

In fact Judith was talking about a real person who did exist. Michael McVerry was known to the security forces in Northern Ireland as the commanding officer of the Crossmaglen unit of the Provisional IRA in South Armagh. Judith claimed to have married him on August 15 1973, but after ten days they quarrelled, together with a man called Joe Coyle. It was on the following day that she was questioned by the police at Euston station, and apparently made no mention there of her recent wedding. The police say she was alone and no mention is made of her being accompanied by Joe Coyle or anyone else.

His was a name which was to be repeated again by Judith in connection with another visit to Euston station, this time on September 10, 1973. Judith claimed that at a shop in Hammersmith run by the National Organiser for Sinn Fein, Brendan Magill, she had been approached by Joe Coyle and asked by him to "suss out" Euston station. Apparently she did not know what this involved so he told her. She was to go there and check up on the times that the police officers changed their rosters and note the sites of the surveillance cameras.

September 10 was a Monday. On that day ten people, including Marion and Dolours Price appeared at Winchester Crown Court charged with conspiracy to cause explosions. In the Special Criminal

Court in Dublin, a member of the Loyalist Ulster Defence Association, Robert Taylor, appeared for trial charged with the murder of Oliver Boyce, aged 25 and Briege Porter, aged 21. This young couple, engaged to be married, had been found shot dead through the head. They were lying across one another, in the form of a cross, in a ditch at Birdstown, near Burnfoot in County Donegal in the Irish Republic.

It was a day when it should have been apparent that the Provisional IRA would resort to further bombings if only for the purpose of drawing the attention of the world's media to the Winchester trial. London would have been considered as the most likely target, and it was. At about 1 p.m. on that day a bomb exploded on King's Cross station not far from London's West End. Five minutes later, a man with what was described as an Irish accent, telephoned the Press Association and using a code word warned that a bomb had been planted and was about to explode in a snack bar at Euston station. This was about a half-mile away from the scene of the first bombing. The warning was accurate and true; about 10 minutes later a bomb did explode there, injuring 13 people.

Later that same day at about 5 o'clock, an officer of the London Metropolitan police was standing at a barrier erected near the scene of the Euston explosion. Sometime between then and 5.30 p.m. he saw two young women standing nearby. They were, according to him, swearing and shouting abuse. One was Elaine Gateley, the other, and much more talkative of the two, was Judith Ward. She shouted "if the IRA had done it, they would have made a bigger and better fucking bang; they would have done it properly." Whether that officer was interested or amused, or perhaps even both, by this unattractive conduct matters little; he did nothing to detain either woman for what was clearly at the very least conduct likely to cause a breach of the peace.

In her autobiography Judith recalls this particular Monday. It was her day off work and she and her room mate Elaine Gately went to the cinema to see the film *High Plains Drifter* starring Clint Eastwood. After leaving the cinema they learned about the Euston station explosion and decided to go there. They travelled on the London Underground system to that station. Judith denied that she was drunk, shouting or swearing, or that there was a barrier erected at the station to keep people away. She said that she and Elaine went together to the station bar and there got talking to two or three lads.

One of them was from Northern Ireland. He told the two women that he was from Belfast and was waiting to catch the Train to Heysham in Lancashire in order to get the ferry back to the North of Ireland. He may not have known it, and certainly Judith and Elaine didn't, but the police were already very interested in this young man, James Patrick Diamond. In the event, a number of police officers approached all three and arrested them, on what grounds and in relation to what offences is not now clear.

At the police station Judith was asked to account for her movements for the time the bomb had exploded at the station earlier that day. She told the interrogating officers that she had been in the London Park hotel at the relevant time, about 1.15 p.m. She says now that the housekeeper at the hotel was able to confirm that fact that to the police since she met both women leaving the hotel on the way to the cinema at that time. It may be that the police checked the accuracy and truthfulness of the statement and found it to be correct.

Whilst this was being done however, at about 11.20 in the evening of that Monday a police officer, Detective Sergeant Brian Vickery (who was later to be involved in the case of the Maguire Seven), arrived at the police station to carry out some forensic tests. Using hand kits issued by the Royal Armament Research and Development Establishment based at Woolwich in London (known as RARDE), Sergeant Vickery swabbed the hands and scrapped under the finger-nails of all three suspects detained under arrest at that police station. The purpose of the test was to try to discover whether all or any of the three, Judith, Elaine or James Patrick Diamond, had been in contact with explosives. In the bombing campaign in 1973 (and indeed in 1974 as well) the Provisional IRA had used nitro glycerine (NG) as an explosive substance. NG is a pale yellow, heavy, oily substance which explodes with great violence when subjected to a sudden shock or detonation. On occasions the Provos' bomb makers added dinitrotulene (DNT) to the NG to give it even greater explosive force. In 1973 Mr John Yallop, a Director and head of the explosives Division at RARDE, had helped to develop a test for the presence of NG. (He was later, after his retirement, to give evidence for the defence in the Maguire family case.) This test involved the swabbing of the suspect's hands.

The samples taken from the hands of the three suspects at Euston police station by Detective Sergeant Vickery were sent to RARDE to be subject to detailed forensic analysis. There, Mr. Walter Elliot, a higher grade scientific officer, was in charge of the test procedure. He carried out the tests on the samples forwarded to RARDE by the police. Thereafter he made a written witness statement, not immediately, but he waited in fact until February 18, 1974, some 5 months from the time the hands had been swabbed. No public explanation for this delay has ever been given.

Whatever the test results on the swabs, which would in any event take some time to be obtained, Judith, Elaine and James Patrick Diamond were released by the police, it appears quite unconditionally, without even being required to report back to the police station to be informed of the results of the forensic tests. That in itself seems an extraordinary decision.

In his witness statement, prepared of course for Judith Ward's forthcoming trial in 1974, Mr. Walter Elliott said of her hand swabs, "all gave positive results for Nitroglycerine and Dinitrotoluene," and that was all the information given to her defence team by the Crown for the purposes of part of their case against her, and that was the evidence they proposed to put before the jury.

One is bound to ask at the very outset, if these results were known to the police soon after the swabs were obtained, and Judith claims that they knew the very next day, then why was she not charged with any offence, at least the possession of a prohibited explosive substance, NG, disclosed by that scientific evidence?

When the Home Secretary sent Judith's case to the Appeal Court in 1991, the chemical analysis sheets compiled during the currency of the testing procedure were disclosed to her defence by RARDE for the first time. They make the most astonishing reading, for they indicate that of the three people arrested at Euston station, both Elaine Gately and James Patrick Diamond were more heavily contaminated with NG and DNT than was Judith Ward. Yet, unlike Judith, they were never prosecuted for the Euston bombing or for any other offence.

In relation to Elaine, the dry swab test on both her hands were recorded in the analysis sheet as "trace". The wet ether swab test also recorded "trace" on both hands. The nail scrapings of her right hand indicate "trace" but her left hand was "negative".

In Judith's case the results were as follows:
right hand – dry swab test – "faint trace"
left hand – dry swab test – "negative"
right hand – ether wet test – "faint trace"
left hand – ether wet test – "negative"

nail scrapings on both hands – "negative."

It is possible to deduce from both these sets of tests that Elaine Gately might have handled explosives, but it was unlikely, whereas in Judith's case the faint trace indicated that she probably had not.

In James Patrick Diamond's case however, the results were much more compelling.

The dry swab test on both his hands was "positive"; the wet ether swab on both hands was "positive". The nail scraping test on both hands were noted in the record as "trace".

Even on the strength of these results Mr. Diamond was not prosecuted for any offence. (It is a matter of record moreover that just over a year later, on December 3, 1974 six of the Maguire Seven had their hands swabbed in the same way, using the same test kits and techniques, and they were prosecuted to conviction when the Crown claimed the results were positive proof of the possession of NG. Those swabs were the only evidence against the Maguires.)

There cannot be any justification for Mr. Elliott's evidence in his witness statement that the tests in Judith's case were positive, when a distinction was drawn between results which showed "faint trace," as in Judith's case, "trace" in Elaine's case, and "positive" in Mr. Diamond's case. It was to lead in due course to a judicial lashing of his reputation, but not until after Judith Ward had spent some 18 years of her life in prison for offences she did not commit. Clearly he was taking a risk in putting his evidence in the way that he did, for if the defence team at Judith's trial had called for and examined the chemical analysis sheets they would have discovered that he was being less than frank with the court.

The defence did know however, that the samples taken from the three at Euston had been sent to the Home Office Research Laboratory at Aldermaston for Gas Chromatography/Mass Spectrometry tests (GCMS) to be carried out, but the samples were rejected as unacceptable and no such GCMS tests were done.

It should be noted however, that at Judith's trial in 1974 the Crown never alleged that either Elaine Gately or James Patrick Diamond were jointly responsible with her for bombing Euston station. Her defence team did however attempt to explain away what may have appeared to be strong forensic evidence by claiming that she could have been accidentally contaminated, directly or indirectly, either by some other person at the scene, or by debris from the bomb explosion still around at the time she and Elaine arrived at Euston station, between 5 and 5.30 on that Monday afternoon.

When the true position became known in 1992, when the analysis sheets first saw the light of day in the Appeal Court for the first time so far as the defence were concerned, the prosecution and Mr. Walter Elliott did not escape lightly. Lord Justice Glidewell said that the Crown should not have served such an uninformative witness statement on the defence on behalf of their witness Mr. Elliott, for it was calculated by them to make it more difficult for the defence to probe the detail of the scientific evidence. As for the scientist himself, the judge said that Mr. Elliott had failed to distinguish between the test results on Judith, Elaine and Mr. Diamond, and his statement that "all gave positive results for NG and DNT" was misleading, and for this he alone was responsible. If the true results had been revealed, the defence might have challenged the conclusion that NG was present on Judith's right hand, because they had in fact accepted it as being accurate and tried to explain it on the ground of innocent contamination. If they had known that it was only a "faint trace," that was stronger grounds for believing it was contamination by someone or something else.

Following their release from Euston police station, Judith and Elaine returned to the London Park hotel. Judith was never questioned again by the police about the station bombing.

The fact of being arrested and detained at a police station and subjected to forensic tests would not have been an agreeable experience for anyone, but it did not deter either Judith or Elaine from contacting the police some six days later, on the following Sunday, September 16, 1973. On that day they jointly reported to the police that some property belonging to Elaine Gately had been stolen from their shared room at the hotel. On any view, if Judith was involved in terrorism (and she was not) this would have been an extraordinary thing to do.

As a consequence, entirely predictable, of this report, a police constable of the London Metropolitan police, P.C. Open, visited the hotel and went to the women's room there, clearly something he would have to do since that was alleged to be the scene of the crime.

On arrival the officer found the room filled with IRA posters and other documentary material relating to that organisation. In spite of the fact that the IRA bombing campaign was continuing in London (even on that very day a man had planted a bomb on the premises of Allen International at Westminster, and had been photographed whilst doing so, and two days after that a bomb exploded at any army careers office at Surbiton in Surrey), Constable Open treated the presence of the IRA posters in the hotel room as some kind to joke. In fact he even joked with Judith about the frequent bomb hoaxes at the hotel.

The officer was however cautious enough to make a written statement about what had happened, noting what literature he had seen in the hotel. He also recorded that Judith told him that there would be no bombs at the hotel while she was there. If that was some sort of coded confession that she was involved in terrorism and there-fore would not be harmed in any way by terrorist activity, that would be serious enough. Judith went several steps further than that. In a general conversation about fingerprints, Judith told the officer "oh yes mate, I had them done in Derry. They said I had planted a bomb but they could not make it stick." Such a statement, lacking any denial that she had in fact planted a bomb, was highly incriminating but it did not result, perhaps to her disappointment, to Judith's arrest. Police Constable Open left the hotel mystified, or perhaps even amused by what he had seen that afternoon.

He probably wrote up his witness statement when he returned to his own police station. It was noted and filed away. Neither the contents of that statement, nor even the fact it had been made, were disclosed to the defence at Judith's trial.

Two months later Judith left her employment at the hotel, on November 10, 1973. It may be that she was sacked after playing a practical joke on the housekeeper there.

On the same day, a Saturday, she travelled by train from London to Holyhead in North Wales, intending to sail on the ferry to Dun Laoghaire near Dublin in the Irish Republic. Whilst going through the embarkation hall in Holyhead, Judith was stopped and searched by a police officer, Constable Owen. There was at that time an extensive and careful screening of passengers travelling between Wales and Ireland. A search of her luggage by that officer disclosed her possession of literature relating to the Irish republican movement, similar, if not exactly identical to that seen by the London police officer Constable Open at the London Park hotel. Also found and examined was a small address book containing a number of names, addresses and telephone numbers, including that of Mr. Brendan Magill. (He was a well known figure in the Irish immigrant community in London. Judith has claimed in the past to have met him in a shop he ran in Hammersmith, West London. He operated openly as the National Organiser for Sinn Fein. In that capacity he was directly involved in making the funeral arrangements for James McDade, a member of the Provisional IRA who was killed in a premature bomb explosion in Coventry on November 14, 1974. It was whilst travelling to Belfast to attend his funeral that five of the six men known as the Birmingham Six were detained, on November 21, and later imprisoned for life. Judith also claimed that it was in Mr. Magill's shop that she was asked by Joe Coyle to "suss out" Euston station sometime before it was bombed two months previously).

Constable Owen questioned Judith Ward about the bombings in London. He must have been taken aback when she said to him "yes, Sean Mac is doing well." At her trial in 1974 Judith explained that remark, which must have conveyed to the police officer her approval of the allegedly successful methods which the Irish republican movement were using to advance its political objectives by a bombing campaign in England. Judith told the jury that this was a reference to Sean McStiofan, who had at one time been the IRA's Chief of Staff. Did the jury regard this evidence from Judith and the possession of the republican literature as a seal of approval for the terrorists and their methods?

On the contrary however, it may be a clue to Judith Ward's knowledge, or rather lack of it, of the workings of the Provisional IRA and its leadership. In November 1973 Sean McStiofan, a second generation Irishman born in Leytonstone in East London in 1928 and baptised in the name of John Stevenson in fact was not doing well at all, nor was he in any fit state to commend or command any IRA bombing campaign in London or anywhere else.

Mr. McStiofan was brought before the Special Criminal Court, a three judge non-jury trial court, and charged with being a member of an illegal and proscribed organisation. He certainly got a speedy trial thereafter; some question whether he would get a fair one. He certainly considered that he would not, and resorted to an old effective Republican method of peaceful confrontation by going on a hunger and thirst strike. The following Saturday, November 26, he was found guilty on the membership charge and sentenced to 6 months imprisonment. Because of his weakening condition he was moved from prison custody to the Mater Hospital in Dublin for treatment. He was held there under armed guard. The day following his arrival a number of men, members of the Provisional IRA, attempted to free him from the hospital by force. Gun shots were exchanged between the terrorists and officers of the Garda Special Branch before the attempt was eventually abandoned. One of the IRA men, one police officer and two bystanders were hit in the cross-fire.

On the following Tuesday, now facing the danger of imminent death, Mr. McStiofan was persuaded to abandon his thirst strike by Father Sean McManus, a Redemptorist Catholic priest, who told him his death would only provoke further and unnecessary violence throughout Ireland. The hunger strike did however continue for a total of 57 days, when the Army Council of the Provisional IRA ordered Mr. McStiofan to discontinue the protest. When he was eventually released from prison he was still very ill and physically extremely weak. His influence and interest in the Republican movement thereafter waned. He never regained the status, power of position in that organisation that he had enjoyed before his sentence of imprisonment. Contrary to Judith's views about him, he was not doing well, or even feeling well, at all.

Whatever the police officer may have thought of her explanations and comments following the stop and search at Holyhead, he allowed her to proceed on her way and travel to Ireland.

What happened next to Judith comes from two separate sources, one of which was Judith herself, offered whilst she was giving evidence in her own defence at her 1974 trial. On arrival in Ireland, she said, she went north to the town of Newry, just over the border. Someone apparently told her that Michael McVerry (whom she claimed to have married) had been shot by the British Army and his funeral was to take place on Saturday, November 17, 1973. (In fact it was true that he had been shot dead on November 15). She arrived in Newry on the Friday evening and soon after arrival she was arrested by the RUC and taken to a police station and detained there. Her address book and two other books were taken from her. On the Sunday night she was questioned by a Sergeant McFarlane of the RUC. Following that, on the next day, Monday November 19, she was taken to the ferry terminal and put on the boat to Liverpool. Some of her property, including her address book and her driving licence, she said, was kept by the RUC. The legal power to retain these documents, like the legal power to effectively deport a British citizen from one part of the United Kingdom to another, is questionable and probably non-existent, at least without the making of an exclusion order under the anti-terrorist legislation. When she told the jury this,

142

did they wonder whether she was truthful about the interview with Sergeant McFarlane of the RUC. Apart from Judith's evidence, they were given no further detail or information about it, so they only had Judith's version, probably a mixture of fact and fiction, to rely on.

In fact she was interviewed by Sergeant McFarlane and the police in Britain knew that she had been. On March 8, 1974, after Judith's arrest and while she was awaiting trial, that officer made a witness statement, the existence of which was concealed from the trial court and Judith's defence team. He must have been asked to make such a statement in anticipation of the forthcoming trial, and then having done so its very existence and contents were not disclosed. Someone had made a deliberate and conscious decision to do that in exactly the same way as had happened in the case of the witness statement being made by Inspector Hyland on May 27, 1974. His statement was requested and then concealed from the defence. The same questions posed in his case apply to the evidence of Sergeant McFarlane. Was it the same person responsible in both instances for that decision to conceal two separate witness statements, and was that person acting alone or in concert with others?

Both statements came to light at Judith's appeal in 1992. No inquiry seems ever to have been made to attempt to discover the identity of the skilful and unscrupulous double suppressor of material evidence.

Sergeant McFarlane recorded in his statement that on November 18, 1973 he questioned Judith Ward about her possible involvement with the Provisional IRA. He did not state the ground that gave rise to the suspicion, if any, reasonable or otherwise, for asking that she might be. At first she told the officer that she didn't know anything about that organisation and she had never been involved in it. After further questions however, she said she had brought guns up to Belfast on several occasions, and even identified the guns as revolvers that she concealed in her handbag. If this interview between the sergeant and the suspect was not under caution and Judith had not been told of her right to remain silent, then, when she volunteered this startling information, clearly a ground had arisen for suspecting her of the commission of a criminal offence, and she should have been told of her rights.

However, shortly after, perhaps to the officer's frustration, Judith reverted to her original denials that she was ever involved with the IRA. When she was asked why then had she boasted about bringing guns to Belfast she made this very significant reply: "It was just something to say; I know that's what you want me to say." This was Judith Ward in her role as serial confessor acting true to type, confess and then deny the confession.

The sergeant's written witness statement dealing with this interview ended with a most significant comment, which if the jury had known about it (and there may have been difficulties regarding their admissibility in accordance with the rules of evidence) then their verdicts might have been substantially different. If that document had been disclosed to the defence as it should have been on any view of the law, their tactics might have been different in their conduct of Judith's case. Sergeant McFarlane noted: "I formed the opinion that Miss Ward is not mentally stable and that she could be easily led to say or do anything."

That observation would have had a devastating effect on any overview of the evidence, where at her trial so much depended on the truthfulness of Judith's self-incriminating statements. Here was a senior and experienced police officer giving an opinion on Judith's mental state, which in the event proved to be extremely accurate, and was later confirmed by expert medical evidence many years after this was first written. Even standing alone, that view of a potential prosecution witness would have undermined, perhaps fatally, the Crown's case against Judith Ward. When added to Detective Inspector Hyland's assessment: "despite being interviewed further with regard to this confession, she continued to profess her innocence and I must concede that I found her to be convincing," any jury would be bound to consider whether they could really convict on the basis of self-incriminating statements alone. Was it not for this reason that the evidence of two RUC officers was concealed from the jury and the defence at Judith's 1974 trial?

As it was, the blatant concealment of two material statements left the trial jury to decide between two conflicting versions advanced by either side. On the one hand Counsel for the Crown, John Cobb Q.C, told the jury that Judith Ward "was an intelligence officer, a gun-runner, a bomb-carrier, bomb maker and even a bomb-planter for the IRA."

Defence counsel Andrew Rankin Q.C. invited the jury to look at Judith in an entirely different light. His words were brutal and must have been extremely hurtful not only to Judith's feelings, but also to her family. Later events have proved him right. He posed these questions: "is this girl a female Walter Mitty; is she a pathological liar?" Would the IRA, he asked, have relied upon somebody of such apparent incompetence and ineptitude, and in particular someone who came to the attention of the police and the army authorities so frequently? The jury paid little attention to those questions. They failed to realise that every claim of fact made about Judith by John Cobb Q.C., was totally wrong.

When Judith's appeal came before the Appeal Court in 1992 Sergeant McFarlane was invited by that court to give oral evidence and he readily agreed to do so.

At the time he first interviewed Judith Ward he had served 20 years as an operational police officer in the RUC and was familiar with, and had insight into, the working of terrorist organisations in Northern Ireland. He told the appeal court judges that he regarded Judith's claim to be gun-running for the IRA as total nonsense. When asked why, he replied: "That particular organisation, my Lord, would not trust a person of the mentality of Judith Ward at any time." He went on to repeat his previously stated opinion that Judith was, in 1973, not a stable personality.

(It may be worth noting that, less than a year after these events in the Court of Appeal in London, the Crown was claiming that the IRA used a 17 year old girl called Carole Richardson as a bomb planter. She was a drug user, had minor criminal convictions, was homeless and lived in a squat. She was prosecuted with 3 others, (they became collectively known as the Guildford Four) for the murder of 5 people who died in a bomb explosion in a Guildford public house frequented by soldiers of the British Army. Sergeant McFarlane's view on her role, based on his experience as an operational police officer who had actually encountered genuine terrorists, would be most illuminating.)

Sergeant McFarlane clearly did not believe Judith had committed any criminal offence, and he told the judges that following his interviews with her she was "helped" on the boat. It appears from that that she was being forcibly removed, without any apparent legal authority, from one part of the United Kingdom to another, and this was for the second time. This could only have been done lawfully if Judith had been served with an Order excluding her from Northern Ireland to England. However this poor, under-nourished, defenceless and friendless young woman had no one to stand up for her and to protect her basic human rights.

Those events took place in November 1973. Judith found herself back in England, willingly or otherwise. At first she got a job which she found dull and unexciting, working in a restaurant in Stockport. Whilst there she saw a newspaper advertisement which led her to apply successfully for a job as a groom with Chipperfield's Circus, then based at Belle Vue in near by Manchester. She took up her new post on January 26, 1974. Once again she was working with horses, one of the loves and stabilising influences in her troubled life.

At the circus she shared a caravan with a young woman from New Zealand, Wendy Claxton. Now was the opportunity for Judith, with a steady job which she enjoyed, settled and independent accommodation away from home, to lead a more mature and normal lifestyle. Judith however could not stay silent; she had to talk, mostly about herself. The confessions began. Wendy Claxton told the jury at Judith's trial in 1974 that Judith maintained she was involved in terrorism, that "we" had made bombs, or a bomb, and that she had had a boyfriend who had been shot dead by soldiers. This was a clear and intended reference to Michael McVerry. Miss Claxton did not believe those claims at the time they were made. It is not possible now to ascertain whether at the time she related these boasts to the jury, that Wendy had a change of mind and believed then what she had not believed previously. Certainly the Crown put her forward as a witness who should be believed in what she recollected being said, and the Crown were inviting the jury to accept not merely that Judith Ward had said these things about making bombs to Wendy, but that these statements were factual and true.

Certainly the news from Northern Ireland continued to carry reports of bombings throughout the Province. On the day after Judith joined the Circus at Belle Vue there were explosions in Strabane, Newry, Newcastle County Down and Forkill in Armagh. Very substantial damage to property was caused, although no one was killed in those bombings.

The last evening performance for Chipperfield's Circus in Manchester took place on Saturday February 4, 1974. It was the last of the season and the Circus moved to its winter quarters at Chipping Norton in Oxford, arriving there in the early hours of the Sunday morning. Judith's fellow workers must have had a busy late night and early morning, packing up and loading the equipment and making arrangements to move the animals. There existed within the Circus employees an abundance of evidence, vouched for by numerous witnesses, that Judith Ward was with other members of the Circus staff from that Saturday night and throughout the whole of the next day, the Sunday, from the early morning, throughout the day and the evening. The importance of that evidence was that it contradicted the confession evidence which Judith was to provide subsequently to the police, where she admitted placing a bomb in the boot of a stationary coach at Chorlton Street bus station in Manchester. That coach was waiting to bring service families to the Army Barracks at Catterick in Yorkshire. It was a regular weekly run for soldiers and their families on week-end leave from the army camp. For some time, throughout that Sunday evening, the boot of the coach was left open so that intending passengers could put their luggage inside. The time for departure was always at 11 p.m. Anyone who observed the movements of the coach, its timing and its users, must have known that women and children travelled on the coach along with the soldiers.

Sometime during that evening a fifty-pound time bomb was placed in the boot compartment of the bus by two members of the Provisional IRA. Their identity, that of a man and a woman, the presence of the latter being used clearly to avoid suspicion, has long been known, but proof of their involvement was then, and is now, lacking. In the absence of a confession from either or both of them, there will be no convictions for the most dreadful, cruel and cowardly criminal offences that were shortly thereafter to be committed. Just after midnight, as the bus was travelling along the M62 motorway, the bomb exploded. Eleven people inside the coach were killed instantly. Amongst them were four members of the same family: Clifford Houghton, a serving soldier, his wife Linda and their two children, Lee aged 5 years and Robert aged 2 years. The family may well have been sharing the back seat of the bus, and if so would have taken the direct upward impact of the exploding bomb.

Another young soldier, Private Stephen Walley, aged 18 years, died of his injuries three days later.

The bombing caused a feeling of outrage throughout Britain. (It has long been my view that in response to it, the shadowy military intelligence unit based at Castledillon in Northern Ireland, planned and executed, with the help of loyalist paramilitaries, the car bomb attacks in the city of Dublin and the town of Monaghan. These were carried out some three months later, on May 17, 1974, when a total of 33 people died. Amongst the Dublin dead were another young family, John O'Brien, his wife Ann and their children, Jacqueline aged

17 months and Anne Marie, aged 5 months. The bombs were placed in three separate streets in the centre of the city of Dublin and were timed to explode within minutes of each other, at about 5.30 in the afternoon, just as people were leaving their places of work to return home. There was a bus strike in Dublin on that Friday and the streets of the city were crowded with pedestrians. In total, 25 people died instantly and 140 were injured. Ninety minutes later a car bomb in the border town of Monaghan exploded killing 6 people. These bombings were so organised and planned and carried out in such a way, and with such precision, that few people believe the loyalist paramilitaries acted alone. At the time, in May 1974, the whole of Northern Ireland was in the midst of chaos following the Ulster Workers Council strike, aimed at bringing down the power sharing executive headed by Brian Faulkner. This had been set up by the British Government following the Sunningdale Agreement, which for the first time since 1920 had given the Irish Government a say in the affairs of the Six Counties of the nine which make up the Province of Ulster).

There were some who were not even prepared to wait any longer than a week to extract vengeance for the M62 bombing. In what was clearly a revenge attack, carried out on February 11 by the Ulster Freedom Fighters, a loyalist paramilitary organisation as devoid of pity and as savage and barbaric as the Provisional IRA, two Catholics were chosen as random and murdered. Thomas Donaghy, aged 16 years and Margaret McErlean aged 18, were on their way to work when they were ambushed and shot dead as they arrived at Abbey Meat Packers on the Glenville Road at Newtownabbey in County Antrim. Like the Houghton and O'Brien families, they were two more innocent victims caught up in a conflict in which they played no part, except to add their names to the list of the forgotten dead.

Judith Ward left the Chipperfield Circus winter quarters on the morning of February 4. She told Wendy Claxton she was leaving. She bought a brown duffle bag and a rafia bag in which to place all her possessions (which were in fact very few) in Chipping Norton. She took a bus to Oxford City and then travelled onwards by bus to London, arriving that same evening. There she stayed, so she told the jury at her 1974 trial, with a man called Joe Mooney, at 72 Dyne Road in Kilburn, in the north west of the city. During her stay she found, so she claimed, a number of pieces of paper with references to the IRA, written in Irish, and mention of explosives and the names of persons who could supply them. If the latter part of her account was true someone was careless in the extreme in leaving available to prying eyes information which was both incriminating and dangerous.

On Friday 8 February 1974 Judith left the flat where she had been only for a few days. Her intended destination was Euston Station. If she had anything to fear from the swabbing tests carried out on her hands on the previous September 10 after the bombing there, and of course she did not, it would be unusual in the extreme for even the most unsophisticated terrorist to return there, even for a casual visit. This was not what Judith had in mind. At the railway station she met up with a woman, and a man called Ernie Mayall. For a few days following their meeting, they ate and slept where they could, living a hand to mouth existence in the most difficult conditions. If it was available to them they slept in a railway carriage when it was left for the night in the sidings.

On the Sunday night, February 10, Judith left the two bags she had bought in Chipping Norton, and which contained all her possessions, on a train. When she looked for the one in which she had slept the previous night, it had moved from the sidings, taking her bags with it. They were eventually found by a railway guard at York. Such simple possessions were to provide vital evidence at her 1974 trial, where the prosecution proposed to adduce scientific evidence proving Judith had been in contact with explosives.

At her trial Judith told the jury that on the afternoon of Monday February 11 1974, she had purchased a platform ticket at Euston Station, hoping to spend the night sleeping there. There was prosecution evidence against her that on that very same afternoon, between 3 and 3.30 p.m. a red Audi motor car was seen parked close to the entrance of the National Defence College at Latimer in Buckinghamshire, that is some 40 miles away from the railway station. Shortly after the car was first spotted, a similar one (no one was able to state categorically it was the same vehicle) was seen inside the College grounds. The driver was described as a person with long shoulder length hair. If Judith was being truthful in her sworn evidence about her presence at Euston Station that afternoon, it was unlikely that she was that person in the red Audi car; there was in any event no direct evidence from any independent witness that she was.

There was also evidence from the Crown at the trial that shortly after 7 a.m. on an unspecified morning in February 1974, (neither the day nor the date were ever satisfactorily established) a young couple, a man and a woman, had breakfast in a café some 15 miles from the

Defence College at Latimer. Afterwards they drove away from the premises in a red Audi car. That was all. This very flimsy evidence as it stood carried very little weight against anyone, let alone Judith Ward. That posed no problem to her however; she was ready and willing to make up any deficiencies in that evidence by yet more false confessions. They related to the placing of a 20lb bomb which exploded inside a building at the Defence College at about 9.10 a.m. on the morning of February 12. Ten people were injured, four seriously. A telephoned warning to the College saying "be careful," was given half an hour after the bomb had exploded.

According to the evidence given to the jury by Judith, and in this she was supported by Ernie Mayall, who gave evidence for the defence, she and he went from London by bus to Cardiff in South Wales on that day, Tuesday 12 February, and spent the night in a cheap hotel. Judith did not stay long in the capital city of Wales. The very next day, so she said, she hitched a lift from Cardiff to Liverpool, arriving there at about 11.30 in the evening. She had nowhere to stay or even to sleep.

A few hours later, Constable Barnes, a police officer on foot patrol, saw an outline of a person standing huddled in a doorway and even as he got closer he was unable to determine from the outer clothing and overall appearance what sex that person was. It was only when she spoke that he was able to ascertain she was in fact a woman. It was Judith Ward. Asked to give an account of herself and her movements, she told the officer that she had just arrived from London, and that her luggage had been stolen in that city. It was her intention she said to take the night ferry to Belfast, her intended destination being the border town of Newry.

There can be little doubt that the entire police service was on special alert with regard to anyone going to or coming from Northern Ireland, for only hours before in London the Prime Minister Mr. Edward Heath and senior Cabinet Members in his Conservative and Unionist Government had been forced to evacuate Conservative Central Office following a bomb scare there.

After listening to Judith's explanation about herself, Constable Barnes decided to detain her and take her to a police station. Just exactly what legal power he was exercising in order to do that is not clear. Nor is it clear whether he made it clear to Judith exactly what her status was, whether she was a volunteer assisting the police in their inquiries, or whether she was a detained person under arrest and not free to leave the place in which she then was.

As if to provide the officer with sufficient grounds at least to question her short of arrest she mentioned to him that she had previously been questioned by Army Intelligence and the Royal Ulster Constabulary and she said, "they got nothing out of me." From her track record so far, Judith was setting out on a course of confessional evidence, but this time there was a difference. What she said in custody in a British police station as opposed to her continuous confessions to experienced anti-terrorist officers of the RUC in Northern Ireland, was not rejected out of hand and dismissed as the fantasy it was. In fact in led to her trial, conviction and imprisonment for more than 18 years. She was about to surrender, by her own evidence, the best years of her young life.

Shortly after her arrival at the police station, a search of Judith's meagre possessions was carried out. A driving licence issued in Northern Ireland in her name but with a false address was found amongst them. There was also a letter to her from the RUC. The licence was the document which she later claimed Detective Sergeant McFarland had retained after he questioned her, but later returned it to her through the post. Her explanation for the false address was simple and straightforward. It was the address of a driving instructor who had given her driving lessons. Why his address and not hers should have been used was not disclosed.

The search also turned up a Euston station platform ticket. That, said Judith, had been used when she saw a friend, Joe Coyle, on his departure from that station. Asked to describe him further, she told the police that he was a friend of Jane Rooney's, at whose house at 72 Dyne Road in Kilburn she had stayed until February 13 when she left London for Liverpool.

Since Judith claimed she intended to travel by ferry to Northern Ireland the police were interested in how she would pay her fare, since she had such little cash in her possession. There was an easy answer which apparently the police believed. She was going to telephone a friend in Ireland asking that sufficient money should be sent to her for this purpose. (Perhaps the letter containing the money would have been addressed to her at the doorway in which this sad, bedraggled penniless homeless creature was seen standing by the police officer earlier that morning.)

At their request, Judith provided the police with the telephone number of her Irish friend, but she pleaded with them not to phone at

151

that time, saying "Don't phone now for God's sake". This intrigued the police and they asked why. Even they must have been astounded by her answer. "I've been a member of the IRA for three years and you know what will happen to me if they find out." Perhaps in order to establish further her credentials as a terrorist and reinforce her credibility, Judith added that she was a member of the Roger Casement Cumann (a society or club), based at Kilburn in London. Instead of laughing aloud, since it was being suggested that they had been given a telephone number of someone involved in a terrorist organisation, and then being asked not to use it, the police apparently believed all that she told them and went on to ask her about a small note book that had been found amongst her possessions.

That notebook contained a sketch. This was a drawing of Manchester airport said Judith. No evidence was ever given at her trial or anywhere else that that sketch was worth the paper it was written on. Why Judith was chosen to do it, and what use it would be if it was confirmed to showing an area already open to the public gaze, has never been ascertained. Judith quite willingly told the police that she had been asked to make the sketch by a man called O'Reilly. Not only was she prepared to give the name of a fellow terrorist, but she readily disclosed his home address for good measure as well. In her own interests however, she felt bound to tell the police that she had not made the sketch voluntarily. He had forced her to do so by making threats to harm her brother's child if she would not make the drawing. She did not, apparently, hand it over to Mr. O'Reilly, but left it in her notebook amongst her other possessions for it to be conveniently found there by the police. If she had not linked that drawing to Manchester airport it is probable that the police would have pondered over its meaning from that day to this.

One of the police officers, Detective Inspector Ralphson, who interviewed Judith, asked her whether, in leaving Manchester, and assuming the threats to harm the child were true, had she not put her relatives in danger from Mr. O'Reilly and other terrorists? She made a highly significant reply: "I had to get away" she said, "after the bus, I want out." Asked for a further explanation of that information Judith said "killing children. I just want out."

The Liverpool police must by then have realised in those early hours of February 14 that here was an admission which could well be connected with the bombing of the coach in which the two children died with their parents and others only some 10 days earlier. They decided to detain her.

One is bound to ask whether the police at this stage regarded Judith as one of the bombers of the coach on the M62 motorway, a self-confessed terrorist who certainly liked to talk a lot, mostly about herself. If they did, had her status changed since police constable Barnes had brought her to the police station, when clearly she was not under arrest, for she had never been told of the ground and the fact of arrest? It is doubtful whether, as a matter of law, the police had power to search her possessions at the police station since she was not under arrest there at that time. Nor does it appear that Judith asked for, or was offered, legal advice and assistance from a solicitor at any time up until then. There is no halfway house between arrest and detention. If when Judith was detained she was being placed under arrest, she should have been informed of that fact and the ground(s) for exercising it. At 6.40 a.m. on the morning of Thursday February 14, a Merseyside police officer, Sergeant Scott, told Judith Ward she was being detained. She was no longer at liberty to leave the police station.

At 11 o'clock that morning Judith was seen at a police station by Detective Sergeant Giltrap. He had with him some of her possessions found in the police search after she was first seen by Constable Barnes. Shown the notebook, the Euston Station ticket, the driving licence and the letter from the RUC, she agreed that these belonged to her. As a result, that officer took Judith to another location at police head-quarters in Liverpool and there interviewed her.

Such an interview with a detained suspect should have commenced with the words of the caution that she was not obliged to say anything unless she wished to do so, but that anything she did say would be put into writing and might be given in evidence. It is not clear now whether in fact she was cautioned. She had been at a police station now since 1 a.m. that morning and it seems that Judith had not been given the opportunity to sleep if she so wished.

Sergeant Giltrap, apparently on his own and without a woman police officer being present, asked her to account for her movements during the previous 6 months. She did so as best she could.

At about 6 o'clock in the early evening of that same day, a chemist from the Home Office Forensic Science Laboratory based at Chorley in Lancashire, arrived at the police station. He was Dr. Frank Skuse and he was destined to link his name with the convictions not only of Judith Ward, but also the six Irishmen convicted of the Birmingham public house bombings in 1974, and the Maguire family and their friend convicted of unlawful possession of nitroglycerine, in 1976. (Dr. Skuse told the jury in the Birmingham Six trial that he was ninety-nine per cent certain that two of the Six had been handling nitroglycerine. He told the police officers from Lancashire and the West Midlands Serious Crimes Squad that as well, leading them to believe they had arrested those responsible for killing 21 innocent people.) In 1992 the Appeal Court was to describe his evidence incriminating Judith Ward as demonstrably wrong, even by the state of forensic science in 1974, and added that if the trial judge had known at Judith's trial what that Court knew in 1992, he would have excluded Dr. Skuse's evidence as valueless.

The scientist swabbed Judith's hands to test for any trace of the existence of explosives. He claimed to have found traces of nitro-glycerine under her fingernails, leading another scientist, Mr. Higgs, to deduce that was proof that she had handled and kneaded that explosive. The importance of Dr. Skuse's evidence cannot be underestimated. If the trial jury was in any doubt about the accuracy and truthfulness of the confession evidence, it could find confirmatory, supporting evidence provided by forensic science. If it doubted the strength and validity of that evidence, it could always look to the confession evidence to bolster up the scientific. Judith Ward was caught in a trap.`

Dr. Skuse's career ended three days after the transmission in 1985 of a Granada television programme about the Birmingham Six, where his evidence had helped to prove the case against them. He was 50 years old at the time. He was invited to leave his post by his employers, the Home Office, on the grounds of limited efficiency. Even then, no one considered the importance of his evidence which was so devastating against Judith Ward

On 15 February, at a time following her numerous admissions of responsibility for various acts of terrorism, Judith Ward, perhaps in a moment of lucidity, suddenly changed tack and denied to two Detective Superintendents, carrying out any activities on behalf of the IRA in the United Kingdom. She had not been asked to do so, and if she had been asked she would not have done so. Clearly the defence team ought to have been told about these denials, but they were not. Instead they were deliberately misled. A civil servant solicitor in the DPP's department, acting on the advice of the junior prosecuting barrister in the case, Brian Walsh, wrote to her solicitor saying "I understand that there were interviews with the defendant and senior police officers on Friday 15 February concerning antecedent and certain peripheral matters, details of which I do not propose to adduce at the trial".

At Judith's appeal the court invited the prosecution to call Mr. Walsh as a witness to explain exactly why what was so clearly misleading and wrongful information was provided to the defence in this way. He was not called, for reasons never explained. Instead the hapless civil servant, who had only written what he had been advised to write, was put forward as a witness instead. He was asked to explain, amongst other things, the use of the word "peripheral." Not surprisingly, he could not do so.

The provision of such misleading information which only he could explain but did not do so, and which contributed to a wrongful conviction in a multiple murder trial where the convicted defendant served 18 years in prison, did not the slightest damage to Brian Walsh's subsequent career. He was eventually appointed a Circuit Judge, a post that he held for some years before his premature death. Another barrister, in another case, not involving offences against the State, was not treated so leniently by his profession.

Victor Durand Q.C. was widely regarded as one of the most forceful barristers of his generation, with a criminal practice of some magnitude. In October 1960 he was briefed in a civil case where his client, a police officer, was being sued for damages for assault and unlawful arrest by a photographer, Sidney Charles Meek. The defendant, Richard Fleming, was a uniformed chief inspector in the London Metropolitan police at the time of the incident, that involved a public demonstration in Trafalgar Square in London. Between that date and the trial however, Inspector Fleming was reduced to the rank of station sergeant by a disciplinary board, when it was discovered that a police constable had given untrue evidence that he had arrested a bookmaker, when in fact the arresting officer was Chief Inspector Fleming. The junior officer had attended court and given this evidence of arrest, which most would regard as a pure technicality assuming the validity of the arrest accepted, instead of the more senior officer, who might well have been more usefully employed somewhere else.

The photographer lost his case for damages in front of a jury and then discovered the demotion of the police officer, so he went to the appeal court and obtained an order for a new trial. At the appeal hearing Victor Durand admitted to the court that the decision not to disclose the defendant's change of status was his alone, for which he accepted full responsibility. The court reported him to the Benchers of his Inn of Court, the Inner Temple, for alleged professional misconduct.

The Benchers brought disciplinary proceedings against Durand, and these were found to be proved. He was suspended from practice for three years, reduced on appeal to one year, which he spent extending his house and tending his garden. More importantly, as a result of this suspension he was debarred from any judicial appointment and he remained in practice at the Bar until he died at the age of 86. Clearly he had concealed relevant information that reflected on the credibility of his client, but that was in a civil case where the ultimate question related to damages in money terms, rather than a criminal case where the defendant's liberty and reputation were both at risk. Some may regard his conduct as much less blame-worthy that that of Brian Walsh, but the consequences were substantially different and more punitive in one case than in the other.

Other important and relevant material was concealed from the trial court also. On 24 June 1974, Judith was committed for trial at Wakefield Crown Court. On 5 July 1974, whilst in custody, Judith made an attempt on her own life, using an implement, to cut her wrist. It was later described by the doctor who treated her as a trivial wound, but her desire for death was acute. Judith's family was not told of this, nor was her solicitor, even when she made a second attempt at self-harm whilst awaiting trial. In the result no psychiatric evidence was sought to explain Judith's conduct to the jury at her trial, simply because the defence knew nothing about these incidents, or the denial of her previous admissions. Someone was determined to convict an innocent.

It took 18 years for the truth to emerge and Judith's ordeal was over. She was unfortunate in many ways, except that from one viewpoint it was unlikely that she would have withdrawn from the downward spiral in her life if she had not been imprisoned. The scientists whose evidence convicted her, as well as Dr. Skuse, were castigated in the appeal court.

Of the most senior scientist, Mr. Douglas Higgs from Royal Armaments Research and Development Establishment (RARDE) at Woolwich, the judges said: "......we reject Mr. Higgs' account as a deliberate falsehood." With regard to another RARDE scientist, Mr. Walter Elliott, they said he must have known that the advice given to the prosecution about a test for explosives being absolute was incorrect and misleading….." They went on to say: "We reject Mr. Berryman's evidence as untrue. The consequence is that in a criminal trial involving grave charges three senior government forensic scientists deliberately withheld material experimental data on the ground that it might damage the prosecution case. Moreover, Mr. Higgs and Mr. Berryman misled the court as to the state of their knowledge about the possibility of contamination occurring from the debris of an explosion…..Three senior RARDE scientists took the law into their own hands, and concealed from the prosecution the defence and the court matters which might have changed the course of the trial."

Seldom, if ever, can so many have gathered together to ensure that an innocent person goes to jail for life. It took 18 years for their lying conduct to be exposed, but as in other cases, it proves that truth will out. Many people would have broken under the strain of wrongful conviction and unending sentence, but Judith Ward did not. She was sustained by the fact that whatever the court record might say, she was an innocent woman who had done no wrong to anyone except herself.

CHAPTER 5

ARE YOU SERIOUS?

The *Sun* is the sister newspaper of the London *Times* and the *Sunday Times,* and claims to be Britain's most popular tabloid newspaper, with sales exceeding three million copies a day. It is part of the News Corporation Group, owned by the publishing tycoon Rupert Murdoch, and further claims to have swung public opinion in favour of the Labour Party in 1997; so much so that it won the General Election in that year for Mr. Tony Blair's New Labour Government.

On 11 October 1993, under the heading "Sue Us Challenge to Birmingham 6 by Cops in Clear", one of the *Sun's* journalists wrote: "Detectives have challenged the Birmingham Six to sue them over their bombing convictions – because they claim the truth will come out.....Ex-Detective Sergeant Michael Hornby, a former member of the Squad, said "we would all be happy if the Six sued. It would give us the opportunity to produce all the new evidence we know exists and clear the names of the officers involved in the case once and for all".

In an editorial on the same day, the *Sun* said: "Why hesitate? Police in the West Midlands issue an open challenge to the Birmingham Six: sue us for false imprisonment. Officers are sick of claims that they fitted up innocent people for the 1974 pub bombings. But the only way they can air new evidence is if the Irishmen they helped convict take legal action. Most people wouldn't hesitate if they'd been jailed for a crime they didn't commit. So what are the Six waiting for?"

That was published the day after a High Court judge, Mr. Justice Garland, ruled that the trial of three former police officers charged with perjury and conspiracy to pervert the course of justice in respect of six men, known collectively as the Birmingham Six, should not proceed for four reasons. First, the re-examining of events in 1974, when 21 people died when the Provisional IRA bombed two Birmingham city centre public houses put the defence at a substantial disadvantage. Second, it would be "at best difficult and in practice impossible to isolate the very narrow Crown case involving Mr. McIlkenny (one of the Six), alone from the rest of the case". Third, the volume, intensity and continuing nature of the publicity, with a 'snowball effect', each time a new alleged miscarriage of justice arose, had made the "Birmingham Six" synonymous with "forced confessions". And finally, specific publicity about the three defendants, Detective Superintendent George Reade, Detective Sergeant Colin Morris and Detective Constable Woodwiss, since the successful appeal by the Six in 1991, had created a public perception that the three officers were guilty.

These reasons, either singly or collectively, amount to nothing more than a judicial whitewash. The first reason of delay fails to carry any weight in cases, and amount to a bar to a prosecution, where a man is accused of sexual child abuse, often going back in the case of school teachers or care workers, for twenty years or even longer. Memories of events do fade with the passage of time and the defence is at a disadvantage, but in this case, much of the evidence was to be found in the documents and exhibits, many of which were made at the time.

The second reflected on the decision of the Director of Public Prosecutions to limit the scope and extent of the prosecution against only three police officers, (although a fourth had originally been charged with them) involving only one of the Birmingham Six, whereas it is claimed that there is an abundance of evidence available to charge many more officers in respect of the remaining five men from that wrongly convicted group. The Director has never explained why this course of action was chosen, to prosecute only a few from the many, nor has there ever been an explanation why, even in the limited prosecution, there was no intention to call Richard McIlkenny to give evidence in the case.

The third and fourth reasons are equally invalid. There are many criminal cases which receive substantial media coverage, either because of the nature of the offence or the identity of the alleged offender, where at the subsequent trial the judge simply tells the jury to ignore any pre-trial publicity, and to decide the case only on the evidence adduced before them. That could have been done here.

The judge's approach, following three days of legal argument, was novel and his reasoning unique, but even so the case is not reported in the Law Reports, indicating that it does not establish any principle of law of public importance, or establish any precedent. In addition, of course, in avoiding a trial by reason of the arguments put forward on their behalf, the police officers were missing the opportunity to put before the court the "new evidence" referred to by former Detective Sergeant Hornby. There are some who maintain an interest in seeing what that so called new evidence amounts to, and the source from which it comes.

The *Sun* newspaper, in its editorial on 11 October proclaimed: "police in the West Midlands issue an open challenge to the Birmingham Six. Sue us for false imprisonment. Officers are sick of claims that they fitted up innocent people for the 1974 pub bombings. But the only way they can air fresh evidence is if the Irishmen they helped to convict take legal action. Most people wouldn't hesitate if they'd been jailed for a crime they didn't commit. So what are the Six waiting for?" What the newspaper did not make clear was whether the challenge to sue was issued by serving members of the West Midlands police, or former members like ex-Detective Sergeant Hornby.

Michael Hornby was a member of the West Midlands Serious Crime Squad, and one of its longest serving members, from 1974 to 1989, when it was disbanded by the Chief Constable following a series of cases that caused great public unease. These cases led a member of Parliament, and former Government Minister, Clare Short, the MP for Birmingham Ladywood, to claim on 25 January, 1989, that there was a pattern of malpractice within the Squad, that the forging of confession evidence was widespread, that certain members of the Squad decided who were guilty and simply framed them. The Squad was rotten, she said, and the police themselves knew it. It was a ferocious assault on the police, protected by Parliamentary privilege, but it was one that had to be faced up to, and was not.

The Serious Crime Squad, or "The Serious" as they liked to be known, was first formed in February 1952 in the City of Birmingham Police, as an experimental unit to assist the work of the regular and established Criminal Investigation Department, the CID. Its primary purpose was to use a group of seasoned and experienced officers driving "wireless cars" to combat organised crime. After a number of reorganisations, in April 1974, following the enlargement of the West Midlands police, the Squad was given the name it bore until its disbandment in August 1989.

As early as 1985 however, a series of complaints against "The Serious" led to an investigation headed by Commander Robert Hay of the London Metropolitan police. As James Morton noted in his book *Bent Coppers,* that investigation centred around the case of a man kept for eight months in custody accused of murder. He had confessed to the crime, but was released when another man, subsequently convicted of the murder, was arrested and charged with it. Commander Hay's Report was never made public, but it is known that he criticised the Squad's interviewing techniques, failure properly to use police pocket books for recording relevant information and the inordinate amount of time that officers were allowed to remain with the elite unit. Nothing changed as a result of that Report.

The events which led to the discrediting and ultimate downfall of "The Serious" began in July 1986, with the arrest of four men in connection with a burglary and theft at a cash-and-carry warehouse in Willenhall, in the West Midlands, where property worth some £30,000 was stolen. The four, Clifford Jones, Christopher Turner, John O'Brien and Harry Michael Elwell, were taken under arrest to the local police station where their detention was authorised by the custody officer.

Clifford Jones was interviewed by Detective Sergeant Hornby and Detective Constable Hugh McLelland. Because of the changes in the law following the introduction of the provisions of the Police and Criminal Act, 1984, PACE, (enacted following the recommendations of a Royal Commission) the interview was recorded in writing. It had to be so recorded unless the investigating officer considered it would not be practicable to do so, or would interfere with the conduct of the interview. Mr. Jones admitted knowing the other three men who had also been arrested, but he denied all knowledge of, or involvement in, the warehouse burglary. Following the termination of the interview, Constable McLelland, (an experienced officer who served in the Squad for about 15 years, only slightly shorter service there than Hornby) invited Mr. Jones to read and sign the interview record. This was in accordance with the Codes of Practice made under PACE. Mr. Jones readily read the record and signed it. He was then detained overnight in police custody.

The next morning all four suspects were taken before the

Magistrates' Court in order to apply for bail. This was opposed by the police, who sought their remand in custody. They were so remanded. According to Clifford Jones, Detective Sergeant Hornby told him at some stage that he would probably get five years imprisonment for the offences he faced. He was devastated, for apart from minor convictions for road traffic offences, he was of previous good character.

However, the prosecution now alleged that they had a strong case against him, that in the course of the interview on the previous day, Mr. Jones had confessed to being a party to the agreement to steal from the warehouse.

He was fortunate in the choice of his defence solicitor who took immediate action and consulted a handwriting expert, Robert Radley, requesting him to examine the original notes of the police interview with Mr. Jones. It so happened that Mr. Radley owned an Electrostatic Document Analysis machine, ESDA, and used it to carry out a forensic test known as the ESDA test. The existence of this test was not widely known, since it was of comparatively recent invention, and its purpose was to make it possible to read any imprint or indentation on a document immediately below another piece of paper on which any original writing appears.

The lower sheet of paper is placed on a metal plate and covered with a very thin foil. The plate is given an electrostatic charge and then sprinkled with a fine powder. The effect is that the imprints or indentations, if there are any, show up in black on the ESDA foil, and the writing shows up white. The foil can be photographed and kept as a permanent record for future reference, making it especially useful as evidence in a criminal trial.

Mr. Radley's analysis of the record of Clifford Jones's interview disclosed that pages one, two and five contained denials of any crime whatever. Page five contained the impressions of some of the writing on page one and two, as might naturally follow if they lay in sequence one below the other. Pages three and four however, contained words and phrases that could be construed as partial admissions of complicity in the warehouse burglary. There was not, however, an impression of either of these words or phrases on page five, as would be expected if they had been written in sequence. The very strong inference that could be drawn from this expert evidence was that pages three and four of the interview record had been inserted at a later date and were not written contemporaneously as had been claimed.

The trial of the four accused men began at Wolverhampton Crown Court in June 1987 before His Honour Judge Christopher Stuart-White and a jury. Two police officers, Detective Sergeant Daniel Lloyd and Detective Constable Lawrence Shaw, had interviewed one of the co-accused, John O'Brien, and claimed that he confessed to the crime in the course of an interview that was contemporaneously recorded by Constable Shaw. That written record had been read back to him and Mr. O'Brien agreed with it.

Defence counsel used an interesting ploy to deal with this point. He asked that Constable Shaw simply copy out the record of that interview as the judge, jury, lawyers, the four accused looked on. He did so. It took a total of 21 minutes to write up the record. However, another document, the custody record required by PACE to verify timings of interviews, indicated that the original interview took only 14 minutes. In the light of this evidence and that relating to the ESDA test involving Clifford Jones, the trial judge directed the jury to acquit both he and John O'Brien. In the light of that direction, quite unusual in a criminal trial, the prosecution elected not to continue their case against Christopher Turner and Harry Michael Elwell, and they were also acquitted by the jury.

That occurred on 25 June 1987. When, some six months later, in January 1988, six men were accused of carrying out two robberies at post office premises in the West Midlands, which were denied by the six, defence solicitors must have been interested to note that two of the police officers in the case were Detective Sergeant Michael Hornby and Detective Constable Hugh McLelland. Their interest would no doubt be heightened when it was disclosed that the six men had confessed to the crime, that they had committed the offences with which they were charged. The solicitors knew of the evidence in the case against Clifford Jones and his three former co-accused and asked the Crown Prosecution Service, the CPS, for a sight of the original notes of the confession evidence, no doubt for the purpose of subjecting them to an ESDA test. They never received the original documents. The explanation put forward by the CPS for the failure to furnish the defence with them, was that the documents had been lost by the police officers between two police stations, a matter of some considerable carelessness on the part of someone never identified, but also of some assistance and convenience to the prosecution if they were allowed to present their case relying only on copy documents without the need to prove the originals. In two successive weeks, at

163

two separate Crown Courts in the West Midlands, the judge ruled that copy documents of the alleged confession evidence were not admissible. In the light of those rulings, and in the absence of other evidence, the CPS withdrew the case against the six accused men and they were found not guilty.

The reaction of Detective Sergeant Hornby to the collapse of the prosecution in both of the above cases in which he was involved is not known, and it seems he did not publicly at any rate invite anyone to sue him or the West Midlands police. He might have been on dangerous ground had he done so, especially in the light of another case which fell for hearing between the two mentioned above. On July 11, 1987, just three weeks after the acquittal of Clifford Jones and others, a jury acquitted John Bullivant, Hubert Forbes, Leo Morgan and Wesley Stewart, after their defence lawyers made allegations against the police of fabricating evidence, inconsistent timings of interviews, flawed evidence of visual identification and documentary evidence said to be missing. One of the police officers in the case was Detective Sergeant Michael Hornby; another was Detective Sergeant James Bernard McManus, who served in "The Serious" for some four years between 1985 and 1989, and whose name and activities surface again and again in cases involving the Squad.

That year, 1987, may not have been the most fortunate and happy year in the life of Detective Sergeant Hornby. On 23 October 1987, Paul Harris was arrested on suspicion of burglary and deception. When first interviewed by the police in custody, he made no admissions of any kind whatsoever. When questioned by different officers at a later stage however, they claimed that he confessed to them in the course of an interview that they recorded in writing, but when given the opportunity to sign the notes as an accurate record he refused to do so. The officers who claimed to have obtained the confession, freely and voluntarily made, otherwise it would not be admissible in evidence, were Detective Sergeant Michael Hornby and Detective Constable Hugh McLelland. These two seemed to be most successful in obtaining confession evidence in cases where others failed to do so.

The case was listed for trial in the Crown Court on 25 April 1989. By this date much more was known about the way in which confession evidence was being obtained by officers of "The Serious", and how such evidence frequently surfaced in the complete absence of any other evidence at all which implicated the suspect in the commission of a criminal offence. Accordingly, notwithstanding the existence of the confession, which if it was accurate and true would result in a conviction, the prosecution simply threw the case in and the trial judge directed the jury to acquit Paul Harris, as they were bound since there was simply no evidence upon which they could convict.

Just two months after that, on 22 June 1989, another accused, Ronnie Bolden, a 42 year old car dealer from Hertfordshire, was acquitted of robbery. He had been arrested in August 1987, on suspicion of armed robbery of a security van whilst he was travelling down the M1 motorway after being at a Birmingham car auction, and thus fell within the jurisdiction of "The Serious". That robbery had taken place a few hours prior to his arrest. He was held on remand, as a Category A prisoner, at Winson Green prison in Birmingham for no less than twenty two months before his eventual release. His first trial was stopped during the course of the evidence, and a jury acquitted him after a retrial. Three of the police officers in the case giving evidence for the prosecution against him were Detective Sergeant Michael Hornby, Detective Constable Hugh McLelland and Detective Sergeant James Bernard McManus. Such a combination might be expected to conjure up some confession evidence, and if there were any observers of the practices of these three police officers, they would be more than surprised by its absence than by its presence. It did appear.

After his arrest Ronnie Bolden was taken first to Rugby police station, then on to Queen's Road, which is mentioned frequently in the case of the Birmingham Six. There he was interviewed no less than three times by Detective Sergeant McManus and Detective Constable Ronald Adams (who served in the Squad for three years), and also by Detective Sergeant Hornby and Detective Constable McLelland on two occasions. The police asked him not only about the offence in respect of which he was arrested, but also about an armed robbery at a bank that had been committed some five months earlier.

According to Mr. Bolden, at no stage during the interviews was any written note made by police officers. He signed nothing, admitted nothing and maintained his innocence throughout the time he was being questioned. At some stage he was asked whether he would agree to stand on an identification parade, for it was claimed that there were a number of eye-witnesses who could give relevant evidence in the case. He agreed and did attend such a parade procedure. A total of 16 witnesses attended and of those only two, both police officers, picked him out as being involved in the bank robbery. Not a single identifying witness linked him to the robbery of the security van.

Following that, Mr. Bolden was remanded in custody by the court to await his first trial, which was fixed for October 1988. When his solicitors received advance disclosure of the prosecution evidence against him, they saw that it was alleged that there existed a confession to robbery, and in addition an allegation that he had offered the sum of £10,000 to the police as a bribe.

It so happened that another trial was fixed for October 1988, in Birmingham Crown Court involving Paul Fitzsimmons. He was charged with robbery at a florist's shop where property valued at £1,000 was stolen. The prosecution alleged that Mr. Fitzsimmons had confessed, freely and openly, to that robbery. He told his solicitors, Messrs. Saunders & Co., that was not so. Any confession he might have made had been extracted from him by duress, and what he had admitted was unreliable and untrue. That duress took the following form. He said that, following his arrest and detention, two police officers, whom he named as Detective Sergeant McManus and Detective Constable Adams, had taken him to police station where first he was given food and drink, including a can of Coca-Cola, in the police canteen. Then after that he was taken to an interview room elsewhere in the building. There, in the course of an interview, he was questioned about his alleged involvement in the robbery at the florist's shop. He claimed that Constable Adams told him that a Coca-Cola can had been found in the rear of the getaway vehicle used in the robbery. That can had Mr. Fitzsimmon's fingerprints on it. It was not conclusive evidence of involvement in the offence, since there was no proof when the can had been placed there, but when it was produced for him to see, Mr. Fitzsimmon's may not have taken that point, however strong or weak it might have been. What he did appreciate however was the fact that the police had in their possession such a can with his fingerprints on – left there whilst he was drinking from it in the police canteen. There was worse to follow.

According to Mr. Fitzsimmons, the police officers told him that the owner of the florist shop had died two days after the robbery. That was apparently true, but death was due to natural causes and there was accordingly no link between the robbery offence and the subsequent death that would have made the robber liable in law for causing the death of the owner. There simply was no chain of causation between the two events. The significance of this point would not have been apparent to Paul Fitzsimmons, who is semi-illiterate, and he said that the two officers offered him a choice of three charges. Which one he might face was up to him. In order of seriousness they were murder, manslaughter or robbery. No one will be surprised to learn he quickly chose the latter and made a short one page statement confessing to robbery.

When the case was listed for trial in the Crown Court, it may be that the prosecution anticipated a plea of guilty to the charge of robbery to which the accused had confessed. It was not to be. Paul Fitzsimmons denied the charge and the case proceeded with evidence being called before the jury. After hearing legal submissions, the judge ruled that the confession was not admissible in evidence since he could not be sure that it had not been obtained by duress as the defence claimed. There being no other evidence against the accused, the jury, in whose charge he was, were directed to find him not guilty and they did. He was discharged and released by the court.

Mr. Fitzsimmons did not however fade into the obscurity from which he probably wished he had never emerged, for he was later to allege that whilst he was in Winson Green prison, where he had been remanded in custody awaiting trial, he had an unexpected visitor. It was Detective Sergeant McManus. It was claimed that officer told him that unless he agreed to give evidence for the prosecution against Ronnie Bolden, he would be re-arrested on release from custody. That evidence that he was invited to give took a somewhat unusual form, for it was not directly connected to the offence of armed robbery, but it was suggested that Mr. Fitzsimmons should say that the solicitors acting for Ronnie Bolden, Messrs. Saunders & Co., had attempted to bribe him to give evidence for the defence at his trial. This most serious allegation, if it was true, may give some indication of the determination of some officers in "The Serious" to obtain a conviction against Ronnie Bolden, and the extreme lengths they might have been prepared to go in order to achieve that result.

After fourteen months spent in custody awaiting trial, the case against Ronnie Bolden alleging armed robbery began. It came to a sudden halt when Detective Sergeant McManus said on oath in evidence that the solicitors in the case acting for the accused had attempted to bribe Paul Fitzsimmons, and a statement to that effect supporting the officer's allegation was in the possession of the Crown Prosecution Service. He said that two men employed by Messrs.

Saunders & Co had offered the bribe. The Sergeant then produced the prison visitor's book for the purpose of proving that two representatives of that firm of solicitors had actually been at Winson Green prison on the relevant date and time. He was subjected by defence counsel to a fairly severe cross-examination on his credibility as a witness. The Sergeant had to admit that he had been the subject of a number of complaints of alleged fabrication of evidence, and that he had been under investigation himself on no less than six occasions in the preceding five years.

In the light of all this, the trial judge decided he had no alternative but to discharge the jury from returning a verdict in the instant case, and he ordered a new trial. Ronnie Bolden was remanded in custody and remained there for another eight months until his second trial began.

The truth about Detective Sergeant McManus's allegations of attempting to obstruct justice and fabricate evidence made against the defence solicitors turned out to be somewhat different from what he claimed. The two legal executives from Messrs. Saunders & Co., James Montgomery and Paul Baker, certainly did have a pre-arranged appointment to see Paul Fitzsimmons in Winson Green on the day in question. Their purpose was to try to establish whether he could assist their client's defence regarding the evidence gathering techniques of "The Serious" in general, and Detective Sergeant McManus in particular. They would have been interested to learn about the Coca-Cola can and the fingerprint evidence and the way in which it was obtained.

Both legal executives had submitted to the prison authorities, as they were required to do, a written and signed application for the granting of a Visitors Order to enable them to enter the prison to see Paul Fitzsimmons. On the day of the proposed meeting there however, it so happened that Paul Baker was suddenly and unexpectedly called away from Birmingham at the very last minute, in order to see another of his firm's clients who had sought their advice following his arrest and detention at Golders Green police station in North London. Accordingly, James Montgomery carried out the prison visit at Winson Green on his own. For some mysterious reason which has never been explained, Paul Baker's purported signature appears, together with that of James Montgomery, in the Visitors' Book at the prison in Birmingham, when it could be conclusively proved he was many miles away in the London area, attending a client in a police station there. That was a fact that could be proved because it was recorded in the client's custody record, as required by PACE, in Golders Green.

Ronnie Bolden's trial on two counts of armed robbery began at the end of May, 1989. Amongst the prosecution witnesses were Detective Sergeant McManus and Detective Sergeant Hornby. Evidence of various interviews between the accused and the police officers in the case was adduced by the prosecution. The defence claimed that some of the phrases attributed to Mr. Bolden by the police had an air of unreality about them. One point the defence, took in addition, related to a telephone number at Mr. Bolden's home in Hertfordshire. When he was taken under arrest to Queen's Road police station he was brought before the custody officer, a sergeant, who was told of the grounds of the arrest and who then had to decide whether to charge him or to detain him for questioning or securing further evidence. He was informed that he was being detained and given the reasons and told of his rights to free legal advice, to have someone informed of his arrest, and a copy of his rights under the Codes of Practice made pursuant to PACE.

The custody sergeant opened a custody record as he was lawfully required to so. In that record, one digit of the telephone number provided by Mr. Bolden was inadvertently omitted by that officer. When the first interview in that station began, an identical mistake was repeated on the first page of the record of the interview. This suggested that the number had been copied from the custody record rather than being furnished by Ronnie Bolden as the officers conducting that interview claimed. It seemed very unlikely that exactly the same mistake relating to the missing digit would be repeated by different police officers on two separate occasions.

This in itself may not be a very strong point, for it may be that it was Mr. Bolden, who on two separate occasions, provided the wrong information about the number. But the fact that the point was taken at all may indicate the degree of suspicion and distaste with which the evidence of some of the police officers in the case was regarded. In the event, the trial judge, the Recorder of Birmingham, His Honour Judge Richard Curtis, described some of the police evidence as "unattractive" and "totally misleading". In the light of that it may be somewhat surprising, not that Ronnie Bolden was acquitted by the jury, but that it was by a majority verdict on both counts of armed robbery.

In early August 1989, the name of Detective Sergeant Michael Hornby was mentioned again and again in the case of a prosecution against two brothers, Gerald and Ronald Gaul and others on charges of assault and the unlawful possession of a firearm. From the time of the arrest of Gerald Gaul up until the commencement of the trial, his solicitor was endeavouring to obtain a copy of the original statement of the victim of the alleged assault. The defence were entitled to see that as a matter of right, not discretion, in accordance with the Advance Information Rules then in force at that time. The statement had a high degree of relevance to the issue in the case which involved disputed visual identification that the defence alleged was mistaken. They wished to see that statement which contained the victim's description of his attacker, in order to compare it with Mr. Gerald Gaul's actual appearance, or indeed any of those arrested with him.

The Crown Prosecution Service and the police said they were unable to trace the file containing the original statement. One officer, Detective Sergeant James Milligan, told the court in evidence on oath that the file had been missing since 1988. It was not known who might have been responsible for removing it. However, during the lunch-time mid-day adjournment on Tuesday 8 August 1989, the file suddenly and rather unexpectedly surfaced. It had apparently been found in a box by Sergeant Milligan. When the relevant record book was produced, it was found that the file had been signed out to Detective Sergeant Michael Hornby.

That officer told the court that he was not responsible for the missing file and that someone else must have booked out the file in his name for what was termed "an administrative convenience". What useful purpose this would have served seems not to have been explored, and why someone should use Sergeant Hornby's name rather than his or her own remains a mystery to this day. The description of the attacker in the assault bore no relation to the description of Gerald Gaul or anyone charged with him, which probably explains why the file went missing in the first place.

The prosecution called as a witness a man called Paul Joseph Jarvis. His character and conduct are described by Dr. Tim Kaye in his book *Unsafe and Unsatisfactory – the Report of the Independent Inquiry into the working practices of the West Midlands Police Serious Crime Squad.*

Dr. Kaye relates how Mr. Jarvis was arrested by the Squad after he and two other men carried out an unsuccessful robbery at a supermarket. He did "a deal" with officers from the Squad in order to get bail and avoid being remanded in police or prison custody. He failed to answer to his bail and absconded. He was arrested in Devon after a robbery there. On his return to Birmingham he became a protected informant and kept in police custody for eight months. He was cultivated by the police as a supergrass, i.e. an informant ready to implicate other criminals on a massive scale in the commission of criminal offences. During all that time he was provided with alcohol, allowed to watch television and his girlfriend was allowed to sleep with him in his cell.

When he appeared at Lincoln Crown Court he pleaded guilty to seventeen offences, including armed robberies, aggravated burglaries and a contract shooting. Since he also admitted, in addition, no less than 1,510 other offences that he asked the court to take into consideration when sentencing him, one would expect that even a compliant supergrass would receive a substantial prison sentence. He was ordered to be imprisoned for four years, of which term he served about sixteen months.

The prosecution called Mr. Jarvis to give evidence against the Gaul brothers and their co-accused. He got into some difficulty when it became apparent that he could not, because he was in prison at the time, have committed 203 of the 1,510 other offences which he had asked Lincoln Crown Court to take into consideration.

In spite of the fact that the trial judge described Paul Jarvis as "a compulsive liar," and despite the saga of the missing file, the jury convicted the accused on the very same day that the Chief Constable disbanded the Serious Crime Squad.

On 21 October 1991 those convictions were quashed in the Criminal Division of the Court of Appeal. The case is referred to in another, that of Derek John Treadaway, whose appeal was before that Court in November 1996. That case arose in this way.

Mr. Treadaway, then aged 27 years, was convicted of two offences of robbery and two of conspiracy to rob post office premises and vans, by a majority jury verdict at Leicester Crown Court on 10 March 1983. He was sentenced to 15 years imprisonment. He claims that officers from the West Midlands Serious Crimes Squad refused him access to legal advice at the police station, handcuffed his hands behind his back and placed a series of plastic bags over his head so as to suffocate him. He faced a stark choice – sign or suffocate. He signed a confession statement which had already been prepared for his signature by police officers.

In 1985, he took the most unusual step of suing the West Midlands police and was met with stringent attempts by them to block the case at every turn. The first attempt to have the case struck out on the ground that it was so preposterous and without merit, failed and the case was permitted by the court to continue. When it was set down for trial in 1989 however, there was a further attempt to strike the case out on the ground that the passage of time was so great that the police would not get a fair trial, and this did succeed before a part time deputy district registrar, the lowest and most junior judicial officer in the British legal system. An appeal by Mr. Treadaway against that decision was refused by a West Midlands circuit judge, but he persisted and obtained an order from the appeal court that the case be allowed to proceed to trial.

On 28 July 1994 Mr. Justice McKinnon ruled in favour of Mr. Treadaway and awarded him compensatory damages of £10,000 and exemplary damages of £40,000 for assault, against five officers of "The Serious". He concluded that Mr. Treadaway had been cynically denied access to a solicitor when it was plain he wanted one, and the judge rejected the police suggestion that the handcuffing had taken place at Mr. Treadaway's home; that had happened when two officers had gone into the cell at the police station, handcuffed him behind his back prior to placing the plastic bags over his head. The judge said he did not believe the evidence of the four identified officers, Brown, Pickering, Russell and Price, who gave evidence before him. Detective Inspector John Brown (his rank at the relevant time, he later was promoted to Superintendent) was described as "a most unsatisfactory witness", whose "stock in trade was ambiguity and he simply did not tell the truth". This officer, Superintendent Brown, had also been involved in the Gaul case. He had expressed confidence in the total reliability of the supergrass Paul Jarvis, who gave evidence as a witness for the prosecution in that case.

One of the original witnesses at the Treadaway criminal trial was a supergrass named Morgan, who said he and another man called McKay had taken part in four offences together with Mr. Treadaway. Mr. Morgan had absconded from Britain and was found in Gibraltar. A court order for his extradition was obtained and he was returned here. The police officer who first suggested that he might give evidence for the prosecution was none other than Detective Sergeant Michael Hornby.

Furthermore, Sergeant Hornby signed, as a witness, no fewer than 53 witness statements made by Morgan, relating to Mr. Treadaway's prosecution and he also escorted Morgan on a number of drives in a police vehicle to identify various locations.

Would it be unfair to Detective Sergeant Hornby to claim that he was deeply involved in preparing the prosecution evidence against a man whom a High Court judge believed was abused and misused in the most oppressive way in a police station in Britain?

When Mr. Treadaway's case was referred back to the Criminal Division of the Court of Appeal by the Home Secretary pursuant to section 17 of the Criminal Appeal Act 1968 on 28 July 1994 for his long standing conviction to be considered, as it was bound to be after the findings in the civil case, the prosecution decided to try to uphold the safety of the conviction. It was a not a case, they said, of which the West Midlands Serious Crime Squad can be proud. However, they further said they relied on the evidence of the two accomplices, Mr. Morgan and Mr. McKay, who incriminated Mr. Treadaway in the offences. This may have been put forward with the tongue in both cheeks, because the prosecution well knew that both men had what the Appeal Court called "a vast criminal record," and Mr. McKay had a history of psychiatric illness as well.

The prosecution realised they needed the evidence and the attendance at court of Superintendent Brown and Detective Sergeant Russell, and perhaps because of their reluctance to attend, the Crown applied for, and were granted, witness summonses to enforce their attendance. Both failed to appear in court. This is what appears in the transcript of the appeal court hearing on Monday 18 November 1996, in the judgment of Lord Justice Rose. "Prior to the hearing before this court today, witness summonses were served on Brown and Russell. Neither of them attended this court today. We are told that within the last 72 hours, and that must be after the witness summons was served upon him, Brown has gone to Egypt. We are told that as far as Russell is concerned, although he too appears to have had a witness summons served upon him, there is in existence a note from his general practitioner, dated 14 November, which states no more and no less than that Russell is not fit to attend court."

This discloses the most astonishing state of affairs. A senior police officer refusing to obey a court order to attend court and instead leaves the Country, while another simply sends a sick note to say he can't attend, without giving the slightest detail of the purported illness that keeps him away. The one safe deduction one can make from this is simply that neither Brown nor Russell wished to give evidence, and since this was their opportunity to vindicate their reputations that had been so damaged in the judgment in the civil case, their absence and subsequent silence is difficult to understand.

(One very interested spectator to the developments in the Treadaway case was George Keith Twitchell. He was arrested in 1980, and charged with the murder of a security guard and robbery, which he denied. He was convicted on 26 February 1982, of manslaughter and robbery and sentenced to 20 years imprisonment on the first charge and 15 years concurrently on the second. He alleged that a signed confession had been obtained from him by officers of "The Serious" after a plastic bag had been placed over his head whilst he was in their custody in Willenhall police station in the West Midlands. He said "Somebody put this bag over my head and it was clamped tight around my mouth and eyes. I remember struggling and heaving and then I must have gone unconscious." Even whilst serving his sentence he maintained his innocence. He was released from prison in 1993, but his convictions stood. He and Mr. Treadaway do not know each other. When it became apparent that at least one of the officers involved in his case was John Brown, the Home Secretary referred his case back to the appeal court also. His counsel, Stephen Solly Q.C., told that court that "in a scenario that beggars belief", police officers handcuffed Mr. Twitchell's wrists to the back legs of chair he was sitting in, in the police station and then placed a plastic bag over his head. He was threatened with suffocation until he signed the confession. There were about eight or nine police officers present at the time. One officer was alleged to have threatened: "The bastard signs or he goes out feet first." The convictions were quashed on 25 October 1999. He had served more than 12 years in prison.)

Detective Sergeant Michael Hornby's role in the Treadaway case was subject to judicial comment as well. Of him, Lord Justice Rose said: "An officer called Detective Sergeant Hornby, had, as is apparent from this Court's judgment in Gall, been involved in the suspicious disappearance of a file of witness statements and the manufacture of the other offences which Jarvis asked to have taken into consideration......There is other material before the Court, into the detail of which it is unnecessary to go, to show that Detective Sergeant Hornby was deeply involved in the reprehensible activities of the West Midlands Serious Crime Squad prior to its abandonment."

For the avoidance of any doubt, let it be said that one of the most senior judges in the British legal system was stating that this former police officer was, in two criminal cases, involved in the concealment of material evidence in one and in the fabrication of evidence in another, as well as being deeply involved in other reprehensible conduct with other officers in a specialist squad in which they all served.

When the *Sun* newspaper published its invitation to the Birmingham Six to sue the West Midlands police in October 1993, and quoted ex-Detective Sergeant Hornby, they could not have foreseen the criticisms directed at him by the appeal court in November 1994. Those who read that newspaper question whether, even if they had done so, it would have made any difference, since truth and accuracy are so seldom allowed to get in the way of a good story.

The evidence of Detective Sergeant Michael Hornby was vital to the prosecution case against one of the Birmingham Six, Hugh Callaghan. Hornby was the officer who obtained a confession to the public house bombings from him. If the jury that convicted Mr. Callaghan could have seen into the future and learn of the constant and consistent allegations which were to be made against him and his fellow officers in "The Serious," it may be that they would have given much greater credence to the circumstances in which Mr. Callaghan confessed to the monstrous crime of multiple murder he did not commit.

Hugh Callaghan was born in Belfast in 1930 and moved to Birmingham in England in November 1947. He was then only 17 years old. He stayed in various lodgings in the suburbs of the city. He married an Irish girl from County Mayo in 1956. They have one daughter. They lived together happily and peacefully as a family. Why a man who had spent the previous 27 years living a normal family life in Birmingham should suddenly take a decision to commit, with others, a mass murder of innocent people and then return home to his wife and family, seems a question that troubled few if anyone.

He was arrested at his Birmingham home at about 10.45 p.m. on Friday 22 November 1974, just over 24 hours after the Provisional IRA bombed two public houses in the city centre of Birmingham, killing 21 people. The point is often made that if he really had been involved in those bombings on the previous evening, it was exceedingly strange that he should make no attempt either to hide or to flee the country where he had spent almost the whole of his adult life, especially when it was known that five other men, all either friends or acquaintances, had been arrested at the ferry terminal at Heysham on their way to Northern Ireland.

Mr. Callaghan was interviewed in the early hours of the following morning by Detective Chief Inspector Powell, Detective Sergeant Higgins and Detective Constable Buxton. He gave an account of his movements, which included going to New Street railway station and seeing off from there the other five men accused of the bombings. He said that he knew James McDaid, who died on 14 November 1974, when a bomb he was planting at the Central Telephone Exchange in Coventry exploded prematurely, and that the five were travelling to Belfast for his funeral. (McDaid was a well known singer and entertainer in the Irish pubs in and around Birmingham. His family also came from the Ardoyne, the same part of West Belfast as Mr. Callaghan). Mr. Callaghan denied he was in the IRA. He denied planting any bombs. According to the police he was distressed and crying and kept repeating "can you help me, can you help me?" He denied this. He said that he was slapped once, possibly twice, across the face by Sergeant Higgins. At about 1.45 a.m. on 23 November, Mr. Callaghan was taken by car to Sutton Coldfield police station, about three or four miles away from Queen's Road. He claimed that having arrived there he was taken straight to an interview room and interviewed during the night. He further claimed that he was shown a statement made by Billy Power, but he did not read it but only glanced at it. There was a lot of shouting but no violence used against him. The police denied any of this happened at all; there was no interview. Hugh Callaghan said he did not sleep during the night "because one of the officers was sitting inside the cell, just looking at me all the time…..An Alsatian dog was coming out all the time".

On the morning of Saturday 23 November, the police claimed that there was a further interview between him, Detective Sergeant Higgins and Detective Constable Buxton. Mr. Callaghan cannot remember that interview taking place. The police version was that he described to them how he and three of the others, McIlkenny, Walker and Hunter, all went by bus to New Street railway station where Power was waiting for them. It was not long before Paddy Hill arrived at the station and they all had a few drinks. At that point, according to the police, Mr. Callaghan started to sob, put his head in his hands and said "listen, I shall need some help. God forgive me. I want some help." Shortly before this his hands had been swabbed by a scientist with negative results.

Hugh Callaghan's version of the sequence of events and their content was entirely different. He said that sometime on that morning, even before the taking of the swabs, he was moved by Sergeant Higgins and Constable Buxton to a room and told his particulars were to be recorded. Whilst that was being done, Constable Buxton was kicking him on the shins under the table. Both officers denied that interview ever took place or that anyone kicked him on the shins.

Leaving to one side the dispute as to the number of interviews and their content, and the police conduct during them, it is manifestly clear that at no stage had Mr. Callaghan made any admission or confession to any crime over a number of hours of interviews with police officers. All this was now to change, for onto the scene came Detective Sergeant Michael Hornby. His slogan might well be "When all else fails, get a confession".

At 2.55 p.m. on that Saturday afternoon, three officers, Detective Sergeant Bryant, Detective Constable Davies, and Detective Sergeant Michael Hornby interviewed Mr. Callaghan. According to the police account they began by telling him what they had been told and Hornby went on: "You know why you are here and I believe you wish to tell us the extent to which you are involved in the bombing incidents in New Street, Birmingham on Thursday 21 November 1974. Do you wish to make a written statement about this? If you do you can write it or I can write it for you at your direction." He was cautioned that he need not say anything unless he wished to do so, but that anything he did say might be put into writing and given in evidence. According to two of the officers at the trial (Constable Davies was said to be ill and did not attend), Hugh Callaghan then asked them: "Is it true sir that all those people are dead and injured?" This seems an extraordinary question, since the news media, both radio and television had, from the Thursday evening, and the newspapers on the Friday morning, been full of accounts of the dead and the dying in the explosions. Hugh Callaghan, unlike the other five men, had access to that information up to the time of his arrested at 10.45 in the evening of the Friday, so he would have known, if not the exact figures, at the very least there were many dead and very many injured.

Sergeant Hornby told the court that he replied: "yes, Mr.

Callaghan, as a result of those explosions there are a large number of people dead and injured. Do you want to make a statement?" He replied: "Yes, I want to confess – Mary, Mother of Jesus, help me and forgive me." He then, said the police, threw his arms around Constable Davies and sobbed on his shoulder.

He was asked if he wanted to write the statement, and he said "no, you write it." Sergeant Hornby then wrote down Mr. Callaghan's statement at his dictation and this was exhibited before the jury as exhibit 112. These exchanges had taken about 10 minutes. The statement commenced at 3.05 p.m. and finished at 4.30 p.m. when it was signed by Hugh Callaghan. Whatever had been said or done by Detective Sergeant Hornby and/or his two colleagues, it had certainly induced a man to admit something he had previously denied, and it is difficult to see why he should have done that if the police behaved towards him in the way they described.

In his summing up to the jury, the trial judge Mr. Justice Bridge said, "there are a number of matters as regards this interview. The first concerns clothing. I do not see any great importance in it myself, but as it was pressed, I think I had better remind you of it. The police admit that when Hornby arrived he mistakenly gave instructions to Callaghan to remove his clothing, not realising that the clothing in which he had been arrested had already been taken for forensic examination."

Hugh Callaghan's explanation of this point was simple. He said that he was made to undress and dress several times. When his clothes had been taken he was just given a blanket to put round him. It was a situation which was calculated to, and did, make him both vulnerable and humiliated. He asked the police repeatedly "please don't beat me up," to which Hornby replied, "not half if you won't make a statement". It was during this process of dressing and undressing that one of the police officers – he could not exactly say which one – shook a fist in his face and said "you're going to make a statement". At this stage, so he claimed, Sergeant Hornby was shouting like a raving lunatic. That officer said to him "if you do not make a statement we will bash you round the cells". He was so frightened he said, and with his stomach ulcer paining him, he had no option but to make a statement.

In that two page statement he said "Whilst I was in the bar I noticed that Walker and Hunter had got some white plastic bags. I hadn't seen them before this. When we were about to leave the bar Hunter gave us all a plastic bag with a bomb in it and told me to go to the Mulberry Bush with him and put them outside. I put my bomb on the main road side of the Mulberry Bush, that's the side where you can walk out of New Street station. After this Gerry and me went back into the station and I went into the bar to finish the drink that I had left there."

This version of events of the public house bombings could not be correct for, unbeknown at that point in time to Hornby and the others, there would be scientific evidence called by the prosecution at the trial that the explosions were probably caused by two bombs side by side, inside (not outside) each pub, bombs that had probably been carried in brief cases, not plastic bags. No witness ever came forward to say they saw anyone of six rather shabby working class men carrying brief cases in the public houses or elsewhere in New Street railway station.

On Sunday 24 November, Hugh Callaghan was taken by police car back to Queen's Road police station. According to the police it was a perfectly normal uneventful journey. He disagreed. He said that during the car journey they pulled up near Salford Park that runs under Spaghetti Junction near the centre of the city of Birmingham. There is a lake in that park. "Let's throw him in the lake," he alleged that Sergeant Hornby shouted. That was denied.

Mr. Callaghan said to the police "you can't let that statement go through. I am involving innocent people, Hunter and myself, in matters we know nothing about." Whereupon the officer in the front passenger seat pointed a gun in his stomach and said "you had better stick to your statement." In response to this allegation, the police denied that anyone in the car was armed, which some may consider a somewhat unusual approach to escorting a man said to have admitted being a dangerous bomber and mass murderer, through the public streets of Birmingham. If there had been an armed attempt by anyone to release him from police custody, the police would have been powerless to resist.

After the convictions and sentences in the case of the Birmingham Six, it was assumed that their case would fade away from public consciousness. It did not. There were other cases as well.

George Glen Lewis is now 38 years of age. He was arrested on 16 January 1987 on suspicion of being involved in a burglary. When interviewed by divisional detectives he denied any involvement and was released without charge. Five days later he was arrested by two officers from "The Serious," Detective Constable Perkins and

179

Detective Constable Reynolds and taken to Wednesfield police station for questioning. Dr. Tim Kaye sets out (in his book *Unsafe and Unsatisfactory* at page 44) what happened next. After being reminded of his right to stay silent, Constable Perkins said: "Firstly let's talk about the burglary that happened last week at Tettenhall." Mr. Lewis was alleged to have replied, "The police have already interviewed me about it. I did it."

Just like that. Nothing could have been easier. The event seems to be somewhat similar to the case of Mr. Callaghan, not admitting anything to anyone for some time, and then suddenly "The Serious" arrive on the scene and the suspect admits committing a crime without delay or hesitation.

The true picture was spelt out at a hearing in the High Court in Birmingham on 19 January 1998 where Mr. Lewis was awarded two hundred thousand pounds in damages for crimes he had not committed. The judge was told that after being arrested by Perkins and Reynolds he was driven by them in a police car to the station. On the way Perkins racially abused him, punched him in the head two or three times and head-butted him. They both falsely alleged that Mr. Lewis admitted in the car to carrying out an armed robbery. At the police station he was refused access to a solicitor, and when he refused to sign blank sheets of paper he was struck again in the head by Perkins. He was also threatened with a syringe.

Mr. Lewis served five and a half years in prison after his wrongful conviction of the burglary and two armed robberies. The judge who awarded him the massive amount of damages told him he had been totally vindicated at the hearing.

Hassan Khan was arrested on 20 November 1987, on suspicion of robbery committed in a shopping precinct in Birmingham. About two months previously, on 12 September 1987, a security guard, Kevin Robinson had a gun pushed into his stomach by an unmasked man as he emerged from a shop carrying a bag containing £10,000 in cash. He threw the bag at the gunman who then ran off. He fired two shots, wounding two members of the public who chased him. He escaped.

Hassan Khan was arrested at his home in Caernarvon. He was then taken from Wrexham in North Wales by officers of "The Serious" and driven on a 103 mile car journey from there to Chelmsley Wood police station in Birmingham, where he was detained. The police alleged he confessed to the robbery in the course of the journey, and the confession was recorded by Detective Sergeant Swinnerton in the front passenger seat of the vehicle, using the light of a fluorescent torch hanging around his neck.

At the trial, the police told the court that on the afternoon of the following day Mr. Khan confessed again to his part in the robbery, but he would not sign a statement to that effect. For his part, and this allegation by now has a familiar ring to it, he denied that such an interview ever took place, and that the evidence was a complete fabrication. He maintained that he was forcibly dragged from his cell, shouting in protest and was told that he was dealing with "The Serious," and that whatever happened he was going to sign a confession.

Hassan Khan relates one most interesting statement. According to him, and there would be no reason for him to invent it, one rather big police officer said: "I dealt with those Irish bastards who did the Birmingham bombings and believe me, when I had finished with them they kissed my shoes and called me 'Sir' every time I asked them a question."

After twenty six months in prison, Mr. Khan's convictions for robbery and two offences of wounding with intend to cause grievous bodily harm were quashed in the appeal court and he was released from custody. This was on 23 February 1990. By this date the Serious Crimes Squad was no longer in existence, for on 14 August 1989, the Chief Constable of the West Midlands Police disbanded the Squad. Their tactics could no longer be tolerated, even by their senior officers.

An investigation into the Squad was set up by the Police Complaints Authority and conducted by the West Yorkshire police. They looked at 97 complaints against the Squad made between January 1986 and August 1989. Some consider that the parameters were set to avoid looking at the activities of the Squad in relation to the convictions of the Birmingham Six in 1975. However, their convictions were quashed on 14 March 1991, in the face of other evidence of malpractice by the police and the collapse of the so-called forensic evidence against them.

Between March 1990 and October 1991, a number of cases were sent by the Inquiry team to the Crown Prosecution Service to consider criminal charges against some of the officers in "The Serious".

In May 1992, the then Director of Public Prosecutions decided that there was "insufficient evidence to prosecute" a single officer from the Squad.

Some may regard that decision as being anything but the truth.

CHAPTER 6

THE CASE OF AGENT 294

The report in the London *Times* newspaper on 22 August 1984 was short and to the point. It was headed "Double Agent's jail sentence cut by Prior" and went on "A double agent who helped to smash dozens of IRA units in the 1970's has had an 18 year sentence reduced by eight years by Mr. James Prior, Secretary of State for Northern Ireland." (That meant his almost immediate release from custody. Questions are sometimes asked why this public announcement was made in the way that it was, rather than allowing the man involved to slip quietly away.)

"Anthony O'Doherty, aged 34, claimed that he saved hundreds of lives, but he turned to crime and in 1981 he was jailed on 47 terrorist charges. O'Doherty is expected to be freed next year from the 'supergrass' wing of Belfast's Crumlin Road jail.

Last January, Sergeant Charlie McCormick, a former Special Branch officer who worked with O'Doherty on anti-terrorist operations had a conviction for bank robbery and possessing weapons quashed on appeal."

This newspaper report concealed much more of the truth than it revealed.

Anthony O'Doherty was born on 14 June 1949, the second youngest in a family of seven and was brought up in the Portglenone area of County Antrim in Northern Ireland. He received an elementary school education, leaving at the age of 15 years and began employment as a trainee fitter-welder. Before long he became involved in crime, quite unsuccessfully, for on 19 November 1966 he was convicted of housebreaking and theft when he was conditionally discharged by the court. He was told if he stayed out of trouble he would hear no more of the offences for which stood convicted. On 23 January 1967 however, for similar offences that were clearly much more serious, he was sentenced to a term of education and training in a Borstal institution. He was at a later date to be accused by a barrister of being a man "of considerable intellectual dexterity". His early education and criminal career belies that description of him.

Thomas Charles McCormick was a serving officer with the rank of Detective Sergeant in the Royal Ulster Constabulary with some 22 years experience at the time of his arrest in Belfast on 7 August 1980, on suspicion of being involved in serious criminal misconduct. He was then 45 years of age. He had been a member of the Special Branch staff attached to the RUC station at Ballymena, Country Antrim for a number of years, during which time he had first encountered Anthony O'Doherty.

The pair had met at a memorial ceremony for Roger Casement, the Irish patriot hanged by the British in 1916 for treason. O'Doherty was selling copies of a republican newsheet *The United Irishman* at Murloch Bay, Ballycastle in Antrim and they exchanged words in a not unfriendly fashion. Shortly after that they met again, in less agreeable circumstances on 9 August 1969, when in a series of dawn raids the British Army arrested 342 men, almost exclusively Catholics, in Operation Demetrius, intending to intern them without trial. Of those, some 105, including O'Doherty, were released within the space of a few days. Whilst held in custody however, he met Detective Sergeant McCormick who told him that if he heard anything about terrorist activity he was to give the Special Branch a ring on the telephone and ask for himself. He agreed to do so.

In January 1972 O'Doherty was arrested again on suspicion of involvement in a wages robbery at a shirt factory, but after being detained for about six months on the Maidstone prison ship and later in the Maze prison in Belfast he was released. After that he met Sergeant McCormick and another Special Branch Officer and there was talk about getting O'Doherty infiltrated into the terrorist scene. That bore fruit and for some two years between 1972 and 1974 both men were in regular contact with each other on a almost weekly basis, and during which time information about the IRA and other republican terrorist organisations like the Irish National Liberation Army was passed from one to the other.

A senior Special Branch officer was prepared to, and did say in court on oath, that the information which O'Doherty passed on, using the cover "Agent 294" through Sergeant McCormick as his "handler" was reliable and had saved many lives.

The relationship broke down however in circumstances which are unclear and in dispute. One version is the conventional one that both McCormick and O'Doherty fell under suspicion by the police, and following his arrest, O'Doherty began to talk, implicating his handler in their joint commission of criminal offences. The other version is less conventional. On 31 August 1984 (i.e. less than 2 weeks after Mr. Prior's decision to release O'Doherty from custody) the Dublin magazine *The Phoenix* claimed that the alleged terrorist had been trained by the SAS and recruited into a pseudo gang of the sort long advocated by General Sir Frank Kitson. (He was a former commander of 39 Infantry Brigade based in Belfast who advocated the use of techniques to terrorise the terrorists.) "The gang consisted of RUC men, British undercover operators and 'native' Irish, i.e. Catholic from republican areas......Like other pseudo-gang members and redundant informers, O'Doherty found that he was not pensioned off, but was set up to be killed. Instead of letting the IRA know about him, however, his handlers arranged to have him carry out a lone ambush on a UDR patrol. The agent provocateur was told to stand in a precise spot under some trees and fire a number of shots at two UDR jeeps which would pass at a given time. The jeeps arrived, but O'Doherty (with the benefit of experience of how his masters operated, stood at a different firing point – and watched the UDR patrol, obviously fore-warned, riddle his planned ambush point with scores of bullets. A terrified O'Doherty then contacted a solicitor and was soon in the relative safety of Crumlin Road jail, having confessed to a number of operations."

Many might be inclined to doubt the truth of that second version. There is some basis for its accuracy. It is known that just before mid-night on 12 February 1974 an Ulster Defence Regiment (UDR) patrol was proceeding along the Gortgole Road in two vehicles, both Land rovers. This road was close to where O'Doherty was living at the time. The soldiers opened fire, but only in response (so it is claimed) to a sustained burst of automatic gunfire from high ground to their right. There were no casualties. This purported ambush had been set up by a Special Branch officer, Detective Inspector Jimmy Blair, allegedly to protect O'Doherty whose identity and role as an informer might have been compromised. The date of this incident is of the most fundamental importance, because if it happened on 12 February 1974 Anthony O'Doherty did not head for a solicitor's office in a state of panic and fear of death, for he continued to be involved in crime, as he admitted, not on his own but with his Special Branch handler, Detective Sergeant Charles McCormick. It was not until his arrest on 3 August 1980 that he began to confess to his part in numerous criminal offences. What is most mysterious about the entire shooting incident however is first whether O'Doherty ever opened fire on the UDR patrol at all, and further whether when the soldiers opened fire they were shooting to kill, or were they part of the charade as well?

Anthony O'Doherty was questioned at Castlereagh police office for at least three days, during which time he made admission after admission. He is alleged to have mentioned not only the above mentioned "ambush" at Gortgole Road, but claimed there was one before that, which the Special Branch of the RUC admit is true and they were involved in setting up that also on 14 November 1973. He further confessed to a shooting at the home near Portglenone of a serving RUC officer, saying he had been asked to do this by Detective Sergeant McCormick who had waited nearby and then driven him away from the scene. He said that on no less than 3 occasions he had fired a ·303 rifle provided by McCormick at the local police station, and all this was done to impress others with his involvement in terrorism and convince them of his bona fides as one of them. Others take the view that he did this, on the instructions of others, to attempt to persuade any doubters, that it was the IRA, not a pseudo-gang that was operating in the area at that time.

By the time his confessions were concluded the police were in a position to charge him with no less than 47 offences involving 13 different incidents or series of incidents. These could be conveniently divided into three main groups, first terrorist offences against the security forces, second, armed robberies carried out at various premises for money and third, murder. Not however any ordinary murder. But it was alleged against Anthony O'Docherty that he was guilty either of being a party to the shooting, or at the very least of withholding information about a crime, namely the killing of Sergeant Joseph Patrick Campbell on Friday 25 February 1977 at Cushendall police station. This is an offence contrary to section 5 of the Criminal Law (Northern Ireland) Act 1967. It was O'Docherty's claim, later repeated in sworn evidence, that the man who shot that officer in a cold and callous killing was a fellow police officer also servng in the RUC, namely Detective Sergeant Cahrles McCormick.

Cushendall is a coastal town in Antrim, some 50 miles from the city of Belfast. At the time the population was small, only about a thousand people lived there. It was a predominately Catholic town. The most senior police officer stationed there was Joseph Patrick Campbell, who was a native of Donegal but was living at Moyle View in Cushendall. He was at the time of his death only 49 years of age. He had been stationed in the town for 15 years and knew practically everyone who lived in it and in the surrounding areas. He was married with eight children whose ages ranged from 21 to 3 years. He was as devoted to his wife and family as they were to him. At his Requiem Mass his parish priest told the congregation that packed the church to its capacity that Joseph Patrick Campbell was "a community policeman rather than an authoritarian, a counsellor and a real advert for the Force. He played very much the fatherly role and was liked and respected by virtually everyone here." Amongst the mourners was the then Chief Constable of the RUC, Sir John Hermon, who had been a personal friend. On the evening of the murder the rector of Cushendall, the Rev. H.D. Heatley called on the Government to bring back the death penalty at once. (Those who knew the Sergeant doubt whether that would have been something he himself would have wanted). The rector said: "I hold the Government primarily responsible for the murder of Sergeant Campbell. He was a gentleman if ever there was one, and a kind hearted Christian officer."

In the weeks before the 25 February 1977 Sergeant Campbell seemed to rather quiet, reticent and in a troubled state. The probability is that he had good reason to suspect that a fellow police officer, Charles McCormick was involved in serious terrorist crime. Certainly, according to O'Doherty that is what McCormick himself believed, for he said to him, so it was claimed "Campbell has twigged on to us, he will have to go."

What they were actually doing together, or so O'Doherty claimed, was to commit a series of crimes which included armed robberies at banks and post offices and the hi-jacking of cars to carry out these offences.

On 29 October 1981 he pleaded guilty at Belfast Crown Court to 47 criminal offences and was sentenced to a series of concurrent terms of imprisonment, the longest of which was 18 years. The scene was thus set for putting Detective Sergeant McCormick on trial for 27 of those

47 offences, and calling as the principle witness for the prosecution his former accomplice in crime, Anthony O'Doherty.

An accomplice in law is anyone associated with another, whether as principal or accessory, in the commission of a criminal offence. The evidence of an accomplice called by the prosecution is admissible but as the law then stood the judge has the warn the jury (if there was one, and himself if there was not) of the dangers of acting on the uncorroborated, unsupported evidence of that suspect witness, the accomplice, who was amongst other things likely to shift the blame onto the shoulders of someone else. The trial judge has to decide whether the witness is an accomplice and the jury (if there is one) has to accept that ruling.

Since the current round of the Troubles recommenced in 1969, the nature and extent of terrorist violence in Northern Ireland has been thought by the British Government not to be capable of being dealt with through the ordinary criminal process of arrest on reasonable suspicion of a specific criminal offence as the first stage in the prosecution process, and trial by jury thereafter.

The whole question of jury trial had been the subject of a Commission of Inquiry conducted by Lord Diplock when he was asked by the British Government to consider legal procedures to deal with terrorist activities in Northern Ireland. The Commission reported in December 1972. They thought that jury trial was unreliable and problematic in respect of terrorist offences because of the danger of partisan verdicts from predominately Protestant juries and also because of the danger of intimidation of jurors from members of paramilitary organisations. They also considered that the main obstacle to dealing effectively with terrorist crime in the regular courts of justice was intimidation by terrorist organisations of those persons who would be able to give evidence for the prosecution if they dared. This problem could not be overcome by any changes in the conduct of the trial, the rules of evidence or the onus of proof, which the Commission regarded as appropriate to trial by judicial process in a court of law.

Lord Diplock accordingly made some recommendations to confront these difficulties. Trials of scheduled offences, broadly defined as those involving terrorist crimes, should only be conducted by a Judge of the High Court or the County Court, sitting alone with no jury. In one swoop, the important constitutional right of trial and to be judged by one's peers was swept aside. In addition, members of the armed services should be given a power to arrest people suspecting of having been involved in, or having information about, offences and detain them for up to four hours to establish their identity. Bail in scheduled offences should not be granted except by the High Court and then only if stringent requirements were met.

A further recommendation was that at the trial process the onus of proof as to the possession of firearms and explosives was reversed so as to require any person found in circumstances to prove on the balance of probabilities that he did not know and had no reason to suspect that arms or explosives were where they were found. A confession statement wherein a suspect admits committing an offence should be admissible as evidence involved in scheduled offence cases, unless it was obtained by torture of inhuman or degrading treatment; if admissible it would be for the court then to decide its reliability on the basis of evidence given from either side as to the circumstances in which the confession had been obtained.

This clearly was a recognition of the difficulties the RUC had in gathering sufficient admissible evidence through normal policing methods. Expert and careful examination of the crime scene was difficult and sometimes impossible in areas known to be hostile to the security forces and where their presence might induce violence or even an ambush. Gathering evidence was fraught with difficulty because it might be destroyed or disposed of before the arrival of the RUC, and if it was not they had to be extremely wary of booby trap devices as they endeavoured to collect it. That was only one area of difficulty.

The decision to abolish trial by jury for scheduled offences was bound to cause trouble in the area of accomplice evidence, and experience proved that it did. In December 1983 the leading Belfast solicitor and Irish scholar Paddy McGrory wrote (in the Belfast Magazine *Fortnight*, no. 200 at page 12) that "….. the use of an accomplice's evidence is not something imported into the system to deal with politically motivated crime in Ireland, but has long been an accepted part of the system in the United Kingdom for a very long time. And just as it was the judges who decided that such evidence was acceptable, so it was the judges who recognised the dangers and insisted that the evidence should be used only if certain safeguards were observed. Of these, the most important was that a jury should be warned by the judge that, although they could accept the evidence of the accomplice as sufficient proof without corroboration, it was regarded as dangerous to do so. Given that such evidence has been used for so long a time, why should its use now in Northern Ireland have become a matter of concern to many lawyers? First, there is the sheer scale of its use. When such evidence came to be regarded as admissible, subject to safeguards, it cannot have been in the comtemplation of the judges that it would be used is a systematic manner, in trial after trial, and that many of these trials would involve large numbers of accused, and that its use would become a dominant feature of the legal system, rather than an occasional and fairly rare occurrence. Few people now doubt that the use of accomplices is now a system and that the police actively seek out such witnesses. Police spokesmen, although they tend to attribute to their new friends or 'converts' motives of nobility conspicuously missing on investigation, scarcely veil their reliance on this new phenomenon as a vital element in law enforcement policy. The Lord Chief Justice was recently at pains to point out that if it is a system, it is a system of prosecution rather than conviction. That may be so, but there are very real dangers in the use of such evidence systematically rather than fortuitously. There was never a system used but it was abused. The temptations to terrorists and policemen alike to abuse this system are enormous."

Clearly, in the light of these trenchant criticisms of the use of accomplice evidence by the prosecution, the Crown faced an uphill task in the attempt to prove the guilt of Detective Sergeant Charles McCormick at Belfast Crown Court, before Mr. Justice Murray, sitting alone without a jury where the main witness for the Crown was Anthony O'Doherty, a self confessed criminal.

Count 1 in the indictment, the document setting out the written charges facing the accused man, alleged possession on 10 February 1974 of a sten gun and ammunition in suspicious circumstances. This charge arose out of the gunshots fired at the house of an RUC Constable Eugene Kearney in the early hours of that day. He was the chosen target apparently because McCormick had asked that officer "to square" a motoring case and he had refused to do so. At least according to Anthony O'Doherty when he admitted his involvement in that offence as he did in those set out in courts 2, 3 and 4 in the indictment alleging possession on three separate occasions between 31 December 1973 and 1 January 1976 of a ·303 rifle and a quantity of ammunition in suspicious circumstances. All three cases involved the use of rifle fire directed at the Portglenone RUC station, committed for the purpose of boosting O'Doherty's reputation in the eyes of the

Provisional IRA and to convince them that he was a genuine republican militant. (The reader will recollect that the date in count 1, 10 February 1974 related to events said to have taken place only two days before the shooting charade, if such it was, when the UDR patrol fired shots at Anthony O'Doherty).

He gave his evidence to Mr. Justice Murray in open court. He said that "the accused was decent to me. Very decent. He would give me money, fed me, gave me clothes and was generally good to me….. we were like brothers at that stage because I was depending on him and he was depending on me. He didn't seem to have any other agent working for him."

O'Doherty then went on to describe, without much reference to any detail, how he would like to leave Northern Ireland to live in Scotland, because the Provisional IRA had a death squad looking for him, so he claimed, because he was known then by them to be a Special Branch informer, a post usually but not always well paid, and which carried with it the penalty of death.

He told the judge, "I still planned to go to Scotland but had no money and Charlie had no money and we were just touring around and he asked me out of the blue could I do a robbery. He said 'there is an answer to the problem.' He asked me could I hold up seven or eight people. We were in the Special Branch van. My first reaction was 'what about the police in Cushendall, the Ballymena police, the UDR and the Army in the area? We drove into Cushendall and on the way we talked about the bank and the post office. He guaranteed me 100 per cent that there would be no Army or police – definitely no police. There were I think 2 policemen in Cushendall although he did not say this to me at the time. He said he could look after the police and there would be no Army and he would find out what the UDR were going in relation to patrols. This was about a week before the robbery. He suggested robbing the bank and post office on the same day as the town was 'wide open'. That was Charlie's idea because I knew nothing about Cushendall. We were to steal a car and it was set for the following Monday. The car would be dropped off at a spot used when the Provies had done the bank previously." Within that wealth of information was one most distinctive feature. It was true that on that day, Monday 25 November 1974, when the sum of £3,048 in cash was stolen in a robbery from Timothy Aloysius Boyle at the Northern Bank, Cushendall, the town really was 'wide open'. The entire police contingent stationed at Cushendall, including Sergeant Joseph

Campbell, was in Belfast, attending Belfast Crown Court to give evidence as witnesses at a trial. Obviously another police officer would have access to this confidential information relating to a commitment which had to be fixed sometime in advance of the trial hearing, if he wished to obtain it. O'Doherty, who probably would not have been privy to this information unless it was provided to him by some one else, went on with his evidence, "I never stole a car before but Charlie got a bunch of keys out of the police station that the police used if somebody loses the keys of their car – the keys were handed over on Friday evening. A pistol, a hand grenade and a pillow case were used in the robbery. On Friday or Saturday we left in the van or car with the grenade, gun and pillow case. We hid the stuff a quarter of a mile outside Cushendall. I placed them in a quiet spot at 5 or 6 p.m. wrapped in polythene bags. On Sunday we met to steal a car. We tried car parks in Ballymena and we tried a Church service up the Doury Road, but it was no good. I had not stolen a car before. We decided the only way to get a car was to hi-jack one. We went over to Portglenone to get a car. Charlie dropped me off at Lisnahunshin. I was armed with a ·303 Bennett gave me'. (There was a Special Branch officer of that name in that area at that time. Apart from O'Doherty's word for it, there is no other evidence that he was the source of the firearm.) 'I needed a red light. There were some road works and I lifted a red light. I was wearing Army gear – combat jacket and scarf and a balaclava. I waited about half an hour. Two cars approached both from the Rasharkin direction. I waved the red light. The car stopped. There was a lady in it'. (She was a retired tobacco worker, Mrs. Martha Quinn.) 'I went forward to the car door and I think she was under the impression that it was an Army checkpoint. I told her to get out. I got in and tried to start the car and nothing happened'. (There was a simple reason for this: O'Doherty tried to start the car using an ignition key. Because of the age of that model of that car, the starter was a push button situated on the floor between the driver's and front passenger's seat.) 'The woman was sort of distressed and I told her to get in and I went back to the next car. There was a man in it'. (His name was David Workman.) 'I told him to get out and keep on walking down the road. I drove off towards Culleybackey and dumped the rifle about two miles away. I parked the car in a quarry outside Cushendall at Gault's Road. I sat there all night until the next morning as the time to hit the bank was 10 or 10.30. I toured around the village just to see there were no police cars or security forces and drove out to where the weapons were. I picked up the weapons, the mask and the pillow and drove to Cushendall. I parked the car outside the bank and went inside with the pistol and grenade. I pulled the face mask over my face. I demanded money and passed the pillow case through the drawer'.

There were a number of men working behind the counter in the bank and a number of customers waiting to be served. They saw the man wearing the black stocking type mask and a green or khaki anorak. He was carrying a pistol and demanded money not merely from the tellers' tills but also from the bank's strong room. As the robbery unfolded a young woman entered the premises and the robber, Anthony O'Doherty, ordered her to stand with the other customers. When she told him that she had left her baby in a pram outside the bank she was allowed to collect the child, re-enter the premises and stand with the others until the robber ran from the bank with the stolen cash. He claimed in the course of his evidence that "I threatened them with the grenade".

Although he also claimed that he and McCormick had planned that he should rob the post office in Cushendall, if that was ever agreed between them, it was not carried out. Instead, immediately after leaving the Northern Bank with the cash, O'Doherty drove some three miles down the coast to the village of Knocknacarry and there he robbed the elderly post mistress of £145 cash. McCormick was never charged in respect of this offence, since clearly on this occasion Agent 294 was engaged in what lawyers sometimes call "a frolic of his own."

He told the judge that after that he abandoned the car about two miles from Knocknacarry in a laneway off the Cushendall/Ballycastle Road and took from it the stolen cash and the implements he had used in the two robberies. He met up with Detective Sergeant McCormick and spent the night at his house in Ballymena.

That officer was charged in counts 5, 6 and 7 in the indictment with the hi-jacking of Mrs. Quinn's and Mr. Workman's cars on 24 November 1974 and possession of a rifle in suspicious circumstances, where on any view his accuser Anthony O'Doherty was the principal actor and he took, if at all, what can only be described in fact and in law, a secondary role. The actual offence in law is Intimidation, contrary to section 1 of the Protection of the Person and Property Act (Northern Ireland) 1969, causing the car driver to surrender control of the car.

Count 8 alleged his participation in the Northern Bank robbery where the £3,048 cash and where again O'Doherty was the prime mover.

Count 9 alleged an attempted armed robbery at a small branch office of the Northern Bank in the village of Armoy in County Antrim on 14 April 1975. The gunman who entered the premises fled without a penny piece when the manager sounded the panic alarm inside the bank.

Count 10 alleged another robbery at a Bank, but on this occasion it was a return to what was becoming familiar territory, the branch of the Northern at Cushendall, committed on 7 May 1975 when a man wearing sunglasses and carrying a handgun and a grenade entered the premises about mid day. The person who was robbed on this occasion was John Brendan Black. The robber ordered the staff to fill a pillow case with cash. With some reluctance they did so, handing over £3,525.00, obtained not only from the tellers' tills but also from the strong room when the robber called out "what about the back". It was the prosecution's claim at the outset of the case that it was on this occasion that a grenade was used to commit the offence. That was not how the evidence unfolded.

On 18 November 1975 there was a further robbery at the Cushendall branch of the Northern Bank. On this occasion two gunmen were involved. On this occasion £2,563 was stolen in the raid. O'Doherty said he and McCormick were the robbers. They had returned there, so he said, because some four days prior to the bank robbery they had together carried out an armed raid on the Century Twenty One furniture store outside Portglenone and only got away with the sum of £10, so they needed further cash after such a disappointing outcome involving some considerable effort. A plastic bag, rather than a pillow case was used on this occasion, and again there was reference to the handing over of cash held in the strong room at the back of the premises. This clearly pointed to the same person or persons being involved in all the robbery offences.

Anthony O'Doherty had admitted his part in three other post office robberies, the first committed on 19 November 1976 when £34 was stolen at Killgarn, the second on 23 November 1976 when £240 was stolen at Glenravel and a white pillowcase was used to transport the money away and finally on 4 January 1974 when £294 was stolen from the same post office. He tried to implicate Charles McCormick in their commission in his evidence, claiming that he had been driven to and from the crime scene on each occasion by his police handler.

When he concluded his examination in chief he braced himself from the storm that was to come from defence counsel, Desmond Boal Q.C. He is a former Unionist politician who, on 30 October 1971, formed the Democratic Unionist Party with the Rev. Ian Paisley, claiming that their policies would be "on the right on constitutional issues and on the left on social issues." He is also a most experienced member of the Northern Ireland Bar and a most formidable cross-examiner. He had a great amount of material upon which to challenge O'Doherty's evidence. He was compelled to admit to defence counsel that for the past number of years he was sitting on a knife edge, playing a double dangerous game and that he was a practised liar who on occasion had to lie to stay alive.

It was in relation to his claim that Detective Sergeant McCormick actually shot Sergeant Joseph Patrick Campbell that he found himself on the most dangerous ground, not least because in 1978 he had told an RUC superintendent that he believed another man, whom he named, had killed that officer. His description of the event however has a ring of truth about it, even if he is lying about the identities of the personnel involved.

He related to the court that McCormick told him that Sergeant Campbell had spotted them after the commission of one of their crimes, which led O'Doherty to believe that the officer might have seen one of their pick-ups after a robbery, but he was not given any further details by his handler. If it was true that the Sergeant knew then Detective Sergeant McCormick's future in the RUC was non-existent and his career as a police officer would be over, and he was not going to allow that to happen. The only solution was to get rid of Sergeant Campbell. Soon afterwards, according to O'Doherty, the thought became the deed. On the night of Friday 25 February 1977 both men set out from Ballymena in a car containing a rifle and a ·38 revolver with the intention of silencing the man who perhaps knew too much.

It is known from independent sources that Sergeant Campbell did not work on that fateful Friday and was off duty over that week end. Sometime in the early evening however he received a telephone call at his home of which he gave no details to any member of his family. This was not unusual, for he kept his professional life and his family life separate and apart. Shortly after that he left his home in order to walk the short distance to the police station in Cushendall only a few minutes away. He was seen by his wife and older children to take his police firearm with him. They clearly recollect that for that was unusual.

On his arrival at the station the Sergeant spoke to the uniformed constable who was alone on duty there, and when that officer left the premises at the conclusion of his shift Sergeant Campbell began to close and lock the gates of the police station premises. As he did so an unidentified gunman came out of the shadows and shot him the head.

According to the evidence of Anthony O'Doherty however the gunman was another police officer, Detective Sergeant Charles McCormick. Had he been the person who had made the telephone call to the Sergeant at his home, asking him to meet at the town's police station? McCormick denied that he was the killer or had any involvement in any way in his death. He said: "I didn't kill Sergeant Campbell. I never arranged to get a gun or anything. There is no way Joe Campbell is in his grave because of me." There came a time in the course of his sworn evidence at his trial that he could not resist the temptation to blacken the character of the murdered officer. Such conduct might give an insight into the devious, self-serving, unscrupulous character that McCormick is. He claimed that he had suspicions that Sergeant Campbell was leaking Special Branch intelligence to the IRA. That outrageous, false and defamatory statement directed against the reputation of a man who could no longer defend himself was not allowed to pass unchallenged. After the case concluded the Chief Constable of the RUC, Sir John Hermon, to his eternal credit, condemned the allegations as a slur on an innocent man who was a fine policeman. One is bound to ask why, if McCormick really suspected what he claimed he did, he did not stand up and proclaim it when Sergeant Campbell was alive and in a position to challenge it, as he would have done. Again, I call for a change in the law to enable the family of a deceased person to have a right of action in civil law to bring proceedings to protect the reputation of the dead.

O'Doherty's description of the events prior to the killing was both graphic and chilling. He claimed that McCormick asked him to carry out the shooting, saying it would be easier than robbing a bank. He refused. McCormick and he both got out of the car and a rifle with a telescopic sight and a revolver were taken from the boot of the vehicle. The Detective Sergeant put a balaclava hood over his head and face and set off towards the town. O'Doherty stayed with the car. After about half an hour he heard the sound of either one or two shots. McCormick returned, out of breath and said words to the effect that this was either the end of the trouble or the beginning of it. The car was driven away from the scene by the police officer and he dropped his Agent off in the town of Ballymena.

Desmond Boal Q.C. had an abundance of verbal ammunition to fire at the person whose evidence, if believed by the trial judge, would result in the imprisonment for life of Charles McCormick. The barrister trailed the witness's character all over the courtroom in his attempt to destroy his credibility as a witness of truth. He called him "a killer, a liar, a hypocrite, a play actor, a devious and plausible villain, a maker of bargains with the police and a person of considerable intellectual dexterity which he frequently used to attribute to other people crimes which he himself had committed or in which he had been involved."

After the trial judge refused to uphold a defence submission that the accused had no case to answer (and of course if O'Doherty was in fact a truthful and accurate witness then the accused had no answer to the case), the Detective Sergeant went into the witness box to give his sworn evidence in his own defence. He denied all the 27 charges against him, saying he had been framed and that he was the victim of a Provisional IRA plot to bring him down as a Special Branch man and so discredit the RUC.

Amongst the witnesses in the case was Inspector Jimmy Blair, the police officer responsible for the two "ambushes" involving, so it was said, Anthony O'Doherty. As Martin Dillon relates in his book *The Dirty War* this officer found himself in serious difficulty when questioned by Desmond Boal Q.C, about the workings of the Special Branch. He was asked whether he had encouraged persons other than policemen to shoot in what was described as "unwarranted circumstances," This presumably meant was he encouraging special branch agents or others to commit a crime. Inspector Blair at first declined to answer the question at all, then said he could not do so on the grounds of security and then after a pause said that to do so might incriminate himself. After a short adjournment the trial judge decided he did not have the answer the question. However the damage was done. The failure to deny the suggestion was as good as admitting it. One of the many reasons why the British Government will never agree to a Truth and Reconciliation Commission similar to that in South Africa is that it is known that many dark secrets lurk in the black shadows cast by the security forces over their conduct in the

North of Ireland over the past 35 years.

After the trial Inspector Blair was compelled to retire from the RUC. In April 1989 he took his own life. The only statistics I can ever recollect seeing on this issue show that between the years 1976 to 1986 officers in the RUC were committing suicide at the rate of one every 13 weeks, disclosing on any view a most disturbing and tragic picture.

In the event Mr. Justice Murray decided to convict the accused on only 4 counts in the indictment, namely, 5, 6, 7 and 8, and acquit him of the remaining 23. He was thus found guilty of the offences of hijacking the motor cars on 24 November 1974, the possession of a rifle in suspicious circumstances on the following day, and the armed robbery on the 25 November 1974 where £3,048 was stolen from the Northern Bank in Cushendall. The judge said in the course of his judgment, giving reasons for his decision, that he had to decide if the evidence given by O'Doherty was in itself credible and if yes then he was bound to look for corroborative or supporting evidence from an independent source, and which implicated McCormick in the commission of the crimes charged. That is a perfect summary of the legal position.

Mr. Justice Murray said the evidence that O'Doherty gave on that robbery and the related firearms charge was in itself perfectly credible and indeed was given by him in an impressive and apparently honest way. He said at one stage that he did not wish to hurt the accused but he had been "broken" in the course of being interviewed by the RUC at Castlereagh police office and there was nothing he could do about it. He then had to go on to look for the supporting evidence. The judge said he found that corroboration in the following clear and compelling evidence.

First, the accused's financial position was worsening over the period August to November 1974 and by the 25 November his overdraft was up to £474, the highest figure it had reached since January of the previous year. Since he was being paid between £350 to £400 after tax and insurance deductions each month the state of that overdraft must have been a matter of some consequence to him. In addition, a hire purchase company was pressing him to pay the arrears of the payments on his Datsun motor car, threatening that in the event of non-payment it would take against him. That would probably include the repossession of the car, which would no doubt place him in great difficulty.

There was evidence in the course of the trial that in December 1974 that in December 1974 Sergeant McCormick paid between £650 and £750 in cash for the purchase of a brown coloured Ford Escort car from a garage proprietor Mr. T.J. Robinson in Kells, and further that on 15 December 1974 a lady called Mrs. Nan McLaughlin was released from hospital where she was treated for injuries following a car accident. Her car had been "written off" in that accident. When she returned to her sister's house in Coleraine she found that Ford Escort car waiting there for her. She is a lady who first met Anthony O'Doherty in 1972 and between the years 1975 to 1980, whilst separated from her husband, they lived together as a couple.

Whilst being interviewed by his fellow police officers at Castlereagh police office on 9 August 1980 (how ironic that was the anniversary day of O'Doherty's arrest and internment without trial nine years previously, when both men met up at that police office) McCormick made and signed a written statement, exhibit 65, if which he admitted buying the Ford Escort Car from the dealer in Kells. But he said, the car was obtained for O'Doherty to give to Mrs. McLaughlin and she was the source of the cash that was paid for the car, passed from her to Agent 294 to give to the police officer. That was the way the evidence seemed to unfold.

Mrs. McLaughlin gave evidence at the trial and denied either paying any money for the car herself or that anyone paid money on her behalf for that vehicle. Mr. Justice Murray accepted her evidence as being entirely truthful. He ruled out the possibility of collusion between her and O'Doherty to injure the accused. She had been fond of her former man friend but was no longer so. The judge therefore found as a fact that McCormick was lying when he said the money from the car came from Mrs. McLaughlin. In law, a lie which is proved by independent evidence or admitted to be a lie, which is deliberate and relates to a material issue and where the motive for the lie is a realisation of guilt or fear of the truth, that is capable of being corroborative evidence. The judge found it to be so.

In view of the state of his personal finances in December 1974 Detective Sergeant McCormick was not in a position to pay cash for that Ford Escort car and if he admitted to his fellow officers that he did they would have sought an explanation as to its source, so he lied in order to divert suspicion away from himself. The truth would have pointed to his involvement, as O'Doherty claimed, in the robbery at the Northern Bank in Cushendall on 25 November when the ready cash then became available.

That was not the end of the corroborative material available to the court.

The judge recalled O'Doherty's evidence that in the course of the bank robbery he had threatened the people in the bank with a hand grenade. A lady called Margaret Given told the court that during 1975 the accused has lodged with her at her house in the Gracehill area of Ballymena, following the breakdown of his marriage and his separation from his wife. Sometime during that time she had found a hand grenade in Detective Sergeant McCormick's room in her house.

When questioned by the police about this mater he vigorously denied it, but in evidence admitted it was true. His explanation for lying to his police colleagues was that he was terrified to tell the truth since he was under suspicion for the murder of Sergeant Campbell. He went further in his evidence to the judge, who rejected his additional explanation, describing it as "a cock-and-bull" story that he did not believe for an instant. McCormick claimed that the grenade was a dummy one, taken from which a police source in order to give to O'Doherty to enable him to switch it for another in a terrorist's box of grenades. That was not done is the way desired, for he claimed O'Doherty bungled the job, but he was not given the grenade back nor did he make a police report about it.

The judge then made reference to what he described as very significant evidence from Detective Sergeant Murray who related that a grenade was recovered from a terrorist source in 1972 and thereafter McCormick admitted taking that grenade from a security cabinet in the Special Branch office at Ballymena police station.

This was regarded therefore as another corroborative lie. Against the background of O'Doherty's evidence that he used the grenade and that it was provided to him by his handler, the judge considered it highly significant that such a weapon was found by Miss Given in the accused's room at her house and that the reason McCormick lied about it was his fear of the truth. If he admitted it was found there, as he eventually had to, this would have pointed to his having made criminal use of that grenade.

Mr. Justice Murray then proceeded onto what in the event proved to be a difficult and controversial area. He referred to O'Doherty's deposition, that is his previous statement made for the purpose of representing the evidence he intends to give at the trial, rather than the trial court evidence itself, in this way. He said, "I note that in his deposition O'Doherty said that in the course of the robbery on the

Northern Bank on 25 November 1974 he 'had a gun in my right hand pocket and a pillow case and grenade in my left......I put the pillow case down where the money was served. I had the gun out at this stage.' This account of what happened coincides with the accounts of the Bank staff and customers in their evidence, but it is at variance with that part of his own evidence where he says 'I threatened them with the grenade.' My view is that the grenade stayed in his pocket and he used his gun to do the robbery. O'Doherty had at least 47 crimes behind him when he was giving evidence before me and recollection of all their details was obviously difficult for him at times. I attach no importance to the conflict in detail over the use of the grenade and the gun. I take the view that the accused's possession of the grenade and his lying denial of that possession provide further and most compelling corroboration of his involvement in the robbery on 25 November 1974."

Mr. Justice Murray then moved on what may be considered to be new and safer ground. He referred to Detective Sergeant McCormick's official diary and the entry for Sunday 24 November 1974, the date before the bank robbery on the Monday. In that diary for that date McCormick had written "... met Agent 294 and also conversed with Sgt. Linton PG. Since O'Doherty had given evidence that he had met his handler on the Sunday, when the officer had dropped him off from his car in the Lisnahunchin area on the night before the robbery, and since the RUC station at Portglenone (PG) is only about a mile away from that location, the judge ruled that the diary entry placed them together as O'Doherty described and provided some corroboration for his evidence of the events of that day.

Mr. Justice Murray thereupon sentenced Detective Sergeant McCormick to 5 years imprisonment in respect of the two intimidation charges and the possession of the firearm in suspicious circumstances, and to 20 years for the first bank robbery committed on 25 November 1974. All the sentences were ordered to run concurrently with each other, meaning that the lesser terms would be subsumed in the longer sentence of 20 years. That sentence was passed on 2 April 1982.

On 9 January 1984 McCormick's case was listed for hearing in the Court of Appeal before the then Lord Chief Justice, Lord Lowry and Mr. Justice McDermott. There were four grounds of appeal against conviction. First that the trial judge misdirected himself as to the meaning and significance of a "credit worthy" witness in relation to the possible requirement of corroboration of an accomplice's evidence. Second, that the judge did not apply the proper principles in assessing the credibility of the witness O'Doherty. Third, that the judge found to be corroboration matters which were not capable of being so and finally that the verdict was unsafe and unsatisfactory having regard to the admitted association between the chief investigating officer and the suspect witness O'Doherty while the accused was in custody awaiting trial. (It was claimed at the trial that on a number of occasions a police officer had interviewed O'Doherty for the purpose of schooling him in his evidence for the forthcoming McCormick trial). There was also an appeal against sentence on the ground that it was manifestly excessive.

The appeal court accepted at the very outset that the evidence which was independent of O'Doherty, that is any emanating from anyone else but he, and which was claimed by the prosecution to be the corroborating evidence, could not of itself be sufficient to prove the guilt of Detective Sergeant McCormick.

The court further accepted that the case being put forward against him was that he obviously was in no position to purchase a motor car from Mr. Robinson from his own precarious finances, and therefore put forward a false account of how he obtained the money and in doing so provided against himself evidence which supported O'Doherty's evidence that he was a party to the first bank robbery in Cushendall on 25 November 1974. The court did however question how this evidence was though to relate to that particular offence rather than the other robberies in which Agent 294 implicated his police handler.

One only has to look at the date of the car purchase transaction, sometime in December 1974, and the evidence was that it was available to Mrs. Nan McLaughlin on her release from hospital on 15 December 1974, to realise that this was a serious and fundamental mistake on the part of the court. All the other robbery offences could therefore not possibly have had any connection with the money used for the payment for the Ford Escort. The attempted armed robbery at the Northern Bank in Armoy was not committed until 14 April 1975, that is some 4 months after that date; the armed robberies in Cushendall (the second bank raid), the furniture shop in Portglenone and the third bank raid in Cushendall, were committed in May and November 1975. Two of the three post office robberies were committed in November 1976 and the third in January 1977. How the judges could possibly consider that the proceeds of these later offences could have been used in December 1975 defies comprehension.

There is likewise some mystery about the related point of the primary source of the money used to buy the car. According to the trial judge "O'Doherty wanted to provide Mrs. McLaughlin with a replacement car and he explained what happened in these words: 'Charlie said I can take you out to this garage proprietor in Kells and he can fix you up with a car on the QT.' O'Doherty went on to describe how the accused (McCormick) did then arrange to get him a brown Ford Escort from one Robinson, a Kells garage proprietor, and without ever coming face to face with Robinson he (O'Doherty) drove the car from a spot near the garage to Coleraine and gave it to Mrs. McLaughlin. He also described how the accused then gave him a lift back to Ballymena. O'Doherty was quite firm on the point that he paid no money for this car." I take that to mean that he was denying that he had handed over any money, whatever its source, to McCormick in order to purchase the car.

The two appeal court judges looked at the point differently. They relied on exhibit 65 referred to above, the statement McCormick made under caution at Castlereagh police office on 9 August 1980. They quote in their judgment from that statement. "He (meaning O'Doherty) said he would get the money from Nan and arrangements were made to go out to Jackie's for the car.... Tony handed me Nan's money in an envelope. I asked him was it right. He said yes that she had counted it."

On any view this is a self-serving statement that might have been totally untrue, manufactured and tailored in order to bolster his own version of events. For some reason he was not asked questions about the source of the money by his own counsel or cross-examined on it by the prosecution. That might have been an important omission on their part, for the appeal court said that the only reference to "Nan's money" came from McCormick's statement, exhibit 65. In other words only he introduced it into evidence and it worked greatly to his advantage. The trial judge said McCormick's lie about the source of the money provided the necessary corroboration of the suspect accomplice's evidence. But, said the appeal court judges, "we respectfully but firmly take the view that the evidence could not justify a finding that the appellant (McCormick) lied about the source

202

of the purchase money; this would mean that, knowing that Mrs. McLoughlin did not provide the money he deliberately stated that she had done so, whereas the only legitimate inference from his written statement is that the information about the source of the money was conveyed to him by O'Doherty. Therefore there is no guilty contradiction between Mrs. O'Loughlin and the appellant. Furthermore, if O'Doherty had robbed a bank without the appellant's complicity, he would have been likely to give him an 'innocent' explanation when handing over the money. Therefore there is no reason to apply the principle of corroboration by means of a false statement on the part of the accused and this alleged corroboration falls to the ground."

I disagree with this reasoning. If O'Doherty told McCormick that he "wanted to provide Mrs. McLaughlin with a replacement car" as the trial judge Mr. Justice Murray noted at page 11 of his judgment, then how would he be doing so if she was the source of the purchase price? He might be obtaining the car for her with McCormick's assistance, he certainly would not be providing her with it.

I consider that the judges fell into error here, for the second time. They had already been mistaken about the dates of the robberies, and now they were accepting that although McCormick paid Robinson the cash for the car, it was not his own money but it was cash given to him by O'Doherty, something which I consider on the evidence O'Doherty denied. Furthermore, said the appeal court, McCormick did not say that Nan McLaughlin was the source of the money, he simply said, in exhibit 65, the self-serving statement, only that O'Doherty had told him that she was – and consequently he wouldn't know whether that was true or not. That was why there was no contradiction between his account and hers.

There was more to come. The court said: "The next point which the judge treated as corroboration is the evidence about the hand grenade. But assuming the appellant's explanation to be fabricated, we do not consider that this fact tends to connect him with the robbery alleged in count 8. There is no evidence that O'Doherty used the grenade in the course of that robbery."

That is difficult to understand. O'Doherty did say in his evidence before Mr. Justice Murray that he threatened the staff in the Northern Bank in Cushendall on 25 November 1974 with the grenade. The trial judge seems to have accepted he had the grenade with him, but not in his hand but in his pocket. He claimed McCormick gave him the grenade. When Miss Given said she saw a grenade in McCormick's room at her house he first denied it, then resorted to the cock-and-bull story. There was also the evidence of his admission of taking a grenade from the security cabinet in the Special Branch office in Ballymena Station. Apart from his lies, why and for what innocent purpose did he do that?

Lord Lowry and Mr. Justice McDermott were prepared to accept that an absurd and presumably false explanation about the grenade pointed (although not inescapably) to McCormick having made or encouraged a criminal use of it at some time, but they said "we cannot identify that use or encouragement with the alleged or proposed use of a grenade in the robbery committed by O'Doherty on 25 November 1974."

They gave fairly short shift to the suggestion that the entry in Detective Sergeant McCormick's official diary for 24 November could constitute corroborative evidence, for it did not tend to show that he was a party to a plan to hijack a car or rob a bank. They found nothing untoward in the suggestion that O'Doherty had been schooled in his evidence by the investigating police officer who had interviewed him 26 or 27 times. Lord Lowry said it was acceptable in a complicated case that an officer should go back repeatedly to check his facts as well as monitor the witness's state of mind. Searching cross-examination could be a most effective weapon against schooling.

That disposed of the prosecution case against McCormick. His appeal was allowed and he was set free. Outside the court he is reported to have said: "It is frightening to think that if it was not for my defence counsel, Mr. Desmond Boal, proving O'Doherty is a liar and a scoundrel, I could have spent the rest of my life in prison." His girl-friend, Miss Roberta Gray, said: "We knew he was innocent. It is nice to see there is still justice in this country."

Charles McCormick was the first police officer to be charged on the basis of "supergrass" evidence given by an accomplice on behalf of the prosecution. The National Council for Civil Liberties welcomed the quashing of his convictions, saying that they hoped that the same standards would be applied in the forthcoming supergrass trials following this case.

Between 1981 and 1988 at least 27 supergrasses agreed to give evidence for the prosecution against their former comrades. One was a woman, Angela Whoriskey. 15 of the 27 were members of the

Provisional IRA, 5 were from the Irish National Liberation Army. Another 5 were from the Loyalist Ulster Volunteer Force and 2 were from the Ulster Defence Association. At least 600 suspects were arrested on the basis of evidence provided by these supergrasses. On 26 February 1985 the Secretary of State for Northern Ireland told the House of Commons that the total direct expenditure on the protection of individuals who gave evidence against former accomplices in terrorist organisations in the last seven years amounted to just over 1.3 million pounds. Sheltering the remorseful clearly does not come cheaply.

Some claim there is a connection between the O'Doherty/McCormick case and that involving other RUC officers accused of murder. The link is a man named Robin Jackson. He was a native of County Tyrone who saw service with the Ulster Defence Regiment. He died from cancer in June 1998. He was widely regarded as one of the most prolific and ruthless killers on the Loyalist side, allegedly being responsible for the murders of more than 50 victims. It was also claimed that he was used by the British Army and the RUC as an agent. The name "The Jackel" was commonly used to describe him and his murderous activities. Shortly before his death Sergeant Joseph Patrick Campbell's eldest son, also called Joseph, went to see Robin Jackson at his home in County Down and asked him if he was responsible for his father's murder. He would not admit that he was.

In April 1980 two police officers, Constable William McCaughey and Sergeant John Oliver Weir, both of the RUC, were put on trial for the murder of William Streathearn. He was a Catholic man, aged 39, married with eight young children. He ran a small shop in the predominately Protestant village of Ahoghill, which was within the jurisdiction of the Ballymena police division. He was shot dead in the early hours of the morning of 19 April 1977 when someone lured him downstairs to open his shop by falsely pretending that an aspirin was needed for a sick child. Two shots in the chest from point blank range killed him instantly. He had a facial injury of many years standing, caused while he was working on a car and he received burns to the face. The subsequent tittle-tattle about that minor defect, which passed for terrorist intelligence amongst some elements in the RUC, linked him with membership of the Provisional IRA. Nothing could have been further from the truth. He was a quiet, decent, respectable, hard working man with no connection with any illegal organisation, but he was still marked out as an easy victim for pitiless slaughter.

At their trial both police officers entered pleas of not guilty. The prosecution evidence was that they used their police vehicle to drive the killers to the killing scene, listening to the police radio to ascertain whether there were any members of the security forces in the area at the time. They waited whilst the murder was carried out and then transported the murderer(s) away. The murder weapon was concealed at the McCaughey family farm on the outskirts of the village. For those who have ever wondered how loyalist murder gangs bestrode the Province of Ulster for years, carrying out the most foul and outrageous killings of Catholics with apparent immunity from detection whilst doing so, should look carefully at this case and wonder whether there were other occasions when those tasked with upholding the law, were helping to bring it down.

Constable McCaughey told his fellow police officers in an interview before he was charged that he and Sergeant Weir had planned the murder and provided the murder weapon, a ·45 pistol. He changed his plea to guilty during the course of the trial and was sentenced to life imprisonment. Sergeant Weir attempted to explain his confession evidence by claiming that his fellow police officers had ill-treated him in Castlereagh police office, something they denied. He was not believed by the trial judge, who convicted him and imprisoned him for life.

During the course of the trial the other two men who accompanied them on their murderous venture were named. One of them was The Jackal, Robin Jackson. Like the other person, he was never even interviewed in relation to the killing. According to David McKittrick (in *Lost Lives* at page 717) Jackson and the other man were never charged because there was no evidence against them. A senior RUC officer is quoted as saying: "Weir offered to give evidence if he was not himself prosecuted but the Director of Public Prosecutions would now allow that to happen. The officer added there would have been widespread protests if a policeman had escaped prosecution in such a way."

Both McCaughey and Weir have now been released from prison. It may be that in appropriate circumstances, such as a Truth and Reconciliation Commission, either one or both of them may be prepared to tell the pure unvarnished truth not merely about the killing of William Streathearn, but Sergeant Joseph Patrick Campbell as well. Did that faithful and dutiful officer know too much about the activities of the Ballymena Special Branch involving not only

Detective Sergeant McCormick, but other officers as well? Was Robin Jackson, working in collusion with the security forces, especially recruited for the killing at Cushendall? John Oliver Weir knows the answer to that, and perhaps William McCaughey does as well. Such a Commission would be a step too far for the British State that is more interested in anything but the truth.

POST SCRIPT TO CHAPTER 6.

On 15 October 1997, Anthony O'Doherty was convicted by a jury in Belfast of two serious criminal offences, first on a count of aggravated burglary and, second of causing grievous bodily harm with intent to do so. The judge, His Honour Judge Smyth Q.C., sentenced him to 12 years imprisonment on each count, the sentences to run concurrently. The prosecution claimed that O'Doherty was involved in a house-breaking incident where the householder was grievously injured by the burglar. So much so, in fact, that the criminal involved, telephoned for an ambulance to be sent to the address to treat urgently the injured victim. A detective sergeant in the RUC, gave evidence that he recognised the caller's voice as being that of Anthony O'Doherty. An auditory phonetician also gave evidence, that in her view it was highly probable that it was he who was the male caller to the ambulance service seeking assistance for the injured householder.

On 30 October 1998, the Northern Ireland Court of Appeal refused leave to appeal against conviction in the case. However on 27 September 2001, the Criminal Cases Review Commission referred the case back to that court, and fresh evidence was put before the judges there. They commented on the poor quality recording of a tape of which only 16 seconds were available for voice identification, and in a 16 page judgment, Lord Justice Nicholson, quashed the convictions and Anthony O'Doherty was set free and released from custody. His present whereabouts are unknown.

BIBLIOGRAPHY

Anderson, Don *14 May Days* Gill & MacMillan, Dublin
Asmal, Kadar & Ors *Shoot to Kill* Mercier, Cork
Bennett, Ronan *Double Jeopardy* Penguin
Bruce, Steve *The Red Hand* Oxford University Press
Callaghan, Huge & Mulready, Sally *Cruel Fate* Poolbeg, Ireland
Clarke, Sr. Sarah *No Faith in the System* Mercier, Cork
Conlon, Gerry *Proved Innocent* Hamish Hamilton, London
Coogan, Tim Pat *The IRA* Harper Collins
Coogan, Tim Pat *The Troubles* Hutchinson, London
Curtis, Liz *Ireland The Propoganda War* Pluto Press, London
Davies, Nicholas *Ten-Thirty-Three* Mainstream, Edinburgh
Dewar, Michael *The British Army in Northern Ireland* Arms & Armour
Dillon, Martin *The Dirty War* Hutchinson
English, Richard *The Armed Struggle* MacMillan
Faul, Mgr, Dennis & Murray, Mgr. Raymond The Birmingham Frame-Up
Fegan, Arthur &Murray, Mgr. Raymond *Collusion* Relatives for Justice
Geraghty, Tony *The Irish War* Harper Collins.
Geraghty, Tony *Who Cares Wins* Fontana/Collins
Hamill, Desmond *Pig in the Middle* Methuen
Hamden, Toby *Bandit Country* Hodder & Stoughton
Hill, Paddy Joe *Forever Lost, Forever Gone* Bloomsbury, London
Hill, Paul & Bennett, Ronan *Stolen Years* Doubleday, London
Holland, Jack *Hope Against History* Coronet
Holland, Jack & McDonald, Henry INLA, *Deadly Divisions* Torc
Holland, Jack & Phoenix, Susan *Policing the Shadows* Coronet
Holyroyd, Fred *War Without Honour* Medium
Kee, Robert *Trial and Error* Hamish Hamilton, London
Maguire, Annie *Why Me* Harper Collins, London
Moloney, Ed *Secret History of the IRA* Penguin
McArdle, Patsy *The Secret War* Mercier Press, Cork
McCann, Eamonn *War & Peace in Northern Ireland* Hot Press Books
McKee, Grant & Franey, Ross *Time Bomb* Bloomsbury, London
McKittrick, David & Ors *Lost Lives* Mainstream, Edinburgh
Mullen, Chris *Error of Judgment* Chatto and Windus, London
Murray, Mgr. Raymond *State Violence* Mercier Press, Cork

O'Brien, Brendan *The Long War* O'Brien Press, Dublin
O'Malley, Padraig *Biting at the Grave* Blackstaff, Belfast
Rolston, Bill *Unfinished Business* Beyond the Pale, Belfast
Ryder, Chris *The RUC Force Under Fire* Methuen
Ryder, Chris *The Ulster Defence Regiment* Methuen
Simpson, Alan *Murder Madness* Gill & MacMillan, Dublin
Taylor, Peter *Loyalists* Bloomsbury
Taylor, Peter *Provos, The IRA & Sinn Fein* Bloomsbury
Toolis, Kevin *Rebel Hearts* Picador
Urban, Mark *Big Boys' Rules* Faber and Faber, London
Victory, Patrick *Justice and Truth* Sinclair Stevenson London
Walker, Clive & Starmer, Keir *J, Ireland*
Clarke, Sr. Sarah No Faith in the System Mercier, Cork
Conlon, Gerry Proved Innocent Hamish Hamilton, London
Coogan, Tim Pat The IRA Ha

INDEX